D0536478

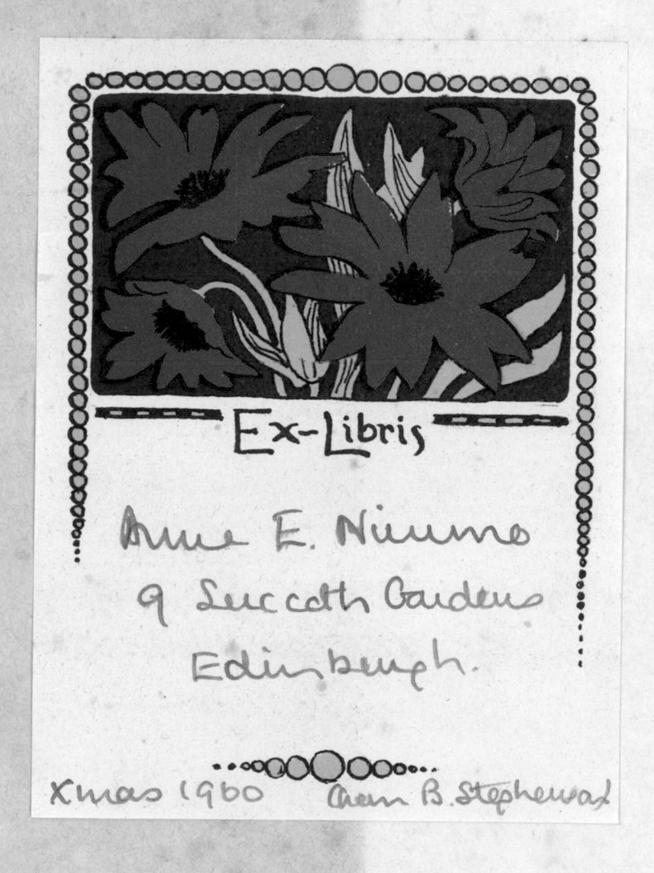
Ex-Libris
Anne E. Nimmo
9 Succoth Gardens
Edinburgh.
Xmas 1960

THE COLLECTOR'S ENCYCLOPAEDIA OF ENGLISH CERAMICS

By the same authors

OLD ENGLISH FURNITURE
Therle Hughes

THREE CENTURIES OF ENGLISH DOMESTIC SILVER
Bernard and Therle Hughes

AFTER THE REGENCY
Bernard and Therle Hughes

ENGLISH PORCELAIN AND BONE CHINA
Bernard and Therle Hughes

LIVING CRAFTS
G. Bernard Hughes

Frontispiece. (*Top*) Bristol porcelain figures of about 1770. (*Centre*) left: Pair of Chelsea figure candelabra; right: "The Maypole", a Chelsea figure group. (*Bottom*) Chelsea figures, early 1750s; left: figure from the Italian comedy series; centre: girl, with red anchor mark; right: craftsman, with red anchor mark.

The Collector's

ENCYCLOPAEDIA *of* ENGLISH CERAMICS

BERNARD and THERLE HUGHES

LUTTERWORTH PRESS

LONDON

First published 1956

To
BERNARD CONWAY

Made and printed in Great Britain by
William Clowes and Sons, Limited, London and Beccles

LIST OF ILLUSTRATIONS

LIST OF ILLUSTRATIONS

INTRODUCTION

THIS book is intended to give all possible assistance to the beginner-collector of English porcelains and earthenwares. The expert has books in plenty for intense study. But the beginner tends to flounder, disheartened, among all the techniques and their terminology, even all the names of potters and their wares generally considered too well known to require description or definition. It is the purpose of this book to make such essential basic information easy to find and clearly understandable. Whether the reader's delight lies in the world of "Whieldon tortoiseshell", "old Spode" or "Chelsea gold anchor", it should give him a sense of confidence in pursuing the ceramics of his choice in museums, in books, even among the fascinations and temptations of places where such lovely wares are for sale.

It is not suggested that such a book can protect him from the innumerable reproductions and fakes that test the ceramic collector's skill; only close study and wide experience can win against the more cunning deception. But it may at least serve to save him from buying, say, "a precious piece of mid-eighteenth-century Bow porcelain" only to discover that it consists of bone china made elsewhere at least as late as 1794. It may warn him that the bellarmine or greybeard bottle which takes his fancy follows a design continuously in production between the 1570s and the 1870s.

Bow porcelain, bone china, bellarmines—such terms as these and some four hundred others are all to be found in their appropriate alphabetical positions in the body of this volume, heavy type indicating that a name or term is given individual definition or description.

In this way, it is hoped, the reader will find the information he requires without tiresome search, whether he has the makings of an ardent collector or is merely one of the very many who have chanced to come into possession of a few pieces of old china and are mildly curious about them.

It must be emphasized, however, that the techniques implied by the terms here listed are essential study for those who determine to collect real antiques. The craft of the potter has grown and developed down the centuries: his materials, tools, kiln facilities have changed. It is not possible here to give more than a brief outline of these developments, as a background to the subsequent references that round out the picture of one of England's notable contributions to the charm of colour and grace of form associated with the eighteenth and early nineteenth centuries.

As early as 1686 Dr. Plot published his *Natural History of Staffordshire*, including a detailed description of Burslem and its current methods of making pottery. As yet there was no porcelain manufacture in Europe, and these earthenware potters were content to work local "throwing clays" on their wheels and paint their vessels with thinner clay slips, breaking the colours into each other with a wire brush, much as paper marblers did, and finally giving them a clear glaze by sifting powdered lead ore—smithum—or better quality calcined lead over them, sometimes blended with manganese to give "the motley colour".

Kiln firing was followed by slow cooling, each potter with his single pot oven making one firing a week and served by no more than some half-dozen men and a few boys. Josiah Wedgwood in 1765 collected data from elderly workmen and calculated the cost of running such a pottery at the beginning of the eighteenth century as £4 an ovenful, including some profit for the master.

Thomas and John Wedgwood were the first to break from such peasant methods, building a far more efficient factory of five ovens in 1743. Indeed, the 1740s may well be regarded as the crucial years when Britain determined what share she should take in the great ceramic developments then stirring Europe. Under appropriate headings the reader will find details of all the major developments associated with the period, of the techniques of such leaders as the Astburys, Whieldon, Josiah Wedgwood, of their stonewares and cream-coloured wares, their basalts and jasper wares, of the salt glaze and galena glaze, and the important Greatbach liquid lead glaze that was a large contributory factor in the success of the famous Staffordshire blue-and-white decoration, whether painted or transfer-printed, and in the fascinating lustre wares.

Even then the reader will have considered only the opaque wares generally classed as earthenwares or pottery. Parallel to these, from the 1740s too, came the great development of translucent porcelains, termed soft paste and hard paste, costly, fragile, but often very lovely, associated with such names as Bow, Chelsea, Worcester, Longton Hall, Caughley, Lowestoft, Derby, Bristol, Plymouth, New Hall, Pinxton, Nantgarw. These, their composition, treatment and decoration, as well as the fundamental differences between porcelains and potteries, and the peculiar contribution of the felspathic porcelains, will be found under later headings.

Meanwhile, however, the beginner-collector must be reminded of England's spectacular contribution to early nineteenth century ceramics and to all subsequent wares, for it is among these bone china manufactures that he is particularly liable to be led astray. Bone china was launched by Josiah Spode only in 1794, but by the early years of the nineteenth century it had transformed ceramic table ware. Translucent, radiantly white, yet comparatively strong and cheap to produce, it meant that beautiful ceramic wares could be enjoyed far beyond the limits of the collector's cabinets, on the tables of an ever-widening class of purchaser. As a result nineteenth century English ceramics offer an extraordinarily rich, varied and delightful field to the discriminating collector, but the possibility of confusion with earlier, rarer fabrics must be appreciated. Little bone china was made on the Continent. Considerable information on this subject may be found in an earlier volume in this Collector's Library, *English Porcelain and Bone China*, which tells how the old porcelain firms adapted themselves to the new medium and further manufacturers became established.

Marks, it must be emphasized, are but little guide to the ceramics collector. In some instances (such as a Chelsea scent bottle, for example) it is almost safe to say that a gold anchor, the most famous Chelsea mark, is proof of spurious work. Almost all the potteries copied the marks of other establishments here, on the Continent and in the Orient, and subsequent imitators have continued the malpractice. It may be mentioned, too, that a date included in a mark is usually a reference to the founding of the factory and not the manufacture of that piece—as, for instance, on Coalport and Adams work. The inclusion of the word ENGLAND in a mark indicates manufacture after the passing of the American Customs Regulation known as the McKinley Tariff Act of 1894. A diamond-shaped mark sometimes used between 1842 and 1883 is described under the heading REGISTRATION MARK. Afterwards a long registration number was used and this too may be noted from time to time.

The more experienced the beginner-collector becomes, however, the less he will tend to look to any marks for guidance in dating his finds. Examining and, whenever possible, handling authentic specimens, he will gradually find that he knows instinctively when a piece is right. He will distinguish unhesitatingly between the naïve original and the modern attempt to be "quaint", between the inexpensive fairing and its modern counterpart that is so often downright shoddy, between the facial expression of an original figure and the empty prettiness that often gives away an otherwise perfect reproduction. But by then, no doubt, this volume will long have been discarded by him: in introducing him to so much beauty and delight its purpose will have been well served.

"ABBOTT POTTER" MARK

John Abbott, Lane End, partner of John Turner in 1786, was in partnership with a dealer named Mist in the early 19th century and made **slip** and **combed earthenwares** and ornamental ware of the **basalt** and **jasper** type. The mark is sometimes ABBOTT & MIST.

ADAMS WARE

The Adams family trace their descent as potters from the time of Edward I, and were established at Brick House, Burslem, in 1657. John Adams was recorded in 1715 as making black and mottled ware. Four of the name William Adams operated as master potters during the second half of the 18th century, as well as several other members of the family. Ware found bearing the mark ADAMS EST[B] 1657, TUNSTALL, ENGLAND is modern.

WILLIAM ADAMS (1745–1805) Greengates, Tunstall: was a highly efficient practical potter, employed by **Josiah Wedgwood** until 1789 when he established his own factory. His products included: deep blue **jasper ware,** both solid and dipped, more violet in hue than Wedgwood's, but considered equal in design, modelling and colour; **basalt**; **cream-coloured ware**, painted and **transfer-printed** with blue underglaze; **stoneware** ornamented with fine **relief**

work modelled by Joseph Monglott, such as jugs displaying all-over scenes of bacchanalian dances and hunting, with characteristic **engine turned** borders, usually interlaced circles, in dark browns. Marks were impressed: ADAMS; ADAMS & CO: W. ADAMS & CO. He was succeeded by his son Benjamin who made similar ware impressed B. ADAMS.

WILLIAM ADAMS (1748–1831) Brick House, Burslem, and Cobridge: great-grandson of John Adams. He founded Cobridge Hall *c.* 1770 and became a specialist in blue **transfer-printed cream-coloured earthenware**, but no mark has been noted.

WILLIAM ADAMS (1772–1829) Stoke-upon-Trent: established in the mid-1790s to make blue **transfer-printed** ware; hand-painted **earthenware** from c. 1800; **bone china** from 1816. Mark: ADAMS, impressed or printed, except on blue printed ware intended for the United States of America which was impressed with an eagle and printed with the name of the subject in a foliated cartouche. After 1829, W. ADAMS & SONS.

WILLIAM ADAMS (1798–1865) Greenfield: made similar wares from the early 1820s. Also ware decorated with sponge-applied colour and painted with a conventional bird.

ADAMS AND BROMLEY: operated at Hanley in the mid-19th century, specializing in **jasper ware** marked ADAMS & BROMLEY; A & B; or, between 1860 and 1880, ADAMS & CO.

AGATE WARE

Dr. Thomas Wedgwood (1695–1737) appears to have introduced to Staffordshire in about 1730 the centuries-old method of mingling batches of coloured clays by rolling and doubling at random, to produce ornamental **earthenware**. Unlike **marbling**, which was merely surface coloured, agate ware was coloured throughout its substance. Ordinary red and buff clays were used to produce broad irregular veining. Vessels were shaped by throwing on the wheel, existing examples exhibiting evidence of this hand manipulation.

Thomas Whieldon in the early 1740s devised an improved agate ware, using white clays stained with metallic oxides, such as brown from manganese, green from copper, and blue from **zaffre**. Flat bats of differently coloured clays were placed one upon the other and beaten to drive out enclosed air and make the separate cakes adhere to each other. The mass was then transversely cut into slices with wires. This process of laying, beating and slicing was repeated again and again, care being taken to preserve the run of the grain. The resulting striated effect resembled the veining of marble.

As potters became more skilled in this work, the layers were made thinner and thinner, and some extremely beautiful effects obtained.

This mass of vari-coloured clay was almost non-plastic and inclined to separate if thrown or shaped by hand-modelling. It does not appear to be generally realized that this difficulty was overcome by pressing it into smooth-surfaced moulds, thus retaining the veining undistorted. A tea-pot, for instance, was pressed into two halves and so joined that the veins continued unbroken across the seam. Veining in handles and spouts was slightly distorted owing to the use of two-part moulds. The ware was polished after firing and before glazing. Until the early 1750s agate ware was **galena glazed**, the rich yellow hue of this glaze toning down the clay colouring; from the mid-1750s the ware was dipped into a transparent liquid lead glaze. After about 1760 the glaze might be faintly tinged with blue so that the ware more nearly resembled the natural stone.

Collectors chiefly associate agate ware with Thomas Whieldon, whose galena glazed agate ware snuff-boxes and knife hafts started him on the road to prosperity. The boxes were sold to Birmingham chapmen who fitted them with gilded brass hoops, hinges and fasteners; the hafts to Sheffield cutlers. Other makers of Staffordshire agate ware were **Thomas Astbury**, Daniel Bird, **Josiah Spode** during the 1770s, and John and Thomas Alders, whose pottery was acquired by **Josiah Wedgwood** and his partner John Harrison in 1752 and operated by them until 1754. Some outstandingly beautiful agate ware was made by

Ralph Browne, Caughley Hall, Shropshire, from about 1755. Josiah Wedgwood perfected the process at Etruria for his costly classical vases, some of which were wonderful imitations of natural agate and other stones.

Among the objects found in agate ware are tea-pots, coffee-pots, cups and saucers, dishes, mugs, sauce boats, pickle leaves, candlesticks, and well shaped toy tea-sets. The manufacture of agate ware had ceased by about 1780 owing to the competition of **cream-coloured earthenware**. Few marked examples have come to light. Modern copies have been made.

ALCOCK, SAMUEL

Established in the late 1820s in **Ralph Wood's** old pottery at Burslem which he rebuilt in 1839, at the same time absorbing the firm of J. and R. Riley. Although primarily making inexpensive domestic ware he issued finely potted and decorated **bone china** and

earthenware. He was celebrated for his jugs in **parian ware** dating from the late 1840s, modelled in high relief by M. Protat, formerly with the firms of **Wedgwood** and **Minton**. The background **colour** was usually lavender or green with the relief work in white and rims heavily **gilded**. The subjects were often named beneath, such as "The Distin Family, the Saxe Horn Performers", each of five panels displaying a three-quarter-length portrait and instrument. Ariadne seated on a leopard was another popular motif, grapes and vine leaves encircling the jug neck. Marks until 1860 were: ALCOCK & CO HILL POTTERY BURSLEM; ALCOCK & CO; or S A & CO. in black letters either impressed or printed.

ALLERTON WARE

Fine **earthenware, bone china**, and gold, silver and resist **lustre** were made by Charles Allerton, established at Longton in 1831. His productions were unmarked until 1870.

ANCHOR MARK. *See* **Chelsea, Chelsea-Derby**, **Davenport**, **Derby**, **Newcastle**, **Liverpool** and **Sunderland**.

ARMORIAL DECORATION

Porcelain, bone china and **earthenware** painted with heraldic coats of arms or crests.

ARROW MARK. *See* **Bow, Pinxton, Shorthose.**

AS (monogram) MARK. *See* **Lacework**.

ASTBURY WARE

The two Astbury potters, John (1686–1743) and his son Thomas, were outstanding contributors to early 18th century progress in English **earthenware**. John established a pottery at Shelton in 1725, operating, as was usual until the 1750s, only a single kiln. His productions were of better shape than those of his predecessors because after throwing he allowed them to stiffen slightly and surface finished them on the lathe. He was first to apply a wash of carefully lawned white **engobe** containing Bideford pipe clay over the interiors of vessels: this provided a smooth, liquid-proof surface, less costly than the tin enamel already used for this purpose. Astbury's next innovation was to harden the body of his earthenware by adding white sand from Mow Cop and Baddeley Edge. This was soon replaced by calcined and ground **flint** as used to-day. With the addition of Shelton marl Astbury produced a hard **white stoneware** suitable for **salt glazing**. John Astbury produced the celebrated Porto Bello ware issued in commemoration of the capture of Porto Bello on the Isthmus of Panama in 1739. Red or buff earthenware was ornamented in relief with ships, fortifications and figures in white: so popular was this decoration that dealers were advertising other versions in the 1760s. The name of Astbury has become a generic term for fine earthenware made during John's period and including the productions of Ralph Shaw, Thomas Wedgwood and Josiah Twyford of Shelton.

It is possible to classify Astbury productions into eight main groups:

Agate and tortoiseshell: made by Thomas Astbury.

Black earthenware: after the style of the **Elers brothers**, with relief ornament in white instead of in self colour.

Figures: men, animals, birds and groups, in the traditional manner, modelled in clay thickly coated with a white **slip** and given decorative details in coloured clay or slip. Astbury arbour groups, such as two rustic lovers seated beneath a fan-like tree, or Adam and Eve beside the Tree of Knowledge, were made years before English porcelain craftsmen acquired the technique which gave them supremacy in this branch of ceramic art. Gradually, however, coloured clays and slips were superseded by white clay decorated in simple glowing metallic oxide **colours** beneath the **glaze.** Musical groups still exist in this medium, each performer a separate piece; also equestrian figures, notably the one now known as "The Grenadier", modelled shortly before John Astbury's death. Figures were also made in salt-glazed **stoneware** including the celebrated pew-groups and copies of Chinese figures.

Glazed earthenware: of exceptionally good quality in reddish brown, buff, yellow, orange, chocolate or fawn, decorated with ornament made by applying pads of white pipe clay stamped with relief designs and occasionally tinged with a purplish brown. Until the mid-1750s these were **galena glazed.**

Sgraffiato: red earthenware covered with white slip and ornamented with scratched design.

Salt-glazed stone ware.

Terra-cotta: hard unglazed red earthenware with **engine turned** decoration made by Thomas Astbury from *c.* 1755.

White earthenware and **Cream-coloured earthenware.**

AUSTIN, JESSE. *See* **Pot-lid pictures**.

AYLIFF, JOHN

The first potter to be granted a patent. This was dated 1635 and covered "Panne Tyles, Stone Juggs, Bottles of all sizes, Earthern Wicker Bottles, which are now made only by Strangers in Forraigne Partes."

AYNSLEY, JOHN

Designer, engraver and maker of **transfer prints** and decorator in coloured enamels. Operated at Lane End, Staffordshire, 1802–26. He both sold the transfers to neighbouring potters and himself applied them to plain **cream-coloured earthenware** bought from the potters, over-painting them in **colours.** His name is found on the transfer and sometimes the ware bears the potter's trade-mark impressed.

B MARK. *See* **Bow, Bristol,** and (incised) **Worcester.**

BADDELEY and FLETCHER (Shelton, Staffordshire)

An unsuccessful **porcelain** venture from 1763 with William Littler of **Longton Hall** as manager. Productions resembled those of Longton Hall, the body being largely composed of ground glass, while **china clay,** the basis of true porcelain, was not used at all.

BAILEY and BATKIN (Longton, Staffordshire)

Makers of **earthenware figures, lustre ware,** etc., in the early 1820s.

BALL BROTHERS. *See* **Sunderland.**

BAMBOO WARE

A dark shade of **cane ware** made to imitate bamboo, introduced in 1770 by **Wedgwood.**

BANDING

Colour lines applied freehand, one finger being used as a guide to regulate the distance of the band from the edge of the article. Since the early 19th century circular articles have been placed on a wheel or whirler, the loaded brush being applied to the rotating object. The hand is steadied by an adjustable rest.

BARNES, ZACHARIAH. *See* **Liverpool.**

BASALT WARE

A uniformly and densely grained black stoneware developed by **Josiah Wedgwood** and issued from 1766. This was Wedgwood's first ornamental ware and was a refinement of the early **Egyptian black,** long made by the Staffordshire potters who stained an ordinary **earthenware** body with manganese dioxide. Basalt was a mixture of ball clay, calcined ochre, and manganese dioxide. The surface was smooth and richer in hue than any other **biscuit,** and required no **glaze.** Until the mid-1790s black basalt was given a coating of varnish which burnt in at red heat. After removal from the kiln it was rubbed with a soft rag which gave to the surface a permanent slightly glossy appearance. Such basalt has no waviness of surface and is devoid of **crazing.** It was soon discovered to be an excellent medium for intricate and sharply defined relief decoration. Basalt made at a later date was finished on the lathe, giving it a dull, soft, unfired appearance, dead black. In the best quality ware the parts in relief were cast in moulds and applied to the basalt body.

The range of ware made by Josiah Wedgwood was wide and included vases, medallions, plaques, busts and tablets decorated in relief with figures, horses, flowers, trees. Tea and coffee sets with trays were made from the beginning: tradition has it that these were used only for funerals.

Following Wedgwood's success with basalt about twenty competitors imitated his productions. **Henry Palmer**, Hanley, made Etruscan shaped vases with medallions in 1770; **Elijah Mayer** and E. Mayer & Sons, Hanley, were celebrated for their basalt ware from the early 1770s to *c.*1830; **John Turner** made exceptionally fine basalt from about 1770; William Baddeley, of **Eastwood**, from 1780; **Edmund John Birch**, 1795.

BASKET WORK

Openwork ware, fashionable during the late 18th century and in mid-Victorian ceramics, made by expressing strips of clay from a wad box and hand-weaving them to the required shape. In fine work symmetry was given to this built-up ware by pressing it lightly into a plaster mould. In **Belleek** basket work the strips are merely laid one upon the other.

BAS RELIEF

Decoration in which the design projects slightly from the background—less than half of its true proportions and without any undercutting. It differs from medium relief in which the raised design represents exactly half the true proportions, with some undercutting, and from high relief in which the motifs stand out boldly.

BAT PRINTING. *See* **transfer-printing**.

BATTAM, THOMAS (London)

Specialist in ornamental red clay work from about 1840 to 1860. The ware, often in imitation of Greek art forms, was decorated with figures and ornamental compositions executed in a dark liquid pigment. This was applied with a quick-drying oil as a medium, effective adhesion being secured by firing at an exceptionally high temperature. In Battam's earliest work the black silhouette figures might be painted upon either a red or a buff ground. The originals from which he made his copies, and which consisted of figures and other ornament in red on a black ground, included historical, mythological and domestic scenes. Every curve in his ware was the segment of a circle, even the most irregular of his lines. Battam impressed his name in full on his work.

BAXTER, THOMAS (1782–1821)

An enameller proficient in a wide range of subjects which he painted in great detail. Until 1814 he worked for his father, a well-known outside decorator in London, employed largely by the London warehouse of Barr, Flight & Barr, **Worcester**. From 1814 to 1816 he worked at Worcester as a painter and teacher of apprentices; from 1816 to 1819 at **Swansea**, after which he returned to Worcester as a specialist painter of feathers and shells.

BB & I OPAQUE CHINA MARK.

Baker, Bevan & Irwin, **Glamorgan Pottery**, Swansea, 1814–39.

BEADING

Encircling bands of hemispherical or other simple motifs sunk or in relief. Made with a revolving wheel in which the design has been embossed or sunk: this is run over the surface of the soft clay, thus impressing a corresponding design on the ware.

BEAR JUGS

Made in **salt-glazed stoneware** at **Brampton, Chesterfield, Nottingham,** and in Staffordshire. They varied considerably in colour which ranged from a pale yellowish buff, through the browns, to specimens so highly charged with oxide of iron as to be almost black. These jugs are in the form of a bear sitting upright and closely hugging a dog that has been set to bait it. A loose ring passes through the nose and a detachable head forms a small cup. The collar may be fitted with a chain ending in a pierced hollow ball containing stones and used as a rattle. The surface of the body may be smooth, but in most instances it is roughened with applied fragments of clay from the turner's lathe. Touches of brown slip suggest eyes and teeth.

BELL, J. and M. P. (Glasgow Pottery)

Established 1842 and continuing into the 20th century to make white and **transfer-printed earthenware.**

Also made **parian ware, terra cotta, pearl ware, granite ware** and **bone china.** Dessert services with perforated borders became a feature.

BELLARMINES

Coarse **stoneware** bottles of a brown mottle colour thickly **glazed**, bearing on the neck a bearded mask of Cardinal Bellarmine (1542–1621) who was disliked in Protestant countries for his opposition to the Reformed Church. Known in England as greybeards, such bottles were being made in London for use in the royal household by the late 1570s. The shape of a bellarmine or greybeard bottle is full-bellied, short in proportion to the small narrow neck that bears the mask, and below which there may be a coat of arms in relief. They were made until the mid-19th century in four sizes: gallonier (gallon); pottle pot (half-gallon); pot (quart); little pot (pint).

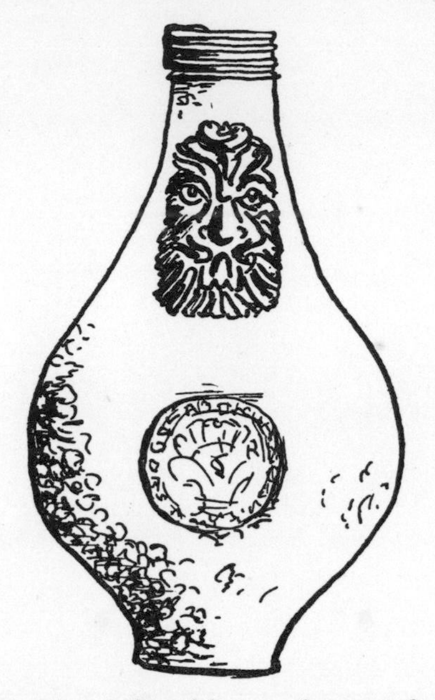

Bellarmines should not be confused with the much more common jugs with masks below their spouts.

BELLEEK (Northern Ireland)

A factory founded in 1857 by Armstrong and M'Birney at Belleek in Co. Fermanagh to produce **parian ware** from local felspar and Cornish china clay. Some extremely fine **figures** were made including Richard Cœur-de-Lion. From about 1865 domestic parian **ware** was made, **lead glazed**. Shortly afterwards came **egg-shell porcelain,** so named because of its delicate thinness and lightness of body, its rich cream-like ivory tones and the pearly iridescence of its glaze. This was basically a **hard porcelain**, the glaze containing salts of bismuth mixed with resin and oil of lavender and coloured with metallic oxides. The body might also be tinted, gilded, or left unglazed. In some rare examples exceptionally skilful modelling was enhanced by the contrast of the unglazed *biscuit* and the sparkling nacrous sheen on a single piece. Much Belleek ware was modelled in the shape of natural objects and a considerable amount of *basket work* was issued. The partners died in 1885, and although the firm continued operating in a smaller way, the nacrous glaze was altered. Two printed marks are found on Belleek ware: a harp surmounted by a royal crown; a harp, hound, tower, and shamrock sprays over the inscription BELLEEK. Jet, red and cane-coloured **earthenware** were also made.

BELLE VUE POTTERY, HULL

Established 1826 and closed 1841, this pottery under the management of Edward Bell and then W. Bell, made **creamware, green glazed** dessert plates with basketwork centres, and **transfer-printed** ware in blue or brown showing landscapes or commemorative scenes. The mark, impressed or blue printed, was BELLE VUE POTTERY HULL in a circle, or the name in cursive scroll-surrounded script about a representation of two bells.

BELPER. *See* **Bourne's Potteries.**

BENTLEY, THOMAS (1730–80)

Josiah Wedgwood's partner in the establishment of Etruria. The partnership indenture is dated August 10, 1769 "between Josiah Wedgwood of Etruria . . . and Thomas Bentley of Chelsea . . . to be copartners or joint traders in the art mistery trade or occupation of making and vending ornamental earthen Ware."

BFB MARK. *See* **Worcester.**

BIANCO-SOPRA-BIANCO

A type of decoration originally depending upon slight relief effects rather than colour, and found on 18th century English **delft ware.** Designs, usually border patterns, were painted in thick opaque white **glaze** on tin enamel which in delft ware was no longer white but lightly tinted to greenish-white or greyish-blue colour, the latter being known as *bleu agate.*

BILLINGSLEY, WILLIAM (1758–1828)

Flower-painter and porcelain-maker. Was apprenticed to **Duesbury** at **Derby** in 1774 and for seven years painted single blooms in the meticulous style then fashionable. He then introduced to Duesbury a new decorating technique in which sharp outlines were abandoned and the colour applied in soft washes. Instead of leaving the ground for high lights Billingsley swept the whole field with a single colour, producing light colour contrast by removing surplus colour with a cotton wool stipple or a clean brush. The effect was more softly delicate than anything previously seen: Billingsley had initiated a new scheme of ceramic painting.

Billingsley's mannerisms in floral groups were almost the equivalent of a signature throughout his career. On fine quality porcelain the roses for which he is famous are painted from countless angles. His favourite appears to have been the Maiden's Blush variety and an outstanding feature of the work is the artist's obvious delight in the graceful play of the long reflex sepals. In many instances the calyx is turned right back from the corolla to emphasize the contrast between massy, rounded petals and feathery sepals. Invariably one rose in each piece is found bending over, leaving the calyx standing out from a deep cavity at the flower base; foliage is often attached to the stem. When painting a small bouquet Billingsley placed one or more rose buds bending over the main flower. Some of his Derby flowers were built up petal by petal and fired after each application of colour, frequently a costly process, for as many as seven firings might be necessary. Foliage is distinctively natural and irregular, and thorns are carefully painted. This understanding of foliage and habits of growth is seldom found elsewhere. His finest floral groups were painted between 1793 and 1795, when he gave an effect of great depth to his work by applying a pale green or delicate brown undertint, painting the stronger translucent colours over this. Most of Billingsley's Derby work was marked with the crown, crossed batons, and script D in puce or blue.

Billingsley left Derby for **Pinxton** in 1796 where he made **soft-paste porcelain** until 1799. A few months later he was established at **Mansfield** as an independent decorator of porcelain and **bone china**. From 1803 to the end of 1807 he was at **Torksey**, again as a porcelain manufacturer, and for a few months early in 1808 he was an independent decorator at **Wirksworth**.

In October 1808 he was with the firm of Barr, Flight & Barr, **Worcester**, engaged in the development of a fine porcelain, and in 1810 Martin Barr reported a "great improvement in the texture, whiteness and beauty of our porcelain". In November 1812 Billingsley sold to his employers "a certain secret relative to a new method of composing a finer and more translucent porcelain" for £200. This was never made commercially, although the trial pieces, marked with the "B" in script, are remarkably translucent. Still fired with the urge to be his own master he left early in 1813 and established a porcelain factory at **Nantgarw**, using the name Beeley. In 1820 he went to **Coalport** were John Rose employed him in a managerial capacity. He died in 1828 at Kemberton, near Coalport, a bitterly disillusioned man, still believing that porcelain manufactured from his costly, impractical recipe outrivalled that of **Sèvres**.

BIRCH WARE

Jasper and **basalt** made by Edmund John Birch and Company, Hanley, from 1795 to about 1820. Mark BIRCH impressed, or the initials EJB.

BIRD TUREENS

Shaped as sitting hens, ducks and drakes, swans, fighting cocks, rabbits, fish, imposing boars' heads, partridges in at least twenty types, and so on, these have been wrongly assumed to have contained food associated with their outer form. Originally, however, they were included in the service of dessert at a period when this was not taken in the dining-room. The vogue for bird tureens was initiated by **Dresden** in the 1740s. They were made in England from the early 1750s and some may date as late as 1775. Those made after about 1763 were inferior in modelling and enamelling.

Chelsea: appears to have been first to copy the Dresden style in England and catalogued them singly and in pairs. Particularly desirable were "tureens in the shape of a hen and chickens as large as life in a fine sunflower leaf dish." The hen is in a sitting position with a chicken perched on her back, three others peeping from beneath her left wing, and three snuggling against her breast. Colouring is in shades of purple, with dashes of brown and blood red. The hen is divided horizontally from the upper tail feathers to the breast, the upper portion forming a lid with a chicken for a knob. The dish upon which it rests measures 21 inches by 15 inches and is composed of three large sunflowers in full relief, several small flowers, and a border of laurel leaves also in relief, all strikingly coloured.

Fighting cocks, plucked, cropped and spurred and in the attacking position; graceful swans appearing to float in their flat oval dishes; crouching rabbits with raised ears; crested ducks and drakes; boars' heads; carp naturalistically coloured in purple and brown with a greenish slime tint around the gills, were all made at Chelsea. Partridge tureens, smaller and less imposing than the others, were made in greater numbers as sweetmeat containers and might be sold already filled: the Chelsea series consisted of two birds sitting on a single dish.

Bow: made pairs of partridge tureens with dishes from 1756, copying a Dresden original and adapting from it several other models and sizes: Bow partridges are less realistically modelled than those of Chelsea, but colouring is more naturalistic. Pigeon tureens were also made.

Derby: made partridge tureens with the birds sitting on plain embossed nests bordered with overlapping rings. These date from 1756 onwards. Pigeon tureens were also made.

Bone china: during the second quarter of the 19th century there was a revival of bird tureens shaped as hens sitting on bowls representing wicker basket nests. Those marketed during the early 1820s were rather smaller than life size and vividly enamelled. These were filled with delicacies and presented to mothers during their confinement. In the 1830s a smaller size was made to contain a valentine gift. Small sitting hens in coarse pottery belong to the 1840s to 1860s when they were filled with sweets and offered as prizes at country fairs.

Life-size sitting hen tureens of finely modelled bone china served a different purpose. They were warmed in the oven and carried to the breakfast-table containing hot boiled eggs in their egg-cups. They were also made in **parian ware** by **Charles Meigh & Sons**, Hanley, and T. J. & J. Mayer.

BISCUIT

Earthenware or **porcelain** materials after being shaped, dried by artificial heat—the first baking—and then fired in a kiln or oven. The term is widely used to include all once-fired unglazed ware.

Biscuit painting or printing: designs applied to the unglazed or biscuit state by means of painting or **transfer-printing**.

Biscuit porcelain: ware heated to a temperature great enough to decompose the clay in its composition and to produce a porous body or biscuit. Also the term used in connection with an unglazed dull **hard porcelain** known to potters as "sculpture body" and used for white statuettes. The methods of modelling and so on were the same as for the ordinary porcelain. Firing required great skill to prevent vitrification which would result in the statuette displaying an unpleasant greasy-looking surface. *See* **Figures**.

BISHOP'S WALTHAM WARE

Ordinary red ware including **terracotta** painted black and decorated with painted figures.

BLANC DE CHINE

White unpainted porcelain originally made at Tehua, China, and ornamented with **sprigged** sprays of prunus blossom. Imitated by **Bow** between 1749 and 1755, probably from St. Cloud and Meissen reproductions. Also copied by **Chelsea,** soft paste **Bristol,** and André Planché's **Derby.** Favourite designs at Bow consisted of simple sprays applied under glaze, and including plum blossom, acorns and oak leaves, and a pair of roses on a single stem. Blanc de chine of Bow is richly mellow, causing other white china to appear harshly crude. The raised work of unmarked Bow is recognized by the sharp edges of the design, only apparent on close examination. Edges are sometimes slightly discoloured. In some later examples oriental flowers in colour might be placed between sprigs and occasional pieces were enriched with gilding. Statuettes in blanc de chine were made in addition to domestic ware.

BLOOR, ROBERT

Proprietor of the **Derby** porcelain factory from 1811. In 1826 he became insane and the works operated under the management of James Thomason until Bloor's death in 1844. The business then came into possession of his son-in-law Thomas Clarke, who acted as manager until the works closed in 1848.

BLUE. *See* **Cobalt; Scale pattern; Mazarine blue; Transfer-printing.**

BLUE DASH CHARGERS

A term given by E. A. Downman

in 1919 to large placques of **delftware** on which the deep rounded rims are decorated with broad dashes of **cobalt blue** applied with a sponge to suggest twisted rope. This style was copied from the Dutch by the **Bristol** decorators. These placques bear crudely painted pictures such as Adam and Eve, English kings and queens from Charles I to Anne, equestrian figures, popular characters and floral designs such as tulips and carnations in blue, green, orange yellow, and purplish brown. Such a placque measures from twelve to eighteen inches in diameter. A point to note is a flat footrim on the back, shaped with a groove or with two holes intended for a hanging cord.

BLUE PRINTING. *See* **Transfer-printing** *and* **Cobalt.**

BOCAGE

A mantelpiece or bracket decoration with a widely spreading background of closely clustered hand-modelled flowers and foliage supporting a **figure**, a tree stem being incorporated into the design to prevent collapse during firing. The ground on which the figure stands may be moulded in rockwork with growing flowers in relief. The back is perfunctorily finished. Made during the 1760s at **Bow, Cheslea, Derby** and **Plymouth.** Bow examples are distinguished by their twisted leaves and petals and are smaller than those of Chelsea in which the leaves are flatter and the outer petals saucer-shaped.

BODIES. *See* **Coloured bodies,** *and* **Dry bodies.**

BODY

The name given to the composite materials of which potters' clay is made. The term body is generally used when referring to **earthenware** or **stoneware**. The term paste is used almost exclusively when referring to **porcelain** or **bone china**.

BOLSOVER (Derbyshire)

Specialized in bright-glazed brown domestic ware either mottled or decorated with trailed or incised **slip**. Operated by T. and W. Robinson, and T. Robinson junior, who dismantled the kilns in 1750.

BONE CHINA

A paste intermediate between **hard porcelain** and artificial or frit **soft porcelain.** Technically it may be considered as a combination of fine **earthenware** and fine **stoneware** made translucent by the addition of calcined bone. Bone china, a non-frit paste, was first marketed by **Josiah Spode**: the firm's old pattern books prove conclusively that the first sales took place in 1794. Spode's paste was made from a basic formula standard to this day: bone ash 6 parts; china stone 4 parts; china clay 3½ parts. The transparent **glaze**, consisting of silica, potash, and lead oxide, was of a texture that enabled enamel colours to sink well into it during firing so that there was no danger of flaking as with porcelain. So widely did bone china differ from all that preceded it, that it acquired an independent status in ceramic technology. Of fine texture and colour, and giving enduring service at a cost far lower than the fragile soft paste porcelains, it achieved immediate popularity, demand outstripping supply for many years. By 1800 **Josiah Spode II** had so improved the manufacturing processes that the new composition had apparently reached perfection of paste, exquisite whiteness, and evenness of translucency. At this time several other potters had started competing in this ware: **Thomas Minton** at Stoke, John Rose at **Coalport, John Davenport** at Longport, William Duesbury at **Derby**, the **Worcester** firms, and the Herculaneum Pottery, **Liverpool**. They were joined by Hollins, Warburton, Daniel & Company of **New Hall** in 1810, the **Wedgwood** firm in 1812, and the Bramelds of **Rockingham** 1820. In addition eighteen lesser known Staffordshire potters were recorded as being in the bone china trade by 1818. Very little of their ware was marked.

BOOTE, T. and R. *See* **Parian ware.**

BOOTH, ENOCH (Tunstall)

Established 1742 as a **salt-glazed stoneware** potter and in about 1750 introduced the method of glazing by biscuiting the ware and dipping it into a **liquid glaze** containing lead oxide and flint. Made **cream-coloured earthenware** from about 1760.

Late in the 19th century the firm's managing director, Charles Bowers, succeeded in reproducing the blue colour characteristic of the period 1750 to 1800, and applied it to the decoration of perforated baskets, plates and dessert services, tea-pots, coffee-pots, leaf-shaped dishes and so on, in designs and made by methods that had been in fashion at that time. These are marked BOOTHS SILICON CHINA with either C B in monogram or the date 1750.

BOREHAM, ZACHARIAH (1738–1810). *See* **Derby.**

BOURNE, SAMUEL (Shelton, Staffordshire)

Maker of **figures** in the style of **Wood** between about 1775 and 1803. His mark was S. Bourne impressed.

BOURNE'S POTTERIES

Makers of domestic articles and

spirit flasks in brown **stoneware.** William Bourne, a potter of Belper, acquired land at Denby in 1809 containing deposits of stoneware clay later recognized as the finest in Europe. Here his son Joseph founded the celebrated **Denby Pottery** still in operation. Mark: BOURNE.

BOW

The first porcelain to be associated with the name of Bow was manufactured in Middlesex, not in the more celebrated china works at Stratford-le-Bow in Essex. This early **soft-paste porcelain** was made under a patent taken out in 1744 by Edward Heylyn and **Thomas Frye**. Porcelain made in accordance with their specification must necessarily have had a white glassy body possibly flawed by fire-cracks, specked, and slightly warped. The project was unsuccessful as production had been abandoned by 1748.

Frye continued experimenting, his intention being to develop a utility ware that could be sold at prices considerably lower than those charged for wares imported from China and Saxony. His researches met with success when he evolved a formula in which calcined bones were a new and important ingredient. His application for a patent was granted November 11, 1749. This new paste was sponsored by the firm of Weatherby and Crowther, who built a factory at Stratford-le-Bow to manufacture the ware. This was known as New Canton, and Frye was appointed works superintendent.

So far as **paste, glaze** and decorations are concerned Bow porcelain may be grouped into three main classes: 1750–56; 1753–63; and 1764–75. Even within these dates there are variations according to the quality of materials available: manufacturing processes were far from standardized.

The dense-textured, cream-coloured paste made at New Canton until 1756 was notable for its freedom from the grease spot or **moon** defects associated with **Chelsea** porcelain. The thinner areas of Bow porcelain are translucent, but normally the ware is thick in section and appears opaque when held to the light, often to the extent of suggesting **earthenware.** By transmitted light the translucent areas may appear yellowish-green, but this tinge is in the glaze and not in the paste itself. Other distinctive features are its great weight and surprising strength: being hard, compact and vitreous, Bow porcelain will chip, but seldom crack. Two types of **lead glaze** were used and both were applied thickly. One was a virtually transparent glaze of the glassy type, with a faintly bluish tinge and soft enough to be scratched easily, applied to underglaze decoration. The other was a thick creamy glaze, either faintly blue or with a slight tinge of greenish-yellow: this appeared on **blanc-de-chine** and also was a ground for painting with coloured enamels.

An improved, softer paste, creamy

yellow in tone, had been evolved by 1756 and this was used until 1763. Transmitted light reveals bright flecks in its texture. The more amenable quality of this paste led to the large-scale production of **figures** and other ornamental porcelain. The glaze had now become smooth and ivory-tinted, concealing flaws and specks in the paste, and providing a richer ground for enamel **colours** and **honey gilding**. The transparent glaze continued in use with blue and white underglaze ware. The centres of some plates made during the second period have the slight central kick found on contemporaneous Chinese work: plate centres might be two or three times as thick as their rims.

After 1763 until the factory closed in 1775 the paste was harshly white, potted with a thinner section than formerly and displaying a faintly brown tinge when held to the light. The glaze was less carefully prepared than formerly and was liable to be flawed with black specks.

Plain white porcelain, known to collectors as blanc-de-chine, and blue and white domestic ware were the mainstay of the first period. It has been estimated that in 1750 Bow issued more than 20,000 pieces of soft-paste porcelain, and output had doubled by 1755. The blue is recognized by its tendency to blur and spread around the edges of the design. During the second period an almost indigo purple was characteristic, in a number of tints. Powder blue (*see* **Cobalt**) grounds with reserves for designs in underglaze blue were frequent.

Enamel painting in colours was used comparatively little until 1753, when the **Japanese** style of chrysanthemum decoration on criss-cross panels came into use. Colours were red, green, blue, and yellow, applied over the glaze with the addition of some gilding. The curious brownish-red enamel on Bow japan porcelain, commonly known as "sealing wax red", is usually lacking in gloss and has a tendency to fall away from the glaze. Blue enamel displays a lifeless opacity. An unpleasant pale mauve-pink, known to collectors as gold-purple, applied in thin washes, was a Bow feature at this time.

Bow introduced the celebrated quail or partridge design composed of a blue-stemmed tree displaying brilliant red and gold blossoms, with two quails or partridges sheltering beneath, sometimes with hedges and wheat-sheaves, all on a white ground with a narrow edge of thick foliage in red.

Famille rose designs appear to have been copied by Bow directly from Chinese export porcelain in thickly applied clear enamels.

Some elaborate table-ware was made after 1764, decoration including raised vine sprigs, enamelled fruits and birds, and blue underglaze reserves containing colourful birds or paintings in the current French manner. Later the blue grounds might be dia-

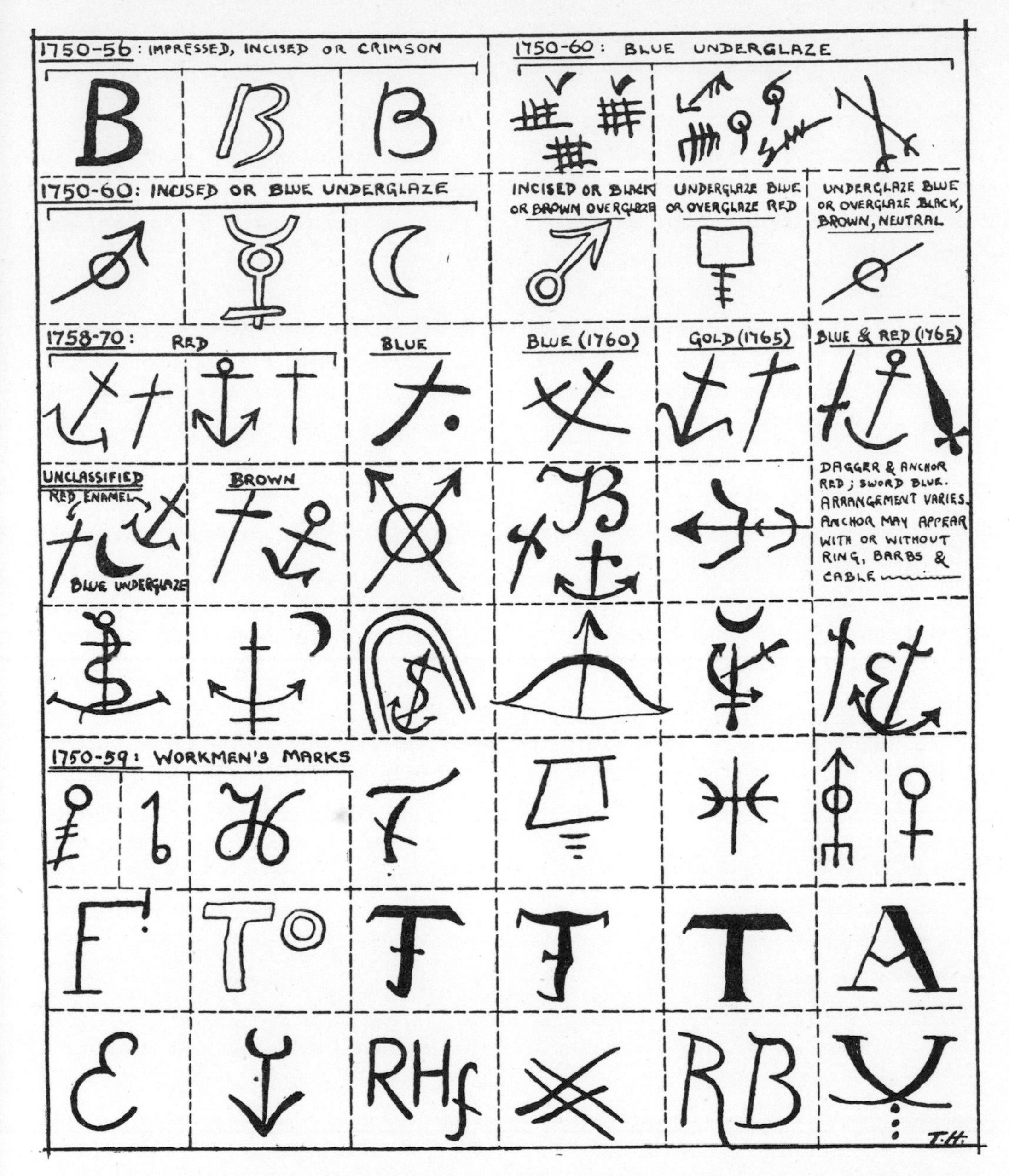

Among marks used until about 1756 were several versions of the letter "B", incised, impressed or in crimson; three thick vertical lines crossed by three horizontal lines, and similar pseudo-oriental marks in blue underglaze.

Contemporary and until 1760 were a circle crossed by an arrow, sometimes modified to a "C" crossed by a stroke; crossed daggers in blue underglaze; a crescent or the sign of the planet Mercury in blue underglaze.

From 1758 to 1770, the sword in blue was used. The anchor and dagger found on Bow porcelain is now attributed to the decorator James Giles. Late in the period the anchor might have a cable. Rebus marks such as a violin bow and a bow and arrow are also known.

Workmen's marks were numerous until about 1760 and included the numerals 1 to 49. Some blue-and-white pieces are marked with "TF", the monogram of Thomas Frye. "R.H.f." is the signature of Robert Hancock, who engraved transfer designs for Frye, probably working as a freelance artist. The mark "T°" is thought to refer to the decorator Thibaud, or Tebo.

pered in gold. A little **transfer printing** was carried out in black, brick red, or dull manganese purple, often enclosed within hand-painted borders.

A high reputation was acquired by Bow for its carefully modelled **figures** after the style of **Dresden**. Few date earlier than 1754, and these are either white or decorated in blue under the glaze. These are characterized by vigorous modelling, but are full of technical imperfections. Early coloured figures are somewhat florid. Copies of Dresden figures began to be made by 1756, their height seldom exceeding eleven inches. Until about 1758 they usually stood upon flat, rectangular bases, either lacking all ornament or with scarcely perceptible scrolls in low relief. By about 1758 a more elaborate stand was evolved with scrolls so designed that the corners of the base became small supporting feet. Small figures generally stood upon round, flat-based pedestals. After 1764 Bow figures became costlier and richer, and their pedestals were designed with gracefully pierced scrolls.

Close examination of the surface of a Bow figure will often disclose marks caused by the modeller's flat knife or other tool used for smoothing the surface and accentuating lines before firing. This is particularly noticeable on drapery. Other factories more simply removed surface roughness by means of a wet brush, as is done to-day.

BRAMELD

A family of potters operating the **Rockingham** factory at Swinton, Yorkshire and associated with **Leeds** 1787–1806.

BRAMPTON (near Chesterfield, Derbyshire)

Established mid-18th century by John Oldfield to make a brown **stoneware** from local clay and usually **salt-glazed**. Interiors of 18th-century examples were sometimes greyish-white; decorations were usually **sprigged** or in moulded relief. Productions included **bear jugs**, posset pots, tobacco jars with thick pressers, **puzzle jugs**, tea-pots, liquor jars, **spirit flasks** and a wide range of domestic ware, continuing until the mid-19th century in forms differing little throughout the period. Marks J. OLDFIELD. CHESTERFIELD; OLDFIELD & CO; J. OLDFIELD & CO.

BRIDDEN. *See* **Chesterfield**.

BRISLINGTON (near Bristol)

A **delft ware** pottery operated from about 1650 to 1752 when it was offered for sale. Its imports of Spanish **lustre ware** have led to the erroneous theory that lustre was made here.

BRISTOL

This Gloucestershire seaport is believed to have produced pottery from the time of Edward I. **Tygs**, jugs and **mugs** are recorded in the late 16th century, but the trade was not fully established until 1671, when pottery apprentices were first recorded in the Bristol apprentice list which was begun in 1593.

Delft ware: late 17th-century examples bear a close resemblance to **Lambeth** productions, no doubt as a consequence of attracting artists and other skilled workers at the time of its first establishment. Numerous delft ware potters are recorded by name, from Edward Ward of **Brislington** who built the Temple Back Pottery in 1683 until the ware was superseded by **cream-coloured earthenware** late in the 18th century. Ward's pupil, Thomas Frank, established a delft ware pottery at Brislington, sold to Thomas Dixon in 1706, when he began to operate another pottery at Redcliff Back in Bristol. Bristol delft has a buff-tinted body, harder, denser, slightly more reddish in hue than the Dutch. The slightly tinted tin-glaze *see* **Delft-ware** is thicker, muddier and harder than that used elsewhere. Hollow ware is characterized by *wreathing*.

Symmetrical flowers are characteristic, and colouring includes a slaty blue, "quaker green", dull yellow, brownish-orange, manganese, and pale turquoise-blue. The tones are softer than London-prepared **colours**. The styles of a few painters have been recognized: the majority of decorators were mere copyists working from a masterpiece painted by the head decorator. John Bowen (apprenticed 1734) is associated with individualistic painting in blue on white, creating scenes in which stately men and women are seen among tall, misty trees and gaunt houses depicted with great economy of line and colour: on the other hand his ships are meticulously detailed.

The Bristol decorators took great interest in Chinese designs. Many were at hand in the dock warehouses that imported porcelains from the East, and ships' captains, too, were commissioned to carry back sample pieces for copying or adapting to speedy reproduction. The early vigorous colours and bold style of painting gave place to softer tones and more delicate lines towards the mid-18th century. Colours continued to be restricted to the underglaze range, fired with the glaze. Much was in blue and white, and more in the Chinese **famille verte** palette. There was also effective use of the **bianco-sopra-bianco** style in imitation of Chinese incised work, the starch blue or lavender blue plate painted with a broad band of white flowers in slight relief around a central ornament consisting of landscapes in blue, or bouquets of flowers in purple-blue, olive green, and brownish-orange.

Among the wide variety of ware made were plates with edges octagonal, foliated, or scalloped. Punch bowls had flattened flaring sides tangential to the curves of the bottoms. Spout cups sometimes had lids in the form of a royal crown with openware bows such as might be found in contemporary flint-glass, with handles in the form of snakes or rolls of clay twisted into the shape of coiled tendrils. Rectangular flower holders were shaped as hollow bricks fitted with loose grids. Such a grid was pierced with a large square hole centrally placed and flanked each side by six, nine or twelve holes for flower stems. **Tiles** were made by most of the Bristol delft ware potters. Brown **salt-glazed stoneware** was made by several Bristol potters but none has been noted with a mark.

Soft-paste porcelain: was made at Bristol between 1748 and 1752, **soapstone** being used as an ingredient instead of kaolin. The resulting porcelain has a hard compact texture and is found in two distinct types:

(a) with a creamy-white tinge, of high translucency and showing ivory if held to the light;

(b) with a greyish tinge, less translucent, and appearing greenish if held to the light.

The thin **glaze**, imperfectly opacified, at first displayed tiny bubbles, quickly improved but always flawed with a multiplicity of microscopic pittings. A starchy blue tinge is characteristic of the glaze in association with blue underglaze decoration. In enamel printed ware the glaze has a warm ivory tint: this glaze receded a little from the foot ring when fired. Blue underglaze decoration is usually badly blurred and frequent in poorly executed *chinoiserie* designs. Enamel painted decoration is in the *famille verte* and *famile rose* styles.

Sauce boats in designs adapted or copied from silver plate appear to have been a principal production: bodies were moulded with poorly trimmed joints; feet and handles were attached with liquid slip. Characteristic features were: rosettes at the body-handle

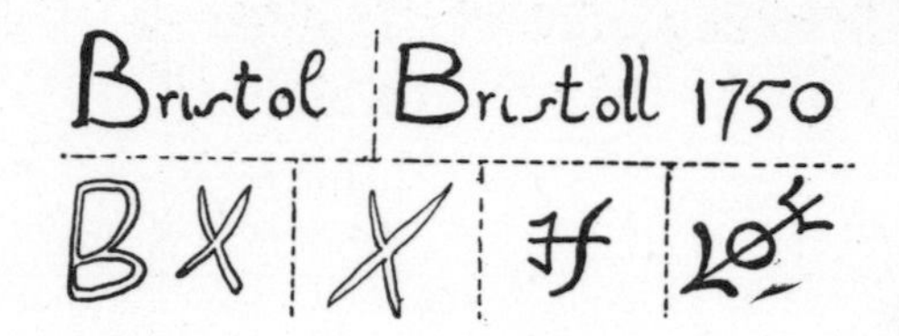

junctions; always a thumb-rest on the handle; an expanded lip usually decorated with flowers or oriental emblems; decoration with running scrolls inside the rim. Exteriors were ornamented with relief work, usually scrolls and festoons, often forming a shallow cartouche on each side of the bowl, framing decoration in blue underglaze or enamels. Examples in the British Museum bear in relief the name BRISTOLL. The top marks in the sketch are impressed in relief; the two bottom left marks are incised; those on right are probably workmen's marks.

This factory is sometimes referred to as Lowdin's Porcelain Factory. Lowdin, the previous occupier of the premises, died in 1745 and his name has been wrongly confused with those of the proprietors—Benjamin Lund

Plymouth porcelain figure emblematic of America.

"Autumn", a Bow porcelain figure of about 1770

Worcester porcelain, gardener and wife. 1770s.

Longton Hall porcelain figures, about 1755.

1. (*Top*) Bow blanc de chine porcelain group of a lady and page, 6 inches high. Early 1750s. (*Below*) Derby biscuit porcelain group of three children representing Minerva crowning Constancy and Hercules killing the Hydra. About 1775. Height 12$\frac{5}{8}$ inches. (*Left*) Bow fortune-teller group, enamelled, inspired by a panel of Beauvais tapestry signed by Boucher. About 1760. (*Right*) Bow shepherdess, about 1760.

2. (*Upper left*) Chelsea tureen in the form of a swan floating on a flat oval dish. Mark: red anchor. Height 14½ inches, length 20 inches. (*Upper right*) Chelsea tureen, sitting hen with a chicken perched on her back, coloured in purple shades with dashes of brown and blood red. Mark: red anchor. About 1755. (*Lower left*) Chelsea parrot and two partridges; mark, raised anchor. (*Lower right*) Chelsea cow and sheep.

and **William Cookworthy** or William Miller. Formulæ, plant, tools and stock were acquired in mid-1752 by **Dr. Wall** and his associates at **Worcester.**

Cookworthy's hard-paste porcelain: William Cookworthy transferred his business from **Plymouth** in 1770. There appears to have been little difference between his Bristol ware and that made at Plymouth: it still remained technically imperfect and inclined to show slight warping. The business and patent were acquired by **Richard Champion** in 1773. The mark at Bristol at first continued to be the chemist's symbol for tin, as used at Plymouth; later a cross in blue enamel or gold with a capital B was used on domestic ware.

Champion's hard-paste porcelain (1773-82): possessed of the exclusive rights to prepare china clay and manufacture hard-paste porcelain Richard Champion envisaged vast profits, foreshadowing a yearly royalty of £100,000 for Thomas Pitt, from whose lands the china clay was obtained. He was fully aware that the quality of the porcelain made by Cookworthy left much to be desired, and he applied for a fourteen-year extension of the patent beyond the expiry date of 1782. This brought about costly litigation, ending in Champion being granted exclusive rights to use Cornish china stone in the manufacture of translucent porcelain: its use was allowed freely to makers of opaque pottery. Thus was created a monopoly which effectively prevented the development of the **bone china** industry until the close of 1796. Financial troubles befell Champion during the next two years, including the capture of his merchant fleet by the French, and active manufacture of porcelain was suspended in the autumn of 1778. Large accumulated stocks of **biscuit** ware, however, were decorated and sold until 1782.

Champion's hard porcelain is white, faintly tinged with grey, and many examples are warped or fire-cracked. If held to the light the tint seen varies from a cold white-grey to a faintly yellowish-green, and small tears are noted reminiscent of **Chelsea moons.** Translucency varies with thickness and quality, the result of variations in raw materials and changes in blending. Its surface appearance, however, is fairly constant. The surface is liable to be marred with brownish specks, and grit is often to be noted in a foot ring. Hollow-ware displays distinct **wreathing.**

On fine quality porcelain the **glaze** is thin, clear, brilliant, and even-surfaced, its colour being almost identical with that of the paste. This glaze, always hard enough to withstand wear and stains, appears to be perfectly fused with the body, rather than as a separate layer in the manner of soft porcelain glazes. Enamels did not sink into it as into frit glazes: rising slightly above the surface they were in danger of peeling off with use. On blue and white and cheap ware Champion used a frit glaze, lustrous and faintly blue in tint.

The greater part of Champion's output consisted of tea ware, for which the heat-resisting hard-paste porcelain

Marks on Champion's Bristol porcelain

was eminently suitable. Dishes and other flat ware liable to sink and warp in the kiln were supported beneath by strengthening ribs. On an oval dish the rib resembled a raised pot hook down the centre of the underside: a plate would be given a supporting ring. Such strengtheners were slightly shallower than the outer rims.

The majority of Champion's porcelain appears to have been marked, with the notable exception of the figures. Four main marks were used, the principal being a cross, painted in blue enamel overglaze or impressed. On blue underglaze ware the cross is also in underglaze, and an occasional gilt cross has been noted. The letter B in blue underglaze was also used. Of the marks sketched, the second from left, top line, is in blue enamel and underglaze blue; the remainder are in blue enamel. On copies of **Dresden** ware the crossed swords, often with a dot between the hafts, might be used in underglaze blue. This might be accompanied by a cross, a letter B, or the artist's name, all in enamel overglaze.

Earthenware: during the mid 1780s the manufacture of **delft ware** in Bristol was being abandoned in favour of the **cream-coloured earthenware** with which potters in other districts were capturing the market. Joseph Ring from 1785 made a fine quality creamware, thin in section, with good edges and slightly yellower than **Wedgwood** or **Leeds**. The latter were cream-coloured throughout their fabric, but Ring's and other Bristol earthenware is characterized by its yellow glaze on a white body. The delft-ware decorators, skilled in blue painting, continued

in this medium which was gradually replaced by enamel decoration in colours. **Transfer-printing** dates from 1797. The mark shown above dates from about 1830 and is printed in blue.

BRISTOL BLUE. *See* **Cobalt.**

BROSELEY. *See* **Caughley.**

BS & T MARK

The impressed mark of Barker, Sutton and Till, of Burslem, makers of **figures,** busts, **lustre wares,** 1833–42.

C MARK. *See* **Caughley, Coalport, Palmer,** and **Worcester.**

CABARET

The name given by collectors to a **porcelain** tea-set fitting upon and including a matching oval porcelain tea-tray.

CADBOROUGH (near Rye, Sussex) WARE

Red **earthenware** coated with a brilliant thick yellow **lead glaze** streaked with delightful effect owing to the presence of iron in the clay. Established 1790 by the Smith family and transferred to the Mitchells in 1840.

Some of the ware was decorated with inlaid **slip** in the manner of medieval tiles: consequently examples are often wrongly pre-dated. Sussex pigs were made here, the body forming a jug and the head a loose cup. These pig drinking vessels are still made at the Belle Vue Pottery, Rye, an offshoot of Cadborough.

"CADOGAN" TEA OR HOT WATER POT

First made by Thomas Bingley at **Swinton.** Modelled from a peach-shaped wine-jug of Indian green ware given to the **Bramelds** by the Hon. Mrs. Cadogan. The characteristic manganese-brown glazed **Rockingham** vessel possessed no lid aperture and apparently lacked any opening for inserting the liquid, except a hole in the base. There was nothing to indicate that this hole was the entrance of a tube spiralling up inside the pot to within an inch of the top. By turning the pot upside down tea, strained clear of its leaves, might be poured into the hole, passing through the tube to the body of the pot, whereupon the vessel could safely be righted. Such tea-pots were ornamented with flowers, foliage and fruits in relief, sometimes gilded. Large quantities were bought by the London dealer Mortlock whose name was impressed beneath.

Tea-pots of the same shape were made by **John Turner** of Lane End and were impressed TURNER, and by **Spode.**

CALLOT DWARFS

Grotesque figures made at **Chelsea,** adapted from **Dresden** examples which

in their turn had been inspired by engravings in the book *Il Calotto Resuscitato* published in Amsterdam 1716 containing caricatures of a miscellaneous assemblage of soldiers, peasants, pedlars and so on. In 1784 they were re-adapted by **Derby** in **soft-paste porcelain** and reappeared again in 19th-century **bone china.** They are known to collectors as the Mansion House Dwarfs because in 1780 similar figures had been placed at the Mansion House for advertising display purposes. The hats of the Derby figures were inscribed with announcements.

CAMBRIAN ARGIL. *See* **Mason Ware.**

CAMBRIAN POTTERY

Earthenware made in Wales but most frequently associated with **Swansea** under George Haynes, late 1770s to 1801. The mark was continued in the early 19th century by L. W. Dillwyn. *See* **Swansea.**

CANE WARE

Tan-coloured fine-grained **stoneware** introduced by **Josiah Wedgwood** in 1770. He refined the clays used by the peasant potters for their buff brown wares into a new and lighter body which he ornamented with embossed decoration in the same colour. The material was found very suitable, too, for busts and statuettes. It was also used by **John Turner** of Lane End for inkstands, bulb pots, wine-coolers, bowls, dishes and jugs. During the early 1800s it was used for imitation piecrusts.

CARPET BOWLS

Pottery balls about four inches in diameter used for the early Victorian game of carpet bowls. Examples are found decorated in all colours and in white, marbled, or painted with conventionally patterned foliage or starry designs in green, red, and black. Made by the **Sunderland Pottery** and elsewhere.

CARVING

Decoration produced by hand cutting into the moulded ware after the first baking and before placing in the biscuit kiln. The operation is usually confined to finishing touches, such as the cutting of fine details and the trimming of contours.

CASTING

A process of shaping hollow-ware introduced from the continent in 1730 by **Ralph Daniel** and first used in connection with **salt-glazed stoneware.** An original model was carved in alabaster: from this a stoneware copy was prepared which in its turn was used in the workshop for making the plaster-of-paris moulds in which the ware was actually cast.

Notching ensured that one part of the plaster mould locked tightly into the other. **Slip** or liquid clay containing **grog** was poured into the dry plaster-of-paris mould until it was filled. The mould immediately began to absorb moisture from the slip, and when this had caused a sufficient thickness of clay to adhere to the inside of the mould the surplus slip was poured out and the mould set to dry. In drying, the clay contracted, permitting the shaped piece to be removed easily. It was then carefully cleaned and the seam marks smoothed. After every fifty castings it was necessary to scrape the moulds to remove a deposit formed on the casting surface.

CASTLEFORD (Yorkshire)

Established in the mid-1790s by David Dunderdale who operated the pottery until 1821. He made a moderately fine **cream-coloured earthenware** in the style of **Leeds,** but less highly glazed and often with enamelled decoration copied from **Wedgwood**; black **basalts** in a wide range of objects with raised ornament in the Wedgwood style; table services and candlesticks in fine white half-glossy vitrified **stoneware** with relief patterns often outlined in bright blue enamel; **tortoiseshell ware** in the **Whieldon** manner. Some stoneware tea-pots had sliding covers: in others a hinged cover swung on a metal pin. The marks were impressed: until 1803 D D CASTLEFORD; then, when he was joined by John Plowes as partner, D D & Co CASTLEFORD or D D & CO CASTLEFORD POTTERY. *See* **Chessmen.**

CAUGHLEY (pronounced Cahflee, Shropshire)

Beds of clay were worked here by the Romans, who made bowls and jugs. The site overlooks the Severn Valley where all the essential materials for pottery making were found.

Earthenware: a pottery was established here 1750 by Ralph Browne of Caughley Hall who appointed John Thursfield as manager. The factory was leased in 1754 to a Mr. Galloway who carried on until his death in 1782. In 1772 he installed as manager Thomas Turner of **Worcester** who assumed entire control. In 1774 he was joined by **Robert Hancock** of Worcester. By 1775, after enlarging and modernizing the premises, Turner began to make **soft-paste porcelain** of the Worcester type, also producing fine **agate** ware, **cream-coloured earthenware**, and pottery or semi-china **figures,** busts and groups. Some of the latter were exceptionally well-modelled and include equestrian figures of "Hudibras", a group representing "The Creation", and a pair of figures "Ceres and Apollo". Caughley pottery of the Turner period was sometimes marked SALOPIAN or with the initials S or C in blue underglaze. The crescent of Worcester may also be noted.

Porcelain: that soft-paste porcelain was in production by 1775 is proved by an editorial comment in the local newspaper in August of that year. This stated that "the porcelain factory is now completed and the proprietors have received and completed orders for a very large amount . . . their productions in colour and fineness are truly elegant and beautiful, and have the bright and lively white of the so-much-extolled oriental". Caughley porcelain was **steatitic** like Worcester and consequently capable of withstanding boiling water. At first it was almost pure white with a cloudy orange or straw-coloured tinge when held to the light. A change was made in the porcelain during the early 1780s, resulting in a grey, hard-looking ware with an "orange-skin" surface, but retaining the straw-coloured tint against the light. **Glaze** was clear and brilliant with a distinct bluish tint entirely unlike the clear glaze of Worcester. Like Worcester, however, paste and glaze were so closely matched that **crazing** was virtually overcome. Caughley used glaze more lavishly than contemporary Worcester, the result being an uneven surface, with small pools of glaze collecting in crevices and sometimes on the bottoms of hollow-ware. Worcester glaze was thinly applied.

Turner controlled Caughley until 1799 when the competition of **bone china** destroyed almost overnight the demand for his soft-paste porcelain. He sold to John Rose of **Coalport,** who continued producing earthenware at the works, sending the **biscuit** to Coalport for glazing and decoration. Caughley was closed in 1814.

Thomas Turner realized the commercial value of decorating porcelain with **transfer-printing** underglaze. At first transfers were printed over the glaze in black, sepia and blue, but by 1776 underglaze blue transfers were being printed with clear vigorous lines in a quality not known elsewhere. Eventually four printing presses were kept continually occupied to produce the transfers. The production of the **willow** and other all-over pseudo-oriental patterns set the seal on Caughley's success.

In 1780 Turner visited the principal porcelain factories of France and returned with a number of experienced ceramic artists. Elaborate polychrome painting and **gilding** now became a feature and enamelled **mazarine blue** and gold a characteristic. These might be in the form of vertical bands of blue edged with gold and separated by white bands of equal width; the blue bands were closely covered with a fine network of geometrical hatchings, while the intervening white stripes might be filled with scrolls or arabesques in gold. There were several variants.

Queen Charlotte's pattern, issued by both Caughley and Worcester, was an elaborated form of the *Strohblumen Muster* design of **Dresden**. In the case of Caughley a plate would be divided into ten radiating panels, compared with eight at Worcester, and six at Dresden. The flowers were large, with scrolls and foliage filling the entire ground, but each was exactly symmetrical. (For sketch *see* **Worcester**.)

Sprays and foliage in blue and in gold, the cornflower, and many other motifs were copied from Chantilly porcelain. The dragon was another popular pattern, printed in two blues —a pure cobalt and lavender—and hand-touched with gold.

Caughley marks have not been greatly counterfeited. The letter S painted or printed in underglaze blue is found in many sizes and shapes and is sometimes preceded or followed by a star: it is sometimes found with the printed letter C. From 1782 porcelain decorated in the French manner was marked with S painted.

The name SALOPIAN impressed is found in several sizes differing by as much as $\frac{3}{8}$-inch on a single service. It was chiefly used on dessert and dinner

In the sketch, the top mark is impressed. The middle line blue (the second from left rarely in gold). The bottom left mark is often mistakenly assigned to Caughley. The others are typical disguised numerals.

services decorated with the mazarine blue and gold.

The crescent, horizontally barred or fully filled in, appears on all classes of Caughley porcelain except those pieces displaying the French influence. The capital C was always printed underglaze. It is found in association with SALOPIAN impressed, the letter S, and the small star. Copies of the Chantilly and Frankenthal marks have been recorded on Caughley porcelain.

CAULDON PLACE. *See* **Ridgway**.

CAULIFLOWER WARE

Cream-coloured earthenware modelled and coloured with green and yellow glazes in imitation of a cauliflower developed by **Josiah Wedgwood** during his partnership with **Whieldon** 1754–59. Such pieces are recognized by a clear orange-brown tint with applied foliage in pale yellow. The term is also understood to include similar wares based on melons, pineapples and maize. These were imitated by many other potters of the period, especially in Staffordshire. Reproductions were made in the mid-19th century, but modelling, colour and glaze were so inferior as to make them easily recognized.

CBD MARK. *See* **Coalport.**

CD MARK. *See* **Coalport.**

CDALE MARK. *See* **Coalport.**

CHAFFERS, RICHARD. *See* **Liverpool.**

CHALK BODY

A white earthenware made by adding chalk to the ingredients of a cream-coloured body.

CHAMBERLAIN

A family of potters operating at **Worcester** from 1783 until 1852.

CHAMPION, RICHARD (1743–91). *See* **Bristol porcelain.**

CHEETHAM AND WOOLEY (Lane End, Staffordshire)

Established late in the 18th century by Mark Cheetham, making pale buff **stoneware** and black **basalt.** In 1818 the firm was recorded as M. Cheetham & Son, and in the mid-1820s became Cheetham & Wooley, inventors of a hard **white stoneware** body resembling **bone china**: this formed a good medium for decoration in relief. The mark was impressed CHEETHAM.

CHELSEA PORCELAIN MANUFACTORY (London)

Established probably late in 1742 by Thomas Briand: a **goat-and-bee jug** incised with the name Chelsea and the date 1743 is the earliest authenticated piece of English **porcelain.** So closely does early Chelsea resemble the soft-paste porcelain developed in France by Baron Réamur that it is possible Briand was formerly employed at St. Cloud. Unlike other contemporary porcelain, Chelsea ware displays none of the uncertainties of an infant industry, although **paste, glaze,** modelling and decoration progressively improved during the 1740s.

It was Nicholas Sprimont (1716–71), however, who became the dominant personality at Chelsea with which he became directly associated late in 1746: a few months later skilled potters from Staffordshire were being attracted to Chelsea by high wages. Advertisements of the period suggest that production consisted mainly of table ware. Sprimont acted as manager, and it has long been conjectured that the Duke of Cumberland and his secretary Sir Everard Fawkener financed the factory: documents exist indicating that the duke invested sums of money in the firm. A temporary cessation of production took place from 1756 to 1758, and when Chelsea re-started it was with Sprimont outwardly as sole proprietor, using a paste strengthened by the addition of bone ash to the **frit**. The use of bone ash as an ingredient of soft-paste porcelain was monopolized until 1763 by **Thomas Frye's** patent of 1749 (*see* **Bow**). It must be assumed, therefore, that Frye licensed his process to Chelsea.

The project does not appear to have flourished financially, and between 1764 and 1769 production gradually "declined and the Porcelain became scarce". In February 1770 the plant and stock-in-trade were acquired by **William Duesbury** of **Derby** who continued the manufacture of porcelain at Chelsea until December 1783. The moulds and materials were then sent to Derby, and Christie's sold "all the remaining finished and unfinished stock of the Chelsea Porcelain Manufactory, with all the remaining buildings and fixtures."

Chelsea porcelain is briefly classified according to the five major changes made in the paste during the factory's existence. Each paste may be distinguished by a different group of marks, but it is essential for the beginner-collector to appreciate that Chelsea marks have been reproduced on all manner of fakes and imitations.

Incised triangle period (1743-47): the paste, creamy in colour and flawed with microscopic specks, has a satin-like texture. If held in the light, irregularly placed small round flecks, more translucent than the rest of the paste, are revealed in the milky white body. These, known as pin-holes, look like floating grease spots and are the fore-runners of the famous "**moons**" of the two following periods. The **glaze** was thickly applied and age has often given it a yellowish tinge. Soft and glossy, with occasional bubbles, it has usually become finely **crazed**.

Chelsea at this time was devoted almost entirely to the production of table ware, such as moulded cream jugs, salt cellars, coffee pots and tea-pots, usually undecorated. Embossed reliefs such as prunus blossom on white porcelain were frequent. Some of the early pieces were adapted from silver models—in fact, the term "silver shape" was later used in various Chelsea sale catalogues. The triangle was incised, beneath the glaze.

Raised anchor period (1747-53): modelling showed distinct technical advances but the paste was faintly greyish in tone. Pin-holes, now known to collectors as moons, were fewer and larger. After 1750 the body was whiter. A creamy glaze was used, thick like candle-grease and inclined to choke the modelling. Owing to its exceptional thickness, small pools of glaze were liable to accumulate in the middle of flat areas.

Domestic pieces still constituted the main productions, but some fine birds and a few **figures** were modelled. Much of the output was directly under the influence of **Dresden** and in the **Japanese Imari** style, such products continuing into the red anchor period. Tea services were made in variety, coloured in delightful pale shades.

The mark used was an anchor in relief on an applied medallion: from about 1751 the relief anchor was painted in red overglaze. This anchor sometimes appears on a circular pad with a raised edge. Occasionally an elaborate blue anchor is found underglaze: even more rare is the crown and trident in underglaze blue.

Red anchor period (1753–56): the paste was thinner than formerly, of finer grain and more translucent, although still possessing an abundance of moons and some exterior blemishes. The glaze was smooth, evenly applied, and seldom crazed. An almost constant feature of pieces of this paste is the appearance of three or four small round **spur marks** on the base.

Soft pastel colours were used to emphasize the delicacy of the sharp modelling. Much domestic ware, still copied from silver, was decorated in the oriental manner, finely painted by skilful artists. The earlier Chinese patterns in blue underglaze gave way to dainty decorations in red and gold. Leaves were now painted in light and yellowish greens, side by side, and veined in black. Applied flowers in full relief were introduced.

Excellent reproductions of the brocade patterns of Imari porcelain were also made, and border patterns in raised work were copied from Dresden. Sprays of flowers and fruit, painted with ornaments in low relief, were sparingly applied. White porcelain imported from the East was decorated by Chelsea artists in this style during a period of temporary closure between 1756 and 1758.

The plain red anchor was painted overglaze in varying forms and sizes, usually small and in a bright hue, but sometimes with a brownish tinge. The Chelsea anchor of this period is also found in brown and purple overglaze, and in blue underglaze. An anchor with a cable is found painted in red and incised: interlocked anchors, one inverted, are also found.

Gold anchor period (1750-69): differs entirely from earlier periods. The paste was now strengthened by the addition of bone ash and consequently was denser of texture, harder, chalky white, more translucent, but tended to suffer from cracking which is visible through the glaze. Mooning was overcome. The limpid, glassy glaze was liable to craze, and gathered in angles and hollows, where it showed a faintly green tinge. Spur marks were still present. This paste was made until 1769.

Modelling of figures became more

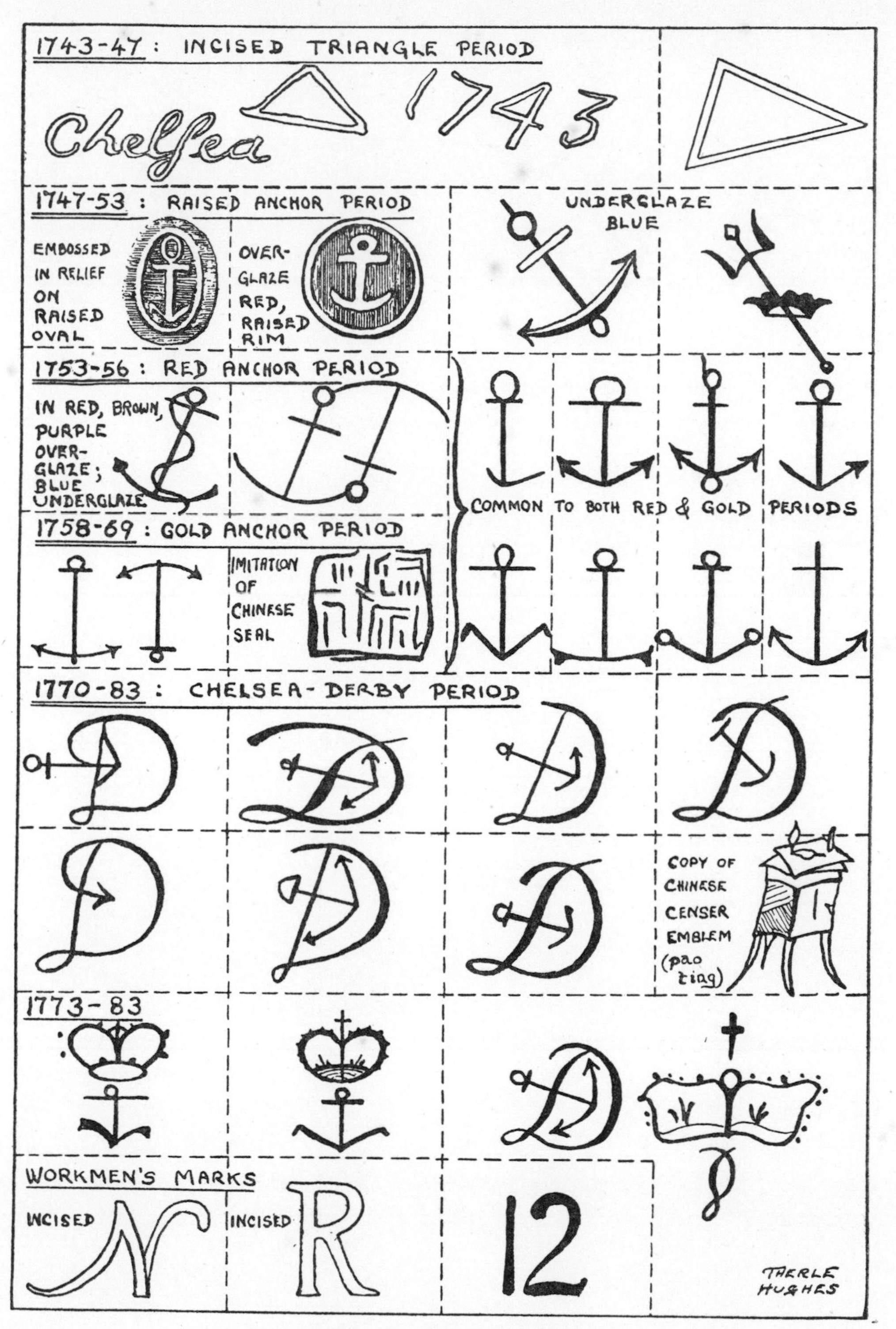

Marks on Chelsea porcelain

meticulous and enamels in pastel shades were replaced by a blaze of vivid colour enriched with **gilding.** Gilded scroll work was now introduced around the decorated panels on the white which formed the central motifs on sets of vases and tea and dessert services whose magnificence largely depended upon their rich and deservedly celebrated ground colours. The beautiful *gros bleu* or **mazarine blue** ground appeared in 1759; pea green in the same year; claret and turquoise in 1760; the rare yellow in 1761. These grounds, too, might be enriched with gold and chased.

The reserves were filled with bouquets, fruit, figure subjects and pastoral scenes copied from the works of artists such as Watteau and Teniers. Exotic birds of brilliant plumage were favourite features. More often than not they were large crested pheasants with sweeping tail feathers and might be accompanied by other equally colourful birds and insects. Yet another distinctively French style was a feature of Chelsea work from about 1765: large elaborate vases were made with pierced necks and covers, and wildly interlacing handles.

Gold anchor marks were in the same designs as the red. A pair of anchors in gold, one inverted but not interlocked, was an occasional mark. The smaller the anchor, either red or gold, the finer the quality of the piece. These marks are sometimes hidden in crevices and may be so insignificant as to be discovered only after careful search.

Chelsea figures have always been the admiration of connoisseurs. Early examples might recline directly upon the table or stand erect upon thin flat square plinths. Rococo scroll stands belong to the gold anchor period. The most charming sets of figures made during the red anchor period represented characters from the Italian Comedy taken from the famous Dresden models. Later there were elaborate shepherds and gallants with their companions, but not until the gold anchor period were vivid colours and gold enrichment used. Figure subjects were copied from paintings by Rubens, Teniers, Van Loo, Watteau, Boucher and others. Statuettes of contemporary celebrities were modelled after oil paintings and engravings. Figure modelling improved during the gold anchor period and those leafy heavily flowered bowers in which small figures were grouped, known to collectors as **bocages**, became highly popular. Some indication of the renown achieved by Chelsea figures is seen in the fact that in 1760 French and German potters petitioned their governments to prohibit the importation of Chelsea porcelain. *See* **Goat-and-bee jugs** *and* **Scent bottles.**

CHELSEA-DERBY PORCELAIN

A term applied to the productions of **Chelsea** during the period it was operated by **William Duesbury** from

1770 to 1783. Seldom were more than a dozen workers employed. Oriental and continental porcelain was lent to Duesbury for copying by the Duke of Newcastle and the Countess Spencer; Lord Lonsdale lent valuable sketches. When George III visited the factory in 1773 he gave Duesbury his patronage with permission to incorporate the royal crown in his trade mark.

Chelsea-Derby **figures** are notable for their interpretation of Louis XVI sentimental groups after the manner of paintings by Boucher, Falcourt, and others. Their scroll bases were more symmetrical than those used under the Sprimont regime. Colours were smoothly bright and included a pale turquoise, brilliant crimson, purple, green, orange, and chocolate. Eyes were given pin-point pupils and pale brown outlines: hair was smoothed on to the head, and cheeks faintly touched with crimson.

Table-ware followed the forms made fashionable by **Sèvres**, and decoration consisted chiefly of centrally placed urns, flower sprays, or cupids, with festoons and swags. The former costly ground colours were discarded in favour of a beautiful though inexpensive red. Edges might be gilt-lined or dotted, and foot rims were usually encircled with single gold lines. Chelsea-Derby leaves were dark green and twisted. Marks were in gold: a Chelsea anchor traversing the downstroke of a script D: from 1773 a jewelled crown was painted above the anchor.

CHESSMEN

Josiah **Wedgwood** was the first English potter to make chessmen. In 1784 he commissioned a set of models from John Flaxman to represent actors playing *Macbeth*. Charles Kemble's interpretation of Duncan, King of Scotland, was used for the king; Mrs. Siddons as Lady Macbeth was the queen. Three differing models of the king and queen are known. One model only was used for each of the remaining pieces, the rooks having square crenellated towers, the knights mounted on rearing horses, and the bishops vested in copes and mitres. The pawns were foot-soldiers, armed with primitive weapons—stones, battle-axes, daggers and bows and arrows. In the sets intended for the French market bishops were replaced by jesters, referred to in Wedgwood's oven-trial books as "Tom Fools".

Wedgwood chessmen are found with three types of bases. Rough mounds serving as footholds for the figures are indicative of the rare 1784 edition in blue and white **jasper**. These were followed by flat, wafer-like bases, in their turn superseded by Attic bases—short, plainly turned classical plinths of jasper. Wedgwood sold chess sets between 1785 and 1795 at five guineas the set in grey, mauve, blue, buff, Flemish green, dark biscuit, and brilliant white. Pieces were usually one colour throughout, sometimes enlivened with gold pencilling; the white were on coloured bases. The mark was always WEDGWOOD impressed, early examples also bearing model numbers and workmen's single initials or fine lines. Flaxman sets in jasper were sold throughout the 19th century.

Jasper chessmen from 1849 might have bases of ebonized and natural boxwood to distinguish the opposing sides. These sold at £3 10*s*. 6*d* the set and **stoneware** chessmen of the same period at £3 1*s*. 6*d*. In about 1880 Flaxman chessmen were made in **queen's ware**, with black inlay on the cream base.

Rockingham issued finely modelled chessmen in **bone china** attired in the Tudor fashion. Also less pretentious sets in the conventional turned design (not the Staunton pattern devised in 1847), in apple green and periwinkle blue enlivened with gilding. These were made between 1822 and 1826.

The **Castleford** pottery is credited with having made porcelain chessmen, but there is no record that porcelain was made there, although a half-glossy stoneware might have been used. In the so-called Castleford chess-sets, dating from 1795, the king and queen represented George III and Queen Charlotte, crowned and in their state robes, the pawns being kilted Scots Guards. Elephants supporting howdahs in the form of square, castellated towers were the rooks. Both sides were from the same moulds, the colours being chocolate brown and grey-green, white and grey-blue, black and white. These pieces were unmarked and have been extensively copied.

CHESTERFIELD (Derbyshire)

A deed in the possession of the Walton Pottery proves the existence of a pottery here in 1830. This was operated in succession by Henry, William, John and Ensor Bridden. Common drinking vessels were made in buff-coloured and brown **stoneware** decorated with applied reliefs. **Bear jugs** and tea-pots have been noted with the impressed mark BRIDDEN.

"CHEVERTON Sc." MARK. *See* **Parian ware**

CHILD AND CLIVE (Tunstall, Staffordshire)

Established in 1783 by Smith Child, a grandson of **Enoch Booth**. They made **cream-coloured earthenware** decorated with painting, **transfer-printing**, and **piercing**, and was in operation until the 1820s. The impressed mark CHILD is often noted.

CHINA

A term applied to a wide variety of ceramics. Technically china means a hard, vitreous **porcelain**, translucent and cold to the touch. Originally the word was used in England to distinguish imported Chinese porcelains from native **earthenware**, but later in the 18th century it was applied to all kinds of white pottery, particularly to blue and white painted wares. In everyday parlance it has come to mean table ware of all kinds, from delicate porcelain cups to rough earthenware mugs, although the terms earthenware and pottery are more generally applied correctly. *See* **Bone China.**

CHINA CLAY

The purest and whitest form of clay. It is obtained in Cornwall and Devon by crushing china clay rock and washing away impurities. It is soft to the touch and feels soapy and is usually regarded as kaolin although differing in many respects. It is used in the manufacture of **porcelain, bone china, earthenware** and **stoneware.** When mixed with ball clay for earthenware it facilitates moulding and gives greater strength.

CHINA STONE. *See* **Cornish Stone.**

CHRISTIAN, PHILIP. *See* **Liverpool.**

CHURCH GRESLEY (Burton-on-Trent)

It is believed that a soft-paste porcelain was made here between 1794 and 1808 but no authenticated piece has yet come to light.

CLEAR GLAZE

A transparent glaze resembling glass. This need not be colourless but is sufficiently light to reveal the material beneath.

CLEWS, JAMES and RALPH (Cobridge)

In 1819 succeeded **Andrew Stevenson** as makers of blue and white **transfer-printed** ware. On a much smaller scale they printed in red, brown and black. The Clews were responsible for three very popular series of transfer prints: the "Three Tours of Doctor Syntax"; "Don Quixote", and the "Pictures of Sir David Wilkie". There were some eighty Syntax designs adapted from Thomas Rowlandson's illustrations to William Combe's books of verse published between 1815 and 1821. Borders were composed of large roses and other flowers interspersed with small scrolls. Each piece was marked in blue with the title of the picture in script enclosed in a decorative rectangle. There were about twenty Don Quixote subjects with borders composed of various flowers with reserves containing prints from the same series. There were twelve Wilkie pictures.

Their English views, totalling nearly two hundred, were issued in three series: "English Views", with borders of bell-flowers and other flowers and leaves, or of foliage and intricate scrollwork; "Select Views", with borders of large aster-like flowers and bell-flowers; and "Picturesque Views", a late series, most examples being found in colours other than blue. Some borders appear on p. 149. These pictures carried title imprints on their backs as well as the name of the firm, which closed in 1834, James Clews going to America where he founded another pottery.

CLOBBERING

Decoration applied to **porcelain** or **earthenware** in which simple underglaze blue transfer-printed outline was enriched by overglaze enamel **colours** and **gilding** such as could not be applied underglaze. Clobbered specimens can usually be detected, for the underglaze blue is seldom entirely covered by the clobbering.

COALBROOKDALE or COLEBROOKDALE. *See* **Coalport.**

COALPORT (Shropshire)

Founded in 1795 by John Rose, an apprentice at **Caughley** until 1785 when he established a small pottery at Jackfield. In 1795 he moved to Coalport and built premises on the canal bank opposite Caughley, which he acquired in 1799 and absorbed in 1814. By 1798 Rose was making **bone china** and until 1830 Coalport was largely engaged in supplying this in the white to London and provincial dealers and enamellers although much decorated ware was issued. From about 1822 Coalport also issued an improved **felspar porcelain.** John Rose died in 1828 leaving the business to his son John Rose II, who died in 1841 and was succeeded by his nephew W. F. Rose.

Coalport bone china was at first flawed with black spots, and possessed little translucency, but nevertheless was whiter and less costly to make than Caughley **soapstone porcelain.** The felspar porcelain was hard, translucent, and brilliantly white. **Glaze** was soft and smooth until 1820 when Rose evolved his celebrated hard, white, highly lustrous **leadless glaze**, but this was used only on costly ware and was continued on bone china until about 1840.

Until the early 1820s decoration was confined chiefly to painting and printing in underglaze blue in the Caughley manner, including the **willow** and dragon patterns: a small amount of polychrome work was produced such as **transfer-printed** designs in pink or purple outline, in which some portions were filled with brushwork, the remainder left uncoloured. Motifs on Coalport domestic ware at this period were more sparsely applied than on competing productions. Flower painting was mannered and **gilding** unusually light in colour. In 1821 Samuel Walker introduced a maroon ground which became a Coalport characteristic. Coalport decoration became richer and more varied during the reign of George IV; splendid dinner, dessert and tea services were issued in brilliant **colours** and highly burnished gilding.

John Rose II went to great expense to emulate the rich ground colours of **Sèvres**, especially turquoise known as "celeste" until 1840 when an improved version was evolved. The claret of **Chelsea** and the deep velvety **maza-**

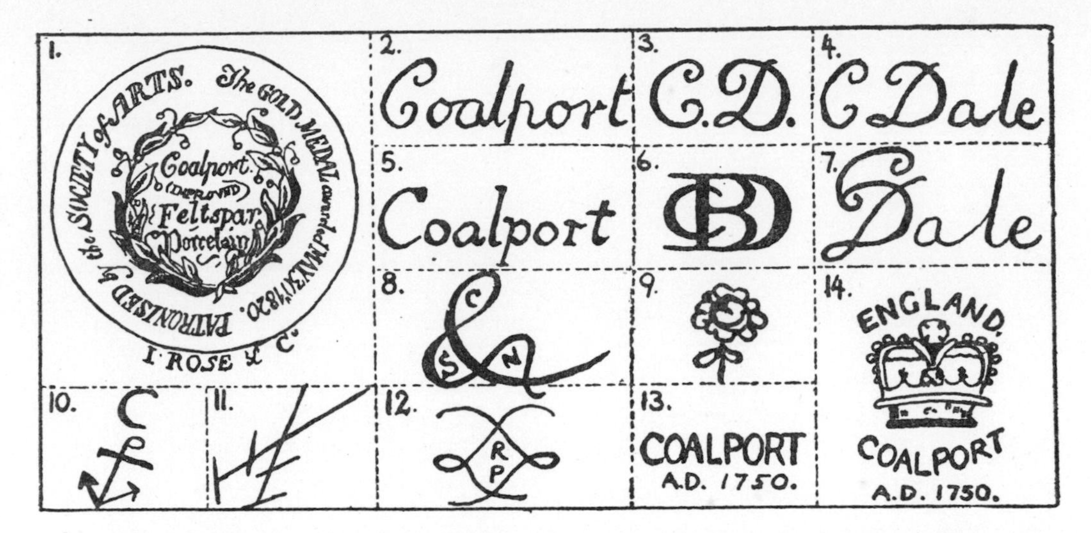

rine of Duesbury's **Derby** were other successful efforts in ground colour decoration.

Coalport by 1830 was recognized as one of the most important potteries in England. Decorative ware such as vases, clock cases, inkstands, and the familiar cottage designs for pastille burners and nightlights might be enriched with masses of tiny flowers modelled in the round (*see* **Flower-encrusted bone china**), and on fine work often enclosing painted landscape panels.

There is no typical Coalport style of decoration, although unmarked pieces may be recognized by their characteristically clean painting in bright fresh colouring. A series of wide-mouthed jugs in various sizes, often painted with large pink roses and inscribed beneath the lip, were a Coalport speciality of 1828–40, but often assumed to be much earlier. From about 1840 flat slabs of bone china decorated with naturalistic groups of flowers and fruits had a considerable vogue. Coalport made particularly handsome examples in the form of trays, wall pictures with burnished gilt frames, furniture and fireplace decorations. **Egg-shell china** of paper-thinness was made from 1845. Coalport was the first English pottery to produce the famous *rose pompadour* colour for which a gold medal was awarded at the Great Exhibition 1851.

Early Coalport bone china was unmarked, but examples of Coalport–Caughley might be marked C, S, or with various disguised numerals in blue underglaze. From 1815 to 1828 the name Coalport was painted in blue script underglaze. Felspar porcelain at first was marked J. R F. S CO. printed in red, suggesting that Rose formed a separate company for its development. More usually the mark was a circle two inches in diameter inscribed "Coalport (Improved) Feltspar Porcelain" within a laurel wreath encircled with the words "Patronised by the Society of Arts. The Gold Medal awarded May 30th 1820". This was printed in red and the inscription might include the name J. Rose. Marks on bone china from 1828 until about 1850 included: JOHN ROSE & CO., COLEBROOK DALE; C.D.; C. DALE.; C.B. D., in blue script of various forms. A monogram C B D in blue or gold was used from about 1851 to 1861. From then until 1875 a C combined with an S scroll forming three loops containing the letters C S N was used in gold, occasionally in red or blue enamel. Between 1775 and 1881 the mark was COALPORT A D 1750; betweeen 1881 and 1895 the same with the addition of a crown. In the sketch on page 47, the marks are: 1. From 1820 onwards, printed in red; 2. 1815–28, painted in blue script; 3–7. "Coalport" and various shortenings of "Colebrook Dale" used 1828 to *c.* 1850; No. 6 possibly to 1861; 8. 1861–75, the letters standing for factories which they claimed to have incorporated—Caughley, Swansea, **Nantgarw**; 9. Rare—for John or W. Rose.; 10–12. Adaptations of other firms' marks—Chelsea, **Dresden**, Sèvres; 13. 1875–81. This mark shows the introduction of the date 1750 which the firm claimed as its date of foundation; 14. A later specimen, used from 1894, when the word "England" was required by law.

COBALT BLUE

Prepared from cobalt oxide discovered in Saxony by Schürer 1545. This he named zaffre and a finer preparation smalt. It was used by the makers of English **delft ware** as their chief source of decoration. In the 18th century the colour was used on **salt-glazed stoneware**, **soft porcelain**, **earthenware**, and, from 1796, **bone china**. When applied to the ware it was a dirty brown in colour: firing at a suitable equable temperature converted it into the celebrated cobalt blue. English importations from Saxony were always substantial, but from 1730 the demand for zaffre and smalt (*see* below) progressively increased so that 180,000 lb. came into the country during 1748 and 286,000 lb. by 1754.

Supplies ceased from 1756 until 1763 when Saxony was involved in war with Prussia. English deposits of cobalt were thereupon worked, encouraged by the Society of Arts. Contemporary opinion appears to have been that English cobalt—a greyish-hued metal faintly tinged with red, brittle and slightly magnetic—was finer than the Saxon, but lack of experience in producing the oxide resulted in a deep hue strongly tinged with indigo, violet or purple. The ceramic industry disliked the violet tinge of English cobalt which was inclined to appear unexpectedly in varying strengths, thus making standardisation of colour on a large service a risky undertaking. English zaffre and smalt ceased to be made from the early 1770s.

3. (*Top*) Worcester porcelain of about 1770: plate marked with four simulated Japanese characters within a double circle in blue; jug, cup and saucer in the style of Japanese Kakiemon ware. (*Centre*) Lowestoft porcelain, 1760s: vases and teapot painted in underglaze blue. (*Below*) Worcester porcelain and two early Bristol vases.

4. A collection of Chelsea and Derby porcelain in the Schreiber collection.

5. (*Top and centre*) Worcester transfer-printed porcelain: the vase, dated 1757, is printed in black from a copper plate by Robert Hancock. (*Below*) Bristol hard paste porcelain.

6. (*Top*) Set of three vases encircled with flowers and fruit in full colours and lavish gilding above and below. Bloor's Derby. (*Below*) Early morning tea-set in jasper, white on blue, designed by Lady Templetown and modelled by William Hackwood. Marked "Wedgwood". 1784.

The finest smalt of Saxony had been monopolized by the government on behalf of the Royal Saxon Porcelain Manufactory, Meissen, near **Dresden** and export was forbidden under threat of severe penalty. Medium quality Saxon smalt cost £11 an ounce in 1733. At the close of the war quantities of superfine smalt were confiscated by the Prussians and some of this was made available to English potters at fifteen shillings an ounce.

Every porcelain factory bought largely of this "Bristol blue", so termed because a wholesale druggist in the town was the sole source of supply. **Dr. Wall** prepared this blue to such excellent advantage at **Worcester** that his decoration more nearly approached K'ang Hsi blue and white than did the work of Meissen: not until the late 1820s was this colour equalled, when the **Copeland** firm reproduced Dr. Wall's blue and white porcelain in bone china.

The cobalt refiners established in London, Liverpool and Staffordshire continued operating, however, importing Saxon cobalt ore in various strengths. With the introduction of blue **transfer** decoration the demand increased.

Powder blue: dry, finely powdered smalt blown through a tube covered at one end with a piece of lawn, on to an oiled surface before glazing, thus producing a powdered sprinkled effect. The method was used at **Worcester** and may be recognized by the resultant granular effect, the bright blue being mingled with pin-points of the steely blue shade.

Smalt: a preparation of cobalt oxide consisting of from two to ten per cent of high quality zaffre added to glass. While still molten this was poured into cold water and pulverized. Melting, cooling and grinding were repeated a dozen or more times, making the glass exceedingly hard. The resulting fragments were finely ground in a series of mullers until of flour fineness. This powder, smalt, was stored in small bags of white leather.

Ultramarine: a colour prepared from the azure stone lapis lazuli, used for decorating **porcelain**. Produced a paler and more delicate sky blue than the Saxon superfine smalt prepared from cobalt. It was used rarely on English porcelain and then sparingly and at great cost. Obtainable in the early 19th century only from Siberia and sold to potters at £20 an ounce in 1848. Artificial ultramarine was discovered in about 1802 by a French chemist and named *bleu de Thévard*. The colour resembled the bright blue of genuine ultramarine, but because of its low price could be applied plentifully, and formed the basis of the lovely blue found on Staffordshire **figures** from about 1840 to the 1870s. By the late 1840s artificial ultramarine had superseded smalt and zaffre for painting ceramics, costing one shilling and three pence at a time when poor quality zaffre was being sold by the refiners at six shillings a pound. It was not used for transfer-printing.

Zaffre: cobalt oxide, produced by roasting cobalt at great heat. At first it contained many impurities. In the late 17th century the blue colour was improved, the oxide being cleansed of insoluble matter by dissolving it in hydrochloric acid and recovering the clean zaffre. This process was several times repeated when fine quality smalt was required. Further purifying treatments were progressively evolved, all tending to produce smoother and bluer blues. By the 19th century all traces of copper, lead, iron, bismuth and nickel were removed. The resulting zaffre gave a less attractive tint, however, and this is noticeable in reproduction decorations of to-day.

COCKER, GEORGE (1794–1868)

A **figure** modeller and **porcelain** maker. Apprenticed at **Derby,** he left in 1817 for **Coalport**, later working at **Worcester** and returning to the Derby factory in the early 1820s. In 1826 he established a porcelain factory of his own at Derby, producing white **biscuit figures**, animals, baskets of flowers and so on. These had a dry chalky surface and were sometimes incised with his name, but more frequently with a cross. In 1840 he transferred his business to London where he worked until 1853 when he was employed by the **Minton** firm.

COCKPIT HILL (Derby)

Site of the Derby Pot Manufactory established early in the 18th century to make **slipware**, and from about 1751 to 1779 earthenware, and later still **cream-coloured earthenware** decorated with **transfer-printing.** The financing partner from the 1740s was John Heath. The ware was seldom marked. *See* **Derby. Porcelain Manufactory.**

COLEBROOKDALE

The name given to the **Coalport** factory in 1828 by John Rose II because of its proximity to the celebrated Coalbrookdale ironworks.

COLLECTIONS

Outstanding examples of English ceramics may be seen in the following museums: British Museum; Victoria and Albert Museum, South Kensington; Public Museum and Art Gallery, Hanley; Glynn Vivian Art Gallery, Swansea; City Art Gallery, Bristol; Yorkshire Museum, York; Birmingham City Museum and Art Gallery; Cecil Higgins Museum, Bedford; Harris Museum and Art Gallery, Preston.

COLOURED BODIES

Self-coloured body obtained by use of colouring oxides of ochreous earths. **Wedgwood's** dry **cane ware** developed in 1770 was the first of such bodies.

COLOURS

The pigments used for ceramic decoration consist chiefly of refined mineral oxides.

Unfired or cold colours were oil paints applied over **glaze** to which no greater heat was applied for fixing than a few hours in a warm oven. In the 1750s **soft-paste porcelain** advertisements distinguished between fired decoration, termed "true enamel", and the cold unfired pigment termed lacquer, japanning, or varnish. Such decoration was short-lived in wear for it adhered poorly to the smooth surface of the glaze and quickly flaked away. White porcelain is sometimes found showing traces of unfired oil colours.

High temperature colours were painted on the unfired surface of the **glaze** on earthenware, or on porcelain under the **lead glaze.** The only colours capable of withstanding the full heat of the kiln were the universally used **cobalt blue,** manganese purple, the rare copper green and, very rare indeed, orange and yellow from antimony or iron, and iron red.

Enamels were used in overglaze decoration. When a pattern called for several colours superimposed, they were arranged to consist of materials which melted at progressively lower firing temperatures, each being given a separate firing. Coloured enamels until early in the 19th century were very costly. The pigments used were hand-ground together with the flux to "such a degree of fineness that the labour of half a day was employed in grinding a drachm". When required for painting they were rubbed in spirit of turpentine or oil of spike lavender which could be volatilized in the oven without charring. Thick oil of turpentine might be added to give body to the paint.

The enamelled decoration was fired for from five to twelve hours in a small muffle kiln at temperatures ranging between 950 and 700 degrees centigrade, according to the colour used. The ware was allowed to cool gradually during a period of about twelve hours.

In 1812 Samuel Walker, then employed by Barr, Flight and Barr at **Worcester**, introduced a more efficient muffle-kiln for enamelling, replacing the square box kilns formerly used. This innovation made enamel decoration a much less hazardous process, producing far finer results. The new type of enamelling kiln quickly made the **bone china** issued by Barr, Flight and Barr celebrated for the brilliance of its fine colouring. By 1813 it was in use at **Nantgarw**: at **Swansea** from 1814; and at **Coalport** by 1820. Its use became widespread during the 1820s.

COMBED WARE

A coarse **earthenware** with a two-colour marbled appearance. The earthenware, while still moist, received alternate lines of red- and white-burning **slip** which while wet were combed together in a wavy or zigzag pattern by means of a many-pointed tool or brush of leather or metal. This method of decoration was developed into its highest form by **Josiah Wedgwood** in 1760. *See* **Marbled ware**.

COOKWORTHY, WILLIAM

(1705–80). *See* **Plymouth** *and* **Bristol hard paste porcelain.**

COPELAND WARES

Made by W. T. Copeland who succeeded the **Spodes**. Productions included **bone china**, fine **earthenware** a modified **bone china** known as **stone china** and **parian ware**.

CORNISH STONE

Sometimes called china stone. This is a weathered felspathic granite containing the fluxing materials essential to give **porcelain** its hard vitreous nature. It has to be blasted and quarried like granite and then ground to a fine powder. Five qualities are prepared. It resembles the Chinese petuntse.

COTTAGES

An early 19th-century style for pastille burners and night-lights issued by the **bone china** potters in tens of thousands. Examples in **soft-paste porcelain**, **felspar porcelain**, and **earthenware** are recorded. Money boxes, tea caddies, tea-pots and tobacco jars were also made in this shape.

Pastille burners: containers for slow-smouldering perfumed pastilles composed of powdered willow wood charcoal, benzoin, perfumed oils, and gum arabic pressed into conical form for burning. These ensured that rooms were kept sweet-smelling in days of perfunctory sanitation.

Slipware pastille burners are recorded as early as 1700 and Thomas **Whieldon** made them during the 1750s and later in the form of hand-modelled half-timbered cottages decorated with mingled-colour glazes. In **soft-paste porcelain** they are extremely rare. Among the several thousand pieces of porcelain sold at **Chelsea's** sixteen day sale in 1756 were only two cottages, each described as "a most beautiful perfume pot in the form of an old castle or pigeon house decorated with pigeons". Similar perfume pots covered with may blossom were made at **Derby** during the mid-1760s. Cottage pastille-burners in thin **hard porcelain** were made at **Bristol** between 1773 and 1778. The walls were decorated with sprays of tiny hand-modelled flowers, and the hard, thinly-applied glaze had an exceptionally high lustre marred by minute bubbles.

In **bone china** cottage pastille-burners represented old-world dwellings surrounded by gay flower beds, minute coloured flowers encrusting the walls and edging the roofs and gilt-touched chimneys from which curled scented fumes. In addition there were turreted castle gateways, circular toll-houses with cone-shaped roofs, clock towers and creeper-covered churches, water mills, thatched farms, flowery arbours, Chinese pagodas, Indian elephants. The majority were rectangular on plan, but circular, hexagonal and irregular shapes were also made. One of their many charms was the profusion of flowers, pressed out in moulds and placed in position by hand. Grass by the doorway and moss on the roof was given a rough texture with shavings of paste scattered on the glaze before firing, and afterwards coloured green. Roofs of china cottages were most frequently picked out in lines of gilt to resemble tiling. Such details as gables, dormer windows, window panes, door knockers, and handles were often outlined in black.

In the majority of cottages, roof and walls were made in a single piece, so that the pastilles could be placed upon the flat plinth and lit before being covered with the cottage. In others the roof lifted from the walls like a lid, but these are less plentiful. Some had a pull-out side giving access to a small bowl-like cavity in which the pastilles were burned.

It is difficult to attribute a cottage to any particular potter unless it is marked: between 1820 and 1850 they were issued by **Rockingham**, **Coalport**, **Spode-Copeland**, **Derby**, **Worcester** and no fewer than twenty Staffordshire potters. The flowers on Rockingham cottages were usually less disproportionately large than those ornamenting cottages made elsewhere, and details such as the many-paned windows flanking the outlined door were meticulously minute. Clean precision of finish was one of Rockingham's most notable features, and the paste was pure white with a hard white glaze. Rockingham cottages with porches are rare: so are all-white specimens.

Rockingham cottages overburdened with applied flowers in the Coalport manner date from 1826. The **gilding** of Rockingham was darker than that used elsewhere and with the passing of years is inclined to display a coppery tinge. Sprigs of flowers in gold are infinitely superior to those found on cottages made elsewhere. A soft, full-tinted mauve particularly associated with Rockingham is found chiefly on small toll-houses smothered with flowers. The so-called Rockingham lavender is a colour found also on some Staffordshire cottages. Purple cottages were a late Rockingham feature, afterwards copied in Staffordshire.

Coalport made pastille-burners in a white clear paste, often with a **leadless glaze** fired at a low temperature to produce fine effects. The majority of turreted castles on rocky bases display this feature, and sweet-pea, carnation, and ranunculus flowers carefully modelled in the round are characteristic of Coalport, although by no means confined to this factory's productions. **Flower-encrusted** cottages are usually known to collectors as **Colebrookdale.**

Spode-Copeland cottages had a particularly rustic air, featuring door porches, climbing roses and a smother of minute pink flowers: walls might be bright blue and the base emerald-green. Some were made in the shape of a circular summer-house with domed or cone-shaped roof projecting beyond the walls and supported by a circle of pillars. A cylindrical cottage, made only by Copeland, had a loose inner lining within the walls and a lift-off lid. Some excellent pastille-burners have been noted in **felspar porcelain**.

From **Worcester** came cottages with flowers, ramblers, and other decorations painted on the walls, which were picked out in gold lines to resemble bricks. Violets and primroses grew out of the grass at the base. Those marked FLIGHT BARR & BARR date pre-1840. Worcester was the only firm to raise cottages on small scroll feet, and such examples are rare. **Minton** made some well-modelled large cottages in pure white bone china, the only touch of colour being a goldfinch perched on the roof. Pastille-burners were made at **Swansea** between about 1818 and 1823. These had roofs outlined in gold to resemble semi-circular tiles arranged in a salmon-scale pattern. A summer-house variety had tall sham-gothic windows and colourful flowering plants enamelled upon the walls; the base was tinted palest green.

Night-light shelters were made in the form of cottages with cut-out windows from which came faint illumination. These were but a development of the centuries-old mortar light, its wick floating in an open container of whale or other oil. Those who scoff at the need for night-lights overlook the fact that in earlier generations the tiniest protected light burning throughout the night obviated the necessity for laborious flint-striking in the morning. Following the invention of the self-consuming wick in 1825 and the development of the slow-burning non-guttering candle-wick a few years later, thus abolishing the need for periodic snuffing, night-light shelters in cottage form were issued by several potters specializing in bone china.

In most of these the night-light was inserted through a semi-circular arch at the back of the cottage. **Derby** made a speciality of night-light shelters in which roof and walls lifted off a closely fitting box-like base: the inner wall can be seen forming a door within the porched doorway, but leaving the windows uncovered. **Lithophane** night-light shelters were made by Grainger, Lee & Company, **Worcester**.

Crime cottages: earthenware models of houses made notorious by their association with 19th-century murders. The earliest noted example is the Red Barn, Polstead, issued in 1828, in connection with the murder of Maria Marten by William Corder. The most popular of all crime pieces came twenty-one years later. This was Potash Farm, the home of James Rush the Cornish murderer of his neighbour, Mr. Jeremy of Stanfield Hall. Several potters issued versions of each, the finest being those issued by Sampson Smith of Longton, and William Kent of Burslem.

CRAZING

A network of thin, irregular lines crossing each other and resembling fine cracks. This might be confined to the surface of the **glaze**, or might go deep so that food penetrated to the ware beneath, causing discoloration impossible to remove. This crazing took place through the years and was due to constant changes in atmospheric conditions, the paste or body and the covering glaze contracting or expanding in response to these changes at differing rates. It was not until 1885 that potters overcame this glazing defect. In fake crazing the lines are widely spaced.

CREAM-COLOURED EARTHENWARE

A fine earthenware developed by **Josiah Wedgwood**, but made possible by **Thomas Astbury's** introduction of white Devonshire clays into his wares with the addition of powdered calcined **flint**. The addition of the latter made it possible to utilize the higher kiln temperatures then being made available, resulting in ware of greater hardness. This body was used for white **salt-glazed stoneware**. In about 1750 Aaron Wedgwood and William Littler adopted a **liquid glaze** applied to the **green ware** before firing. This process was shortly improved by **Enoch Booth** who fired the ware before applying the glaze, and re-fired afterwards, the method now in use.

Josiah Wedgwood began his experiments towards improving this earthenware body in 1759, but twenty

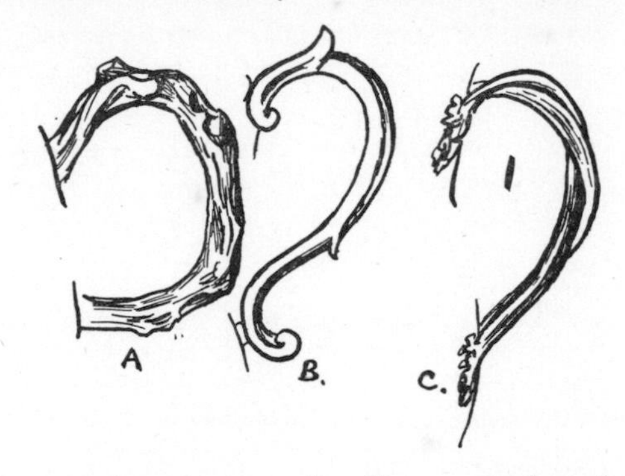

Typical earthenware handles: *a*. Crabstock. *b*. Foliated scroll. *c*. Double interlaced.

years passed before he achieved perfection. For the first few years the ware was faintly yellowish in colour and covered with a hard glaze. In 1764 John Greatbach, employed by Wedgwood at the Brick House Works, Burslem, greatly improved the glaze, and hence the appearance of the ware. In the following year Wedgwood secured the patronage of Queen Charlotte, and named this earthenware **queen's ware**. In 1776 he further improved queen's ware by the addition of **Cornish stone**, producing an earthenware which many competitors tried to copy. In 1780 he reduced the amount of **Cornish stone** in the formula, resulting in the modern cream-coloured body, consisting of almost equal parts of ball clay, china clay, calcined flint, and Cornish stone, the materials being mixed together in the form of **slips**.

The decorations on pre-Wedgwood cream-coloured earthenware resembled that on early white salt-glazed stoneware: painting in high temperature **cobalt blue** and manganese purple was introduced in 1743 and was used almost exclusively until Wedgwood introduced overglaze colours very sparsely applied. By 1765 he was decorating in enamels as lavishly as the porcelain makers. His cream-coloured ware also might be **pierced**, moulded, or decorated with **transfer-printing**.

Queen's ware had a profound effect upon public taste and superseded **delft ware** and white salt-glazed stoneware. By 1790 it was in extensive production by other Staffordshire potters such as **Elijah Mayer** and **Josiah Spode**, and in **Leeds, Bristol** and **Liverpool**.

CRESCENT MARK. *See* **Caughley, Lowestoft, Pinxton, Worcester**.

CRISPE (Bow Churchyard, London)

Allan Cunningham in his life of John Bacon (1833) says that he began his career as an apprentice to Sir Nicholas Crispe, "an eminent maker of porcelain, who taught him the art of modelling various groups and figures, such as the Door and the Holly Tree, the Bird and the Bush, the Shepherd and Shepherdess, and birds of all shapes, and beasts of every kind yet made for show or for use in our manufactories." This was in 1755. No porcelain from this source has yet been identified. It is believed, however, that the manufactory was in Lambeth.

CROCK STREET and DONYAT WARE (Somerset)

A **sgraffiato** slipware, the glaze stained with green patches. Made mainly from the mid-18th century to about 1850, although some specimens exist bearing 17th century dates.

CROSS MARK. *See* **Bristol, Cocker, George**.

CROUCH WARE

Made from a white clay obtained from Crich in Derbyshire, long used at Nottingham for the manufacture of crucibles and melting pots until early in the 18th century. From 1710 it was used in Staffordshire to make the earliest white **salt-glazed stoneware** which was tinged with green owing to the presence of copper pyrites in the clay. Its use was abandoned in favour of **Astbury's** whiter body made from south of England clays and calcined flints.

"CROWN DERBY"

This term should be applied only to the productions of the Crown Derby Porcelain Company established in 1877, and not to the porcelain of Duesbury or bone china of Bloor containing a crown in their marks. "Royal

Crown Derby" dates from 1890. (*See* Derby.)

CROWN STAFFORDSHIRE PORCELAIN COMPANY LIMITED (Fenton, Staffordshire)

This firm was established in 1830 by Henry Green and continued after his death in 1859 as M. Green and Company. The present title dates from 1890. The Green firm specialized in toy tea and dinner services and miniature ornaments. From 1876 they made full-size services in **bone china** with decorations of superlative quality. The firm was also responsible for many of the remarkable reproductions of 18th century **porcelain**. J. F. Blacker wrote of these productions in 1911: "By long and careful experiment their chemists have discovered the exact shades of the marvellous enamels which the Chinese brought to perfection . . . the powder blue on the vases made by the Crown Staffordshire Porcelain Company is the result of some thousands of trials extending over ten years. Each piece is what it professes to be, a copy, which is marked with a crown over 'Staffs' or 'Staffordshire' surmounting two Gs,

one reversed, in a monogram. The flowers that **Billingsley** painted at **Derby** and elsewhere are among the schemes of decoration used by this company."

CSN MARK. *See* **Coalport.**

CUP PLATES

Social custom in some parts of the country from about 1800 to 1870 involved drinking tea from the saucer which was made deep for this purpose. Meanwhile the cup was placed on a small plate provided for it. Such plates, three to four inches in diameter, were of **earthenware** or **bone china** and might match the tea set.

The majority appear to have been made in Staffordshire **transfer-printed** blue, sometimes with an all-over design, more usually a central picture enriched with a printed border. From about 1840 the border might be omitted and the rim embossed in relief and hand-touched with coloured enamels. The majority of cup plates bear the names of **J. & W. Ridgway** or **J. & R. Clews.**

D MARK. *See* **Derby.**

DALE HALL. *See* **John and James Rogers.**

DALE, JOHN (Burslem)

Made cream-coloured earthenware and well-modelled figures and busts impressed I. DALE BURSLEM in two lines. A set of elements in the Victoria and Albert Museum has the name of each figure inscribed on the front of the plinth. Busts of John Wesley are similarly marked. Was at work in the 1790s and early 1800s.

DANIEL, RALPH (Cobridge)

A stoneware potter who introduced to England the secret of **casting** ceramics from plaster-of-paris moulds. Upon his return from Paris with a specimen set of moulds, he demonstrated their use to his competitors. Such moulds quickly replaced the alabaster block and pitcher of porous earthenware, although the plaster lost its sharpness more rapidly. Ralph Daniel is believed to have been the first to develop enamelling in the Potteries, bringing decorators from London and elsewhere in the early 1750s.

DAVENPORT, JOHN (Longport)

Established in 1793 as a maker of **cream-coloured earthenware**, painted and blue **transfer-printed**, achieving outstanding success with openwork-rimmed plates (*see* **Piercing**). By 1800 he was engaged in the production of **bone china** and by 1810 was producing a wide range of domestic ware, vases and a few **figures**. He retired with a fortune in 1832 and the business was continued by his sons until 1887.

Flower and fruit decorations were enamelled in naturalistic colours of exceptional brilliance on a paste that was notably white and translucent, in contrast to the distinctly grey tint of the firm's less costly ware. From about 1830 Davenport made a great use of ground colours and favoured an excellent dark blue. From the late 1830s cups might have sunken panels and gilded feet. **Flower-encrusted** borders might enclose painted landscapes.

Davenport's earliest work was unmarked. The first mark was the name DAVENPORT printed in red with three small irregular circles beneath. Early in the 19th century the name was lettered in an arc shape above an anchor, and from about 1810 was transfer-printed. After 1806 the mark DAVENPORT LONGPORT STAFFORDSHIRE in three lines might be transfer-printed in red surmounted by an anchor. After 1830 the anchor was surmounted by a royal crown. A mark used from about 1850 was the name DAVENPORT in a semicircular ribbon enclosing an anchor. A small flower with six petals is a rare mark of early Davenport. Occasionally Longport in script in red or brown is noted. Some of the principal marks are shown in the sketch opposite.

DAWSON MARKS. *See* **Sunderland.**

DELAMAIN, HENRY. *See* **Dublin.**

DELF

Because several places in the Potteries are so named it has been wrongly

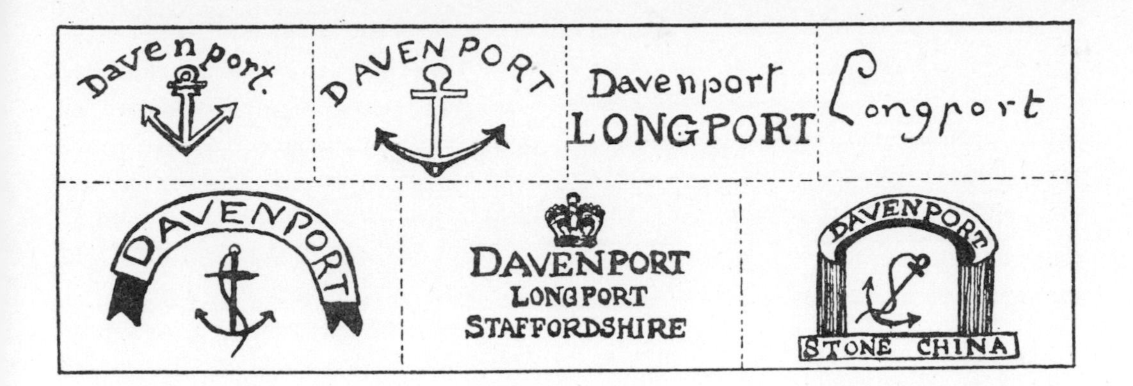

assumed that delft ware was made there. The name is due to the presence of peat which was dug or delved there.

DELFT WARE

Dutch: a blended **earthenware** coated with tin-enamel, decorated and then glazed, named after the town of Delft where a group of potters in this medium established themselves early in the 16th century. Dutch delft has a porous body, yellowish or pale brown in tint, is light in weight and usually soft enough to be marked with a knife.

English: an earthenware intended to imitate Dutch delft, but denser, more vitreous, and consequently less evenly coated with enamel. Sometimes the red or buff body is faintly visible through the enamel. Because the body absorbed but little of the enamel the latter tends to acquire a reddish or yellowish tinge rather than pure white. Owing to lack of harmony between body, enamel and **glaze**, **crazing** is frequent, a fault rarely found on Dutch delft. This **biscuit** was well brushed to remove dust, and then dipped into white tin oxide enamel suspended in water. After drying in a warm room it was fired to a biscuit, painted, then coated with glaze and fired. The addition of a little zaffre (*see* **Cobalt blue**) to the enamel helped to conceal the yellowish tinge of the earthenware beneath. Decoration was usually in cobalt blue under the glaze; manganese purple and yellow were sometimes used and, less frequently, green, puce, brownish red and black. Some ware classified as English delft consists of a buff-burning body covered with a white **engobe** and a colourless **lead glaze**. The ware resembles delft only in general appearance.

English delft was first made at **Lambeth** in 1671 by John Ariens van Hamme, and by 1676 several other delft ware potters were operating in Lambeth. Soon the trade extended to **Bristol**, **Wincanton**, **Liverpool** and elsewhere including Lane Delph in Staffordshire where from 1710 to 1750 Thomas Heath issued a coarse delft ware crudely decorated. Most types of domestic ware were made in this medium until the 1780s.

DENBY (Derbyshire)

Founded in 1809 by Joseph **Bourne** who made domestic drinking vessels, spirit flasks, and other ware in a light-brown **salt-glazed stoneware.**

DERBY. *See* **Cockpit Hill; William Duesbury; Derby Porcelain Company Manufactory; Derby Porcelain**

DERBY PORCELAIN COMPANY

Established in 1755 by William **Duesbury** with André Planché of the **Derby Porcelain Manufactory** as works manager. In 1757 the premises were enlarged to accommodate twice the original output, and in April 1758 he was advertising in the London newspapers "the largest variety of the Derby Porcelain or second **Dresden** Figures". In 1770 Duesbury acquired the **Chelsea** porcelain factory (*see* **Chelsea-Derby**) and in 1775 **Bow.** Duesbury took his son William into partnership early in 1786, the firm then being styled William Duesbury & Son. A few months later he died. William Duesbury II then became sole proprietor until 1795, when he took Michael Kean, a miniature painter, into partnership. When Duesbury II died early in the following year Kean married the widow and controlled the business. Kean retired from the business in 1811, disposing of his shares to William Sheffield, father-in-law of Duesbury III. In 1815 the firm was bought by Robert Bloor who for many years had been the commercial manager. Three years after his death in 1845 the works were closed and the models and moulds, including those taken over from Chelsea, were sold to Samuel Boyle who later disposed of them to **W. T. Copeland.** The subsequent history of china manufacture in Derby is outlined later in this summary.

Five major changes were made in Derby paste:

1. Until 1770 it was made from a white Derbyshire or Dorset clay and a glassy frit. This paste was light in substance, sandy in texture and of creamy translucency, often displaying "**moons**". The white **glaze** was thick and pellucid.

2. Richard Holdship, a former partner in the **Worcester** Tonquin Manufactory, in 1764 agreed to reveal to Duesbury the steatitic formula in use there and to arrange for supplies of **soapstone.** Some porcelain of this period has been found to contain soapstone, but production was soon discontinued.

3. Bone ash was introduced into Derby porcelain after Duesbury acquired the Chelsea factory and continued in regular use until 1798. Cornish china clay was also used. This produced a close-grained soft-paste porcelain of remarkable purity and creamy translucency. The soft glaze, free from **crazing** and easily scratched, was thick and lustrous. So deeply might the enamel sink into the glaze

that it often had the appearance of being under the glaze.

4. Early in the Duesbury-Kean period, 1796-1811, **bone china** was used, made from a non-frit formula. This was whiter and more opaque than the frit bone porcelain formerly made and displayed a greenish translucency when held to the light. The thin hard glaze did not absorb the enamel, which could therefore be applied more thinly than formerly.

5. Bone china of the Bloor period, 1815-48, is somewhat heavy and lacks the translucency expected of such paste. The hard thick glaze has usually crazed and discoloured.

Derby of the 18th century was celebrated for the brilliancy of its ground colours which included canary yellow, apple-green, pale lavender, deep claret, bright orange, coral, and faded old rose. Until 1782 the blue ground so typical of the Duesbury period was an exclusive brilliant overglaze enamel, described in catalogues as lapis lazuli, and known in the factory as Smith's blue in recognition of its invention by an employee of that name. It may be felt slightly raised if the finger be pressed over it, showing it to have been laid on as a thick coat. This was abandoned in 1782 in favour of a less costly underglaze zaffre (*see* **Cobalt blue**) blue. The presence of opaque green indicates a date later than 1796: previously a translucent copper green was used.

Naturalistic painting was introduced in about 1785, notably by **Billingsley** in the painting of flowers, and Brewer with landscapes. This style continued in use until the Bloor period when Edwin Horatio Steele developed a hard formalistic style of ornament with the pattern in bright colours and **gilding** completely covering the ware. Bloor set out to popularize decoration in the **Japanese** taste, introduced by **Josiah Spode II** before 1803. In 1817 Bloor advertised for "twenty good enamel painters who could paint different japan patterns". Derby japan colours include a foxy red, deep orange, deep blue, sharp pink, green, and gold, the latter often forming the outline of the pattern.

In addition to Billingsley, some extremely capable decorators were employed throughout the period. Billingsley was replaced as a leading flower painter by William Pegg whose flowers were almost life-size—much larger than those of any other Derby artist. They were rarely accompanied by arabesques or gilded borders, his only concession being bands of gilding around the rims of domestic ware. The name of the flower, unless very familiar, was painted in red. Edward Withers, a flower decorator until 1790, painted leaves in two shades of translucent copper green over finely pencilled outlines in black or dark brown. One flower always spread out from the group. Two celebrated landscape enamellers worked at Derby: Zachariah

Boreham and "Jockey" Hill. Boreham (1738–1810), who had been chief decorator at Chelsea, arrived at Derby in 1783, and depicted Derbyshire dale scenery in black and brown coloured with low-toned washes. His trees were carefully delineated and he introduced tiny, well-painted figures into his compositions. A pleasant grey tone distinguished his painting, an effect secured by the use of a light yellowish green. He was also an excellent portrayer of exotic birds, usually painted over a transparent copper green background. "Jockey" Hill decorated at Derby throughout the Duesbury era until 1800. He used the same technique as Boreham, his work being recognized by his more vivid colouring, his ochre skies, and his more delicate use of the pencil brush. John Brewer, a former miniaturist, painted landscapes from 1796 to 1810 in naturalistic colours on backgrounds of chrome green. He painted exotic birds equally well. Other outstanding decorators were Richard Askew from 1772 to 1795; George Complin until 1795, and Thomas Steele, who afterwards specialized in fruit.

Solon, the great authority on ceramics, considered Derby **figures** to be "of an excellence unapproached by any kindred productions". Subjects were usually adapted from paintings or engravings. Successful figures were issued in three sizes, the corresponding number 1, 2, or 3 being scratched in the paste beneath. Duesbury's figures were modelled with a sharpness of outline not found in other contemporary figures. Folds of garments were thin, almost knife-edged, this distinctive feature being accentuated by the thinness of the glaze, which did not accumulate in the slight blobs observed on figures by other potters. The bases, which were often flat, usually had three or four dark unglazed patches caused by the pads of clay upon which the figures rested whilst the glaze was fired. Plinths were enriched with painted decoration rather than the more expensive applied flowers used elsewhere. The light, yellow-green leaves forming the **bocages** were appreciably thinner than those of other potteries. During the Kean regime modelling generally deteriorated, colours became gaudy and were accompanied by vast quantities of bronzy-gilding. Bloor's enamels were lifeless, being inexpensive to prepare and applied over a hard glaze.

Duesbury's famous **biscuit** figures date from the late 1760s, moulded with lines cleaner and more distinct than anything known formerly. *See* **Figures.**

Rarely, if ever, was Derby porcelain marked until Duesbury acquired Chelsea in 1770, when he added his own initial to the Chelsea anchor: the mark then used was an anchor traversing the down-stroke of the script D. From 1773 the mark in gold might be a jewelled crown above an anchor.

Porcelain made at Derby might be

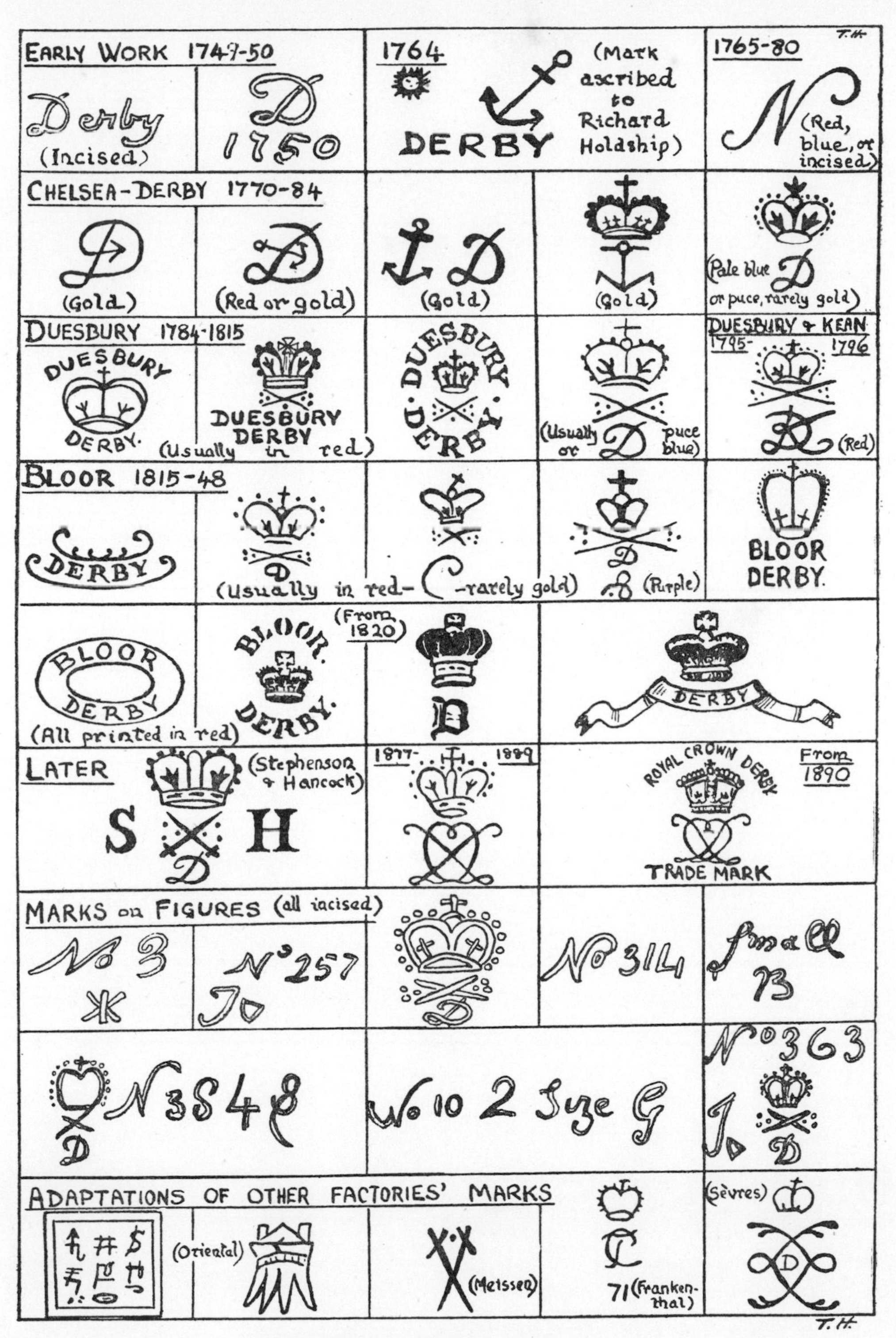

Marks on Derby porcelain

marked overglaze with a jewelled crown above a script D. The earliest were coloured blue, then purple or puce, occasionally gold, light brown or black. Until 1780 a cursive N might accompany the mark, either incised or enamelled in red or blue.

Crossed batons with three dots on each side placed beneath the jewelled crown and above the script D date from 1784 until 1830. Until 1795 this mark was usually in cobalt blue or puce, afterwards in red. A pattern number might be incised below the D. For eight months in 1795–96 the script D was combined with a script K in monogram form. Derby then reverted once more to the crown, crossed batons and script D, now painted in vermilion, and incised on vases or figures where it might be accompanied by the number of the model, the size of the piece, and the modeller's initial or workman's mark. This mark was continued by Bloor on fine quality work until 1830.

The Bloor mark from 1815 to 1820, and used as late as 1830, was a carelessly drawn crown, smaller than previously and without jewels on its bows, two brush strokes to represent crossed batons, and a pattern number below. This mark was in vermilion enamel, rarely in grey. From 1821 until the factory closed in 1848 marks transfer-printed in vermilion included a royal crown over a gothic D or over the word DERBY on a ribbon; two concentric circles enclosing the words BLOOR DERBY surrounding a royal crown; a royal crown superimposed BLOOR with DERBY below.

Locker and Company: when the Derby Porcelain Company closed down in 1848 a new firm was at once created by a group of Bloor's employees who manufactured **bone china** under the management of William Locker, a former clerk. They marked their productions in red transfer "LOCKER & CO., LATE BLOOR" on a band enclosing the name DERBY. In 1851 the firm became Stevenson, Sharp and Company, the mark being the name printed in full. Upon the death of Locker in 1859 Sampson Hancock joined the firm, and the mark reverted to the old Derby jewelled crown and the script D with the batons and six dots, the batons being transformed into swords with hilts flanked by the initials S and H in large capitals. The same mark was continued by Hancock when he became sole proprietor: the firm was still in production during the 1890s.

Crown Derby Porcelain Company: established in 1877 was an entirely new factory specializing in high quality productions. After the visit of Queen Victoria in 1890 the prefix "royal" was added to the name of the company and the words ROYAL CROWN DERBY placed above the mark.

DERBY PORCELAIN MANUFACTORY

Established in 1749 by John Heath

7. Wedgwood: a collection of earthenware made during the partnership with Whieldon, 1754–1759, including red ware, green glaze, cauliflower teapot, combed dish, marbling, and, below, Egyptian black, marbled and agate ware.

8. Mugs and (*lower centre*) delft-ware food warmer. (*Top row*) Fulham salt-glazed stoneware, dated 1761; salt-glazed white stoneware, dated 1739; salt-glazed white stoneware. (*Middle row*) left and right, earthenware with patches of coloured glaze; centre, salt-glazed white stoneware with scratch-blue decoration. (*Below*) left, with combed ornament; right, with transfer-printed and enamelled decoration.

the banker-potter of **Cockpit Hill** who financed André Planché, son of the **Dresden**-trained Planché. From 1750 a long series of **porcelain figures** in the white were made, some of which were decorated in London by **William Duesbury**. The light-weight paste was of poor quality and chalky in appearance. The **glaze** might have a faintly yellow tinge. When Duesbury began operations as a potter in Derby in 1755 it was with Planché as works manager. In the following year the proprietors of the Derby Porcelain Manufactory held a sale of "a curious collection of fine figures, jars, sauceboats, services for desserts, and a great variety of other useful and ornamental porcelain *after* the finest Dresden Models all exquisitely painted in enamel with flowers, insects, India plants . . . and some of the finest of the Derby porcelain." This indicates pretty clearly that Planché had proved himself a capable porcelain manufacturer. Porcelain made by Planché might be incised DERBY or a single script D, occasionally with the date 1750.

DICKER (**Sussex**)

Slipware of an uncommon type made in the late 18th century and early 19th century. Designs were outlined in relief by means of a body slip applied by brush or by a funnel with a narrow outlet. Less frequently decoration was applied by forming grooves or depressions in the earthenware and filling them with slips of different colours. Drops of white slip were sometimes scattered over the surface.

DILLWYN. *See* **Cambrian Pottery, Etruscan ware, Swansea** *and* **Nantgarw.**

DIPPED WARE

A 19th-century type of inexpensive **slip** decoration in which three- or four-colour ornament was applied to **earthenware.** The motifs consisted of slips of similar texture to the earthenware itself and rose slightly above the surface. Skilful workers could apply this decoration in the lathe at a remarkable speed.

The biscuit was rotated horizontally in the lathe. Slips prepared in the three colours required—blue, brown and yellow formed a frequent combination —were poured into a three-section funnel and emerged from adjoining openings. The potter held this over the revolving earthenware in such a way that a fine stream of tri-coloured slip flowed upon it. Manipulation of funnel and lathe speed produced a wide variety of bands, stripes, spots, curves and spirals. Although the three slips left the funnel in a united stream they were received upon the ware in entirely distinct positions. The ware was then fired and afterwards glazed. Several of the well-known potters, such as **Spode-Copeland, Davenport,** and **Adams** of Greenfield, made this ware—much of it for export—as did many of the smaller potters from 1815 to about 1850.

DIXON & CO., DIXON PHILLIPS & CO., MARKS. *See* **Sunderland.**

DON POTTERY (near Swinton, Yorkshire)

Made **cream-coloured earthenware** from about 1790. Acquired in 1800 by John Green while still a partner in **Rockingham** and **Leeds.** Shapes and patterns were identical with Leeds, **pierced** plates and dishes, twig baskets, vases, dinner, dessert and tea services being made. They lacked the fine finish of Leeds and were impressed or printed in red over the glaze DON POTTERY or GREEN DON POTTERY. **Marbled ware** and black glazed ware were also made.

In the early 1820s Green introduced the impressed mark of a demi-lion rampant, holding a flag (or pennon) inscribed with the word DON, and beneath POTTERY. In 1834, following purchase of the business by Samuel Barker of **Mexborough Pottery**, this was modified into a blue-printed **transfer** with the name Barker above the flag. This was followed from 1850 by a shield containing an eagle issuing from a ducal coronet.

DONYAT WARE (Somerset) *See* **Crock Street ware.**

DOUBLE-WALLED JUGS

A Chinese technique copied by **Dwight** in **salt-glazed stoneware** and also later made at **Nottingham.** The outer wall of such a jug was pierced with decorative designs, usually flowers and foliage.

DOULTON WARE

The factory was founded at Vauxhall by John Doulton in 1818 and a few years later transferred to **Lambeth.** At first little more than industrial ceramics were made and some decorated **stoneware** such as tankards, **bellarmines**, **spirit bottles**, motto and **puzzle jugs**, their colourings restricted to the tints of the clays, with, usually, a broad band of rich brown at top and bottom.

By 1870 the firm had become celebrated for ornamental **salt-glaze stoneware** including **sgraffiato** upon ordinary salt-glazed brown stoneware, the scratched lines being filled with colour. In 1872 underglaze painting of fine **earthenware** was begun and became celebrated as Lambeth **faience.** At about the same time Doulton's silican ware was issued—a vitrified unglazed stoneware decorated with coloured clays, bronze, green, brown, blue, chocolate, grey, white and black. In 1887 Doulton began to manufacture **bone china.**

DRESDEN (Saxony)

This **porcelain** is made at Meissen, near Dresden, but it has been called Dresden for two centuries. It is included in this Encyclopaedia because it served as a major challenge, and a major source of styles and designs, to

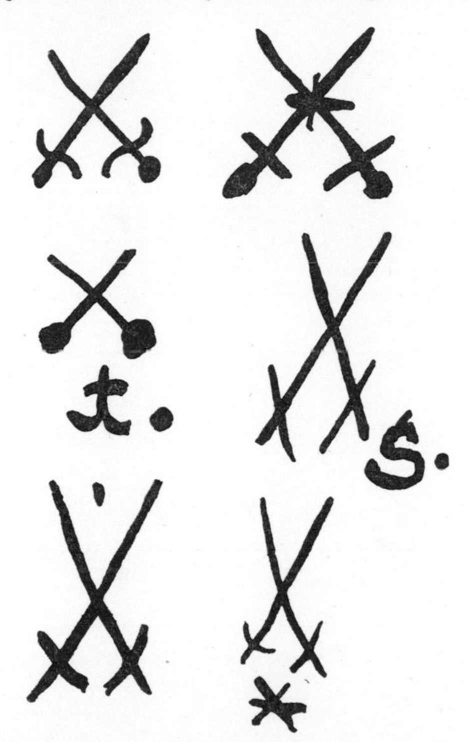

every English porcelain maker. Dresden made Europe's first hard paste porcelain, from 1715. Within twenty years it had become renowned for the magnificence of its productions—**figures**, vases, flowers, and cabinet porcelain of all kinds, marked with various forms of crossed swords in underglaze blue. The English soft paste porcelain potters such as **Bow** and **Derby** closely followed styles originated by Dresden, as did **Plymouth** and **Bristol** in hard paste, and various **bone china** manufacturers of the 19th century. These makers often adapted or copied the Dresden mark.

The first three marks in the sketch are early forms, from 1724 onwards, with pommels and guards carefully depicted: later the mark tended to be more roughly executed, and the sword points closer together. The additional letters, etc., in gold, were apparently for factory use; the star, in blue, was mainly associated with the period 1774–1814.

DRY BODIES

Non-porous **stoneware** requiring no glaze. Made basically of local marls with the addition of colouring oxides or ochreous earths to give the desired hue. The dry bodies included **basalt**, **jasper**, **rosso antico**, **cane**, buff, drab, chocolate and olive. They were made in both ornamental and useful forms.

DRY EDGE FIGURES

Early crudely-modelled figures in white in which the underside was left unglazed, the glaze of the body finishing an appreciable distance above the lower rim.

DUBLIN (Ireland)

A **delftware** plate in the Victoria and Albert Museum is inscribed "Dublin 1735". In 1752 Henry Delamain acquired a delftware pottery which was continued after his death in 1757 by his widow. The ware presumed to be from this pottery was painted in bright blue or manganese purple with landscapes, etc. Marks included DUBLIN, with crowned harp, H and D in monogram, and a painter's initials N. E. Later in the century **cream ware** was made by Edward Ackers and others.

This mark is found on delftware, presumed by Henry Delamain

DUCK EGG PORCELAIN

A fine **soft-paste porcelain** with a greenish translucency made by William **Billingsley** at **Swansea** from the autumn of 1816 to the spring of 1817. E. M. Nance has noted the resemblance of its composition to that of **Spode's bone china**.

DUESBURY, WILLIAM (Derby)

An obscure **porcelain** enameller who became proprietor of one of the most prosperous commercial enterprises of the day. His London account book of 1751 establishes the fact that in that year he enamelled 382 pieces of porcelain from **Bow**, **Chelsea,** and **Derby**. In 1754 he joined William Littler at **Longton Hall**, and a year later established the **Derby Porcelain Company** with financial assistance from John Heath of **Cockpit Hill**. *See* **Derby Porcelain Company,** *and* **Chelsea-Derby**.

DULL FELSPATHIC SOFT PORCELAIN

Invented by Richard Prosser, Birmingham, in 1840. According to Searle this was a mixture of **felspar** and bone ash with a temporary bond such as milk in a solution of boric acid. This was used for making buttons, cameos, mosaic work, and imitation pearl and agate. It was compressed between metal dies and then fired. **Minton** made **tiles** by this process and by 1842 had sixty-two presses making white glazed tiles.

DUNDERDALE, DAVID. *See* **Castleford.**

DWIGHT, JOHN (Fulham) 1637–1703

Celebrated for his fine **stoneware**. In 1661 he was registrar to the Bishop of Chester and there is no evidence that he possessed practical knowledge of pottery making until he established his factory at Fulham, employing stoneware experts from Germany. This was a few months before Charles II issued a proclamation "prohibiting the importation of any kind or sort of stoneware whatever". In the same year, 1671, he was granted a patent (in 1684 this was extended to 1698) for making a "transparent earthenware commonly known by the names of porcelain or china" and of "stoneware, vulgarly called 'cologne ware'". This so-called porcelain was probably a thin, good quality stoneware: examples in the Victoria and Albert Museum do in fact appear translucent in thin sections when held to the light. He also developed a **marbled ware** which was similar to that found on the continent.

Another technique was perfected: that of making **double-walled jugs** with the outer wall pierced in decorative designs. One example is in grey stoneware partly covered with brown salt-glaze, the outer wall being reticulated in flowers and foliage with incised stems. Some **figures** were made by Dwight, of white or slightly buff stoneware, translucent in thinner parts and covered with **salt-glaze** of uneven thickness: others were in dark brown and traces of **gilding** have been observed.

Various notebooks were written by Dwight between 1689 and 1698, and although these are now lost, a manuscript copy is preserved in the British Museum, which shows that he was using "calcined, beaten, and sifted flints . . . instead of white sand, and is rather whiter".

Dwight's productions were listed on June 20, 1693, during the hearing of his action against the **Elers** brothers who were charged with infringing his patent rights: he claimed to have "invented and set up at Fulham several new manufactures of earthenware called White Gorges, marbled porcelane vessells, statues and figures, and fine stone gorges and vessels never before made in England, and also discovered the mystery of opaceous red and dark coloured porcelain and china". After Dwight's death the pottery was operated by his family, who appear to have abandoned figure production and specialized in beer jugs of a grey or buff body. The design was usually cylindrical with rolled and grooved mouldings near top and bottom and a grooved handle pinched where it joined the side near the bottom. **Sprigs** with arched or square shapes, oval or cut to fit the outline of the figures, were used for decoration. From about 1720 there were busts of Stewart royalty and hunting scenes in settings with trees and church spires: other jugs carried representations of their owners. Inscriptions were stamped on. The factory continued in the family until 1864.

EARTHENWARE

An opaque ware porous after the first firing and needing to be glazed before it can be taken into domestic use. It is made from clay selected for its plasticity, hardening qualities and fusibility.

Soft-body: is porous, flaky, and rough to the tongue. It has poor heat resistance qualities. This group includes all **slip** decorated wares, all common white and yellow wares, and all enamelled wares such as **delft**. Appreciably lighter in weight than **porcelain**, of similar section, it may be divided into four groups: unglazed; lustrous, coated with a slight vitreous glaze; glazed with **lead glaze**; enamelled, glazed with a vitreous compound which has been coloured with mineral oxides or sulphates. It is manufactured in three stages: the clay is fired once to produce the biscuit state, then glazed, then fired a second time. Underglaze **colours** and **transfer-printing** are applied to the biscuit before the second firing. If enamel decoration is applied over the glaze, the ware is fired again at a comparatively low heat.

Hard-body: its chief characteristics are hardness and heat resistance. It is occasionally translucent. To this group belong **basalt** and **jasper wares**, **stonewares**, and **agate ware**.

EASTWOOD (near Hanley, Staffordshire)

A pottery established in about 1720. Under the proprietorship of William Baddeley from about 1780 until the 1820s the firm made imitations of Wedgwood ware marked EASTWOOD impressed. The firm was chiefly notable for large flint-grinding mills.

EGG-SHELL PORCELAIN

A celebrated **hard-paste porcelain** of exceptional thinness made in China. It was roughly shaped on the thrower's wheel and finished by turning in the lathe. Imitations were made in Staffordshire and at **Belleek** during the second half of the 19th century.

EGYPTIAN BLACK

Black unglazed **stoneware** first produced in the late 17th century and decorated with flower and foliage designs in relief and incised geometric patterns. This stoneware, probably introduced to England by John **Dwight**, was the forerunner of **Wedgwood's basalt**.

ELERS WARE

A variety of unglazed red **stoneware** made in Staffordshire by the Elers brothers between 1693 and the early years of the 18th century, and by several unknown imitators during the following half century. John Philip Elers and David Elers, silversmiths from Amsterdam, are believed to have arrived in London among the followers of William and Mary. They settled in Fulham as potters and in 1693 were sued by **John Dwight** for infringing his patent by making red stoneware tea-pots. Thereupon they established a pottery for the manufacture of similar ware at Bradwell Wood, Staffordshire. This was controlled by John Elers, his brother David remaining in London at their retail shop in Poultry, London, where he sold the tea-pots at from twelve to twenty-four shillings each. The ware was made from a vein of red-burning clay which produced a dense, hard, red stoneware of fine texture.

Red stoneware tea-pots followed the technique of similar ware in China, and in Portugal under the name of *Buccaro* ware. These were preferred to porcelain as the stoneware withstood boiling water. Caution in using really boiling water in **porcelain** tea-pots led to the belief that only the sturdier pots produced good tea. The Elers' tea-pots display evidence of careful preparation of the body to a homogeneous smoothness. After throwing, the ware was air-dried to leather hardness and then turned in the lathe to make it thin and light and produce a fine surface finish. The high firing produced a stoneware so hard as to be almost solid: it was sometimes referred to as dry red porcelain, and was not glazed.

The surface was ornamented with applied pads of clay impressed in relief with metal stamps and finished by hand-tooling, the prunus blossom being the most frequent, but birds, small figures, and the fleur-de-lys also being found. Stalks, stems, handles, and spouts were made by hand and added afterwards by sticking. Few examples are marked, but three tea-pots in the Victoria and Albert Museum are impressed in countersunk relief with a stag and two square "Chinese" seal marks.

Elers ware is a generic term for all unglazed red stoneware of the period: the brothers' productions are usually lighter in colour than those of later workers in this medium.

ELLIS, JAMES and CO. (Shelton, Staffordshire)

Established before 1830. The name may be found impressed on **parian ware.**

ÉMAIL OMBRANT

Porcelain decoration achieved by applying transparent glaze over designs impressed in deep relief. The technique, long practised by the makers of decorative enamels, was developed on porcelain in the mid-1840s by Baron A. du Tremblay at the Rubelles factory, France. The impressed design was in the reverse of that required for the **lithophane** process, high lights in the design being achieved with projections and the shadows with cavities. This irregular surface was flooded with coloured transparent glaze, usually green, to level the surface once more. As a result the cavities of the design appeared as deep green shadows of varying intensity, while the parts in the highest relief came nearest to the surface of the glaze, giving high-lights to the picture. The **Wedgwood** firm used this process and there was a great demand for tea-sets.

ENAMELS. *See* **Colours.**

ENCAUSTIC PAINTING

A decoration evolved by **Josiah Wedgwood** in imitation of the early Etruscan ware. Special colours mixed with wax were fused directly to the unglazed ware producing a nearly dead or matt surface. It was carried out mainly in red and white on black **basalt**.

ENGINE TURNED DECORATION

Geometric diced and fluted decoration incised on dried but unfired ware of leather hardness by cutting on a lathe equipped with an eccentric motion so that the article oscillated as it was rotated, whilst the cutting tool remained still. This produced complicated patterns usually taking the form of irregular basket work termed rose-engine-turning, used chiefly on Staffordshire red ware.

ENGOBE

A coating of white pipe-clay or other light-coloured earth mixed to a creamy consistency with water, covering an **earthenware** body to conceal its coarse red or buff colour and make a smooth, easily-cleaned surface suitable for painted decoration. *See* **Slipware.**

ETRURIA. *See* **Wedgwood.**

ETRUSCAN WARE

(a) A variety of **Wedgwood** black ware with **encaustic** painting in dull colours imitating Etruscan pottery: also known as **encaustic** ware.

(b) **Swansea** between 1845 and 1850 issued a series of **earthenware** vases, feeble imitations of good examples of the Greek. These had a deep red body upon which etruscan figures and designs were **transfer-printed** and over-painted in shining black enamel. The

mark of L. Ll. Dillwyn, son of **L. W. Dillwyn,** and his wife was DILLWYN'S ETRUSCAN WARE, printed in a rectangular cartouche.

EVANS, GLASSON and EVANS *and* EVANS, D. J. and Co. *See* **Cambrian Pottery.**

EXCISE MARK

Composed of the crown, the monarch's cypher (G.R., WR, or VR), and various numerals which can be interpreted and the date and district discovered. Sometimes lead plugs or bands were inserted into the base upon which the excise officer struck his mark.

EYNSFORD (Kent) STONEWARE

Made **bellarmines** and blue-glazed grey **stoneware**. Eighteenth century.

F (with anchor) MARK. *See* **Newcastle.**

FAIENCE

A term properly applied to French **delftware**, but more recently extended by English potters, collectors, and dealers to include all kinds of glazed ceramics other than **porcelain** and **stoneware**. This has wrongly given the impression that faience is superior to **earthenware**. There is no difference whatever, but the so-called English faience is required to possess a brilliant *glaze* rich in lead oxide and silica. The term *faience fine* for white or cream-coloured lead-glazed earthenware has become well established.

FAKES and FORGERIES

Reproductions of works by celebrated potters so treated as to simulate antiques (made before 1830) and so vastly increase their apparent cash value. It is frequently extremely difficult to distinguish the fake from the genuine article: the deliberate forger is capable of reproducing with accuracy the nature of the ware, the colours and methods of application, and the style of workmanship in such a way as to deceive experts. The majority of fakes are not of this calibre, however, and the collector fully primed with methods of contemporary manufacture and decoration will by careful inspection expose some inconsistency, such as chrome **green** or **lead glaze** of the Greatbach type on pre-1764 **porcelain**.

FAMILLE ROSE

A range of colours derived from the purple of cassius developed on Chinese **porcelain** early in the 18th century and hence a style of ornament in delicate opaque enamels. The bright rose colour was used on early **Bow**, **Chelsea**, and **Worcester** porcelain, and on **bone china** by various Staffordshire firms from about 1820. It is valued because of the long range of rose-colour tints obtainable as well as purple and violet. As the temperature of the enamelling oven increases so does the hue of the enamel, starting at red-brown 650 degrees C.; rose 800 degrees C., through rose-purple, rose-violet, violet, pale violet, very pale violet, until at over 1,000 degrees C. the colour vanishes.

FAMILLE VERTE

Chinese porcelain of the K'ang Hsi period (1662–1722) painted over the glaze with vivid green, red, yellow, manganese purple, blue, black and gold.

FBB MARK. *See* **Worcester**.

FC & AR MARK. *See* **Transfer-printing**.

FELL MARK. *See* **Newcastle-on-Tyne**.

FELSPAR PORCELAIN

Evolved by **Josiah Spode II** in 1800 and made in considerable quantity until the 1830s. He introduced pure felspar into a mixture of Cornish clay and china stone (a lesser quantity of this than in **bone china**) and produced one of the most translucent ceramics ever made in England. Fired at a higher temperature than either **soft-paste porcelain** or **bone china**, the resulting ware was harder than either, less liable to fracture, free from surface flaws and subject to less distortion in the kiln. It was less liable to fracture than oriental hard-paste porcelain. Felspar porcelain was extensively used, particularly for costly table services displaying radiant colours against a brilliantly white body. Pastille burner cottages are to be found marked SPODE FELSPAR PORCELAIN. Chamberlain of **Worcester**, Bloor of **Derby**, and John Rose of **Coalport** issued felspar porcelain as well as a number of small firms in Staffordshire. The fineness of John Rose's improved felspar porcelain induced him to copy **Sèvres** ware complete with the crossed L's mark of that factory.

FELSPATHIC WARE

A fine moderately hard **earthenware** with a white body possessing a slightly yellowish tinge and often slightly translucent. Subsidiary names are **ironstone china**, flint ware, **granite ware**, semi-porcelain, opaque porcelain, and demi-porcelain.

FERRYBRIDGE POTTERY (near Pontefract, Yorkshire)

Established in 1792 by Tomlinson and Company and joined in 1796 by Ralph Wedgwood, who spent his life inventing things and in 1796 discovered the value of borax in making a **glaze.** Ralph Wedgwood was the son of Thomas Wedgwood, **Josiah Wedgwood's** partner. He stayed at Ferrybridge until 1800, during which period the firm was styled Wedgwood and Company, and imitated the ornamental **stoneware** and **queen's ware** made in Staffordshire. The firm then continued until 1834 under its original name. Marks were impressed 1792–96 FERRYBRIDGE; 1796–1801 WEDGWOOD & CO; 1801–34 FERRYBRIDGE—with the D upside down.

FG MARK. *See* **Isleworth.**

FIGURES

In **earthenware** have been made from the 17th century; in **soft porcelain** from the mid-1740s; in **hard porcelain** from 1768; in **bone china** from 1800; in **parian ware** from 1842.

Earthenware: figure ornaments were made long before the end of the 17th century, each being hand-moulded by individual "earth-potters" working local clays and seldom sending their wares far afield. These clay figures were crudely modelled, coated with various coloured **slips,** red, brown, and buff predominating, and **glazed** by dusting with finely sifted lead ore or calcined lead. Innumerable peasant-potters produced figures, but few remain owing to their fragile nature.

As regards modelling technique, the customary method until the 1730s, and still in use about 1760, consisted merely of rapid hand-modelling with the aid of double-ended tools. The clay was mixed to such a consistency that it could be bent and twisted without cracking, while remaining soft enough for a fresh piece to adhere to the mass.

Fortunately, one outstanding contributor to the work of the early 18th century is known and his various styles of work classified. This was **John Astbury**, whose figures of men, animals and birds were produced in the traditional manner, modelled with clay, thinly coated with an off-white **slip**, and given decorative details in coloured slip. Gradually, however, clays and slips coloured by burning were superseded by white-burning clays decorated in simple flowing metallic oxide **colours** beneath the glaze. Astbury also made figures in white **salt-glazed stoneware**.

Figures in **marbled** and **agate ware** were also made in the chief pottery centres at this time, and from about 1750 **Thomas Whieldon** was issuing figures in his celebrated **tortoiseshell ware.** For subjects Whieldon preferred animals and birds to human forms. Among birds he delighted in hawks, parakeets, parrots and ordinary barnyard fowl. His horses were celebrated in his own day.

The first change from this hand-modelling technique was to moulding. In moulding a figure the plastic clay was hand-pressed into moulds, at first of earthenware and from about 1750 of plaster-of-paris. The segments were afterwards joined with a little slip of the same composition. Carving and undercutting were done by hand and minor defects made good.

Few figures appear to have been **cast** until after 1745, when **Ralph Daniel** introduced plaster-of-paris casting moulds to the trade. Casting was brought into use only when a long run of simple figures was proposed.

Some exceptionally clever moulded figures were produced by **Ralph Wood I** from about 1760. At first these followed the traditional Whieldon designs, but soon Wood began brush-applying the metallic oxides in separate colour washes instead of blending one into another. The colours most frequently used were copper green, iron yellow, brownish purple, greyish olive, and a quiet tone of smalt blue. Wood's figures covered a wide range of subjects from fine equestrian groups to farmyard animals. At first he moulded inexpensive single figures but soon elaborate groups were issued.

Ralph Wood II added brown and orange to his palette. By about 1780 he abandoned decoration with colour glazes, substituting bright overglaze enamels. Figures were soon raised upon square or rectangular plinths, usually in white touched with single encircling lines of colour, a style that continued well into the 19th century. Until the early 1770s the majority of figures stood upon rocky bases: it then became usual to superimpose such a base upon a plinth.

Aaron Wood, brother of the older Ralph, influenced the trend of Staffordshire earthenware figures more than any other potter from about 1760. His son **Enoch Wood**, after his apprenticeship as a portrait modeller to **Humphrey Palmer** of Hanley, established his own pottery in 1783 and during the next sixty years there was an increasing flow of hand-made and cast portrait busts from his firm.

Neale and Wilson issued a series of very effective small figures made in two-piece moulds. These were notable for their fine finish and the restrained use of colour (*see* **Humphrey Palmer**). Many excellent figures and groups reflecting contemporary life were made by **Lakin and Poole**. Their enamelling was less garish than most contemporary work.

Numerous other names are found impressed upon earthenware figures from about 1790, many of which are particularly attractive owing to the use of **bocage** backgrounds inspired by **Chelsea** figures of the gold anchor period: **John Walton** of Burslem; **Ralph Salt** of Hanley; Robert Garner of Lane End; **Ralph Hall** of Tunstall; Turner & Abbott of Lane End; potters in **Newcastle, Sunderland** and elsewhere.

Porcelain: at first these were hand-modelled at **Bow, Chelsea** and elsewhere. In November 1753 "The China Works, near Bow" advertised for such a modeller. Others, simple in shape, were cast in a single piece and touched up by hand tooling. These include the early white-glazed figures such as were issued by several porcelain works established before 1753. (*See* **Blanc de chine**.)

These were followed by more complex figures built up by a long, complicated process requiring great skill on the part of all craftsmen concerned. A very elaborate set of plaster moulds was prepared, sometimes consisting of as many as fifty pieces. A lead model taken from the master figure was cut into suitable sections—head, body, limbs, accessories—and plaster moulds made from each. Each segment of the figure was then cast, as many parts as possible being made hollow to reduce loss by firing. The completed parts were assembled and temporarily held in position with a thick slip made of the same composition as the paste. The workman, known as a repairer, then tooled the surface to remove signs of joins, made good defects in moulding, and accentuated lines with a flat knife and sharp tool. Outstretched arms and other projecting segments were propped by an elaborate system of clay scaffolding. This prevented distortion and warping, and might be assisted by the sculptor's skilful arrangement of accessories such as a flowing cloak or a tree stump.

Shrinkage during firing took place to the extent of about one-third, the sections being united by fusion into a perfect whole. Enamels were applied over the glaze, with the exception of the seldom used underglaze blue and yellow. Although many figures were produced from the same moulds, scarcely any two are exactly alike. This was mainly because the slightest deviation in placing shoulders and limbs, the set of a head, the gesture of an arm, created a difference in the whole attitude and even the character of the figure. Some of the finer figures, such as those of Chelsea, were so meticulously constructed that final excellence of finish might be secured by using merely a wet brush before firing.

Characteristic of early **Chelsea** figures until 1756 were flat washes of colour, interspersed with large areas of white, and without any **gilding**. Sets of decorative figures were gracefully modelled and gaily dressed, but not until 1758 were Chelsea specimens highly coloured and enriched with gold. Modelling became more sharply cut.

The high quality of **Bow** figure work was due to the introduction in 1756 of a group of figure makers from **Dresden**. Their influence quickly made itself felt in improved colour work. The dry reds, yellowish grass-green, and other dull colours were superseded by brighter hues including a thickly applied milky blue, and puce in shades varying from pink to crimson. Sometimes the enamels merged to produce marbled effects on the low plinths associated with these figures. From 1764 Bow figures began to display creative individuality, abandoning continental forms and patterns. Modelling became more delicate, colours richer and more daintily applied, decoration more elaborate.

Longton Hall issued some attractive figures, but examples are rare. Distinguishing costume details include the general omission of the flowers which were the delight of other factories, these being replaced with star and diaper patterns. Bases were picked out with a strong, dull crimson, sealing wax red, and a dull dark green.

Derby issued figures from the first year of its establishment. Duesbury was quick to appreciate the mood of the period, copying the popular figures from fashionable engravings. Until the end of the 18th century every figure was meticulously finished and it is this, together, with the mellow and waxen finish of the paste, that constitute their chief merit.

After the turn of the century Derby, and later such other firms as **Coalport**, **Rockingham**, **Spode**, **Davenport**, and other Staffordshire potters continued making figures but in **bone china**. Among these the Derby specimens were distinguished by a greater liveliness and charm: the others had less to recommend them beyond a general gaudy splendour.

Biscuit: an entry in the 1771 catalogue of **Chelsea-Derby** production provides the earliest reference to English **biscuit** figures, moulded with lines cleaner and more distinct than anything known formerly. This soft-paste porcelain was close-textured, velvety to the touch, fairly translucent, and of a light ivory tint. The first of William Duesbury's modellers for this medium was Pierre Stephen, who modelled a long series of national heroes between 1771 and 1795, some having his name incised in their bases. The greatest of Derby biscuit modellers was John James Spengler, employed there from 1790 to 1795. Among the finest of his productions was the four-figure group "Russian Shepherd and Companions". Kean improved the biscuit figures, giving them a delicate surface texture by a new process now termed **smear glazing**. Figures of this type were made until 1811. Biscuit figures were more costly than enamelled figures from the same model. No seconds were allowed to leave the factory, all flawed examples being glazed and enamelled and sold at a lower price.

Biscuit figures were made during the early Bloor period but they were of poor quality and may be recognized by their dry appearance. Eventually they degenerated into ordinary unglazed soft-paste porcelain. **George Cocker**, a former Derby modeller, made biscuit figures on his own account from 1825 to 1840. These were characterized by their dry, chalky surface. Occasionally they were marked with his name, incised, otherwise with a cross.

FINE

A term applied to ceramics made from the purest materials available at the time of manufacture, prepared and shaped by skilled craftsmen. White-burning clays were used.

FINGER-VASE

A flower-vase consisting of five tubular flower-holders placed fan-

wise. In the **Leeds** catalogues they were listed as "Quintal Flower-horns". Made in **bone china** by **Spode** and others.

FLIGHT, THOMAS

Proprietor of **Worcester** 1783–93. Succeeded by his son Joseph.

FLINT

An ingredient of English **cream-coloured** and white **earthenware**. The flints are calcined and ground to a white flour-like silica powder which gives lightness to the ware and makes it possible to obtain greater hardness by firing at a high temperature. It is usually assumed that flint was first used for this purpose by **John Astbury** in 1725 but in fact its use was noted just half a century earlier.

FLINT ENAMELLED WARE

A variant of **Rockingham ware** introduced during 1849 by the United States Pottery, Bennington, Vermont, U.S.A. This had a light yellow or buff body of harder texture than ordinary Rockingham, and was covered with heavy glazes displaying a rich variety of colours, including black, brown, yellow, blue and olive, all in numerous shades and combined to produce **marbled** effects. English collectors will find **toby jugs**, hunting jugs, animal figures, **spirit bottles** in the form of men, picture frames and candlesticks.

FLOWER ENCRUSTED BONE CHINA

The best work of this type was shaped and coloured in close imitation of nature. The leading exponents were **Rockingham, Coalport, W. T. Copeland,** and **Chamberlain of Worcester.** Tiny moulded blossoms had been a feature of **Chelsea, Bow** and elsewhere, but the real development of flower modelling came in the mid-1820s and continued for about forty years in bone china.

Bloor's **Derby** made flower encrustations of a heavier, less translucent paste with a harder glaze more thickly applied than elsewhere, and now often crazed and discoloured. Scented flowers were an exclusive production. A tiny nosegay would be designed to secrete a fragment of sponge soaked in one of the newly invented "artificial essences" or perfumes. An alternative was a standing bouquet with green stalks tied by pink or blue ribbons supporting a variety of herbaceous flowers in which a perfumed sponge might be placed. Vast numbers of encrusted **scent bottles** were made by Derby and elsewhere, those of Derby often resembling those produced in soft-paste porcelain at Chelsea in the 1750s and 1760s and probably from the same moulds which were then in the possession of Derby.

From the early 1830s handsome pot-pourri bowls were made by Rockingham, Coalport and Derby in a variety of forms, the most frequent being (a) shallow saucer-shaped dishes raised on three or four scroll feet; (b) shaped vases on short stems and domed feet; (c) bucket-shaped vessels with foot rings. They were fitted with low-domed pierced covers ornamented with flower sprays in relief. The cover design included a short central handle topped by a finial in the form of a flower spray or single bloom. Dishes bearing expertly modelled garden flowers, full size and in their natural colours, date from the mid-1830s. These were superb of their kind, combining fine modelling, harmonious colours and pleasing arrangement. The majority were from Coalport.

FOLEY POTTERIES MARK

Makers of domestic and ornamental **bone china** at Fenton from about 1820. The mark FOLEY CHINA in a Staffordshire knot dates from 1850.

FOOD WARMERS

Small vessels on stands made in **delft ware, cream-coloured earthenware,** and **bone china** for keeping gruel, etc., warm through the night. The design consisted of a hollow, open-sided cylindrical pedestal holding a night-light and supporting a covered cup set into its top. From about 1825 there was a deep inner bowl containing hot water into which the cup fitted. A series with fully enclosed pedestals was made: these supported and kept warm pots of tea—forerunners of the tea cosy.

FORD MARKS. *See* **Sunderland.**

FRIT. *See* **Porcelain, soft paste.**

FROG MUGS

Drinking **mugs** intended to provide fun in convivial company. A full-size, well-modelled and naturalistically coloured frog or toad, with a wide open mouth, was so fixed inside the mug that it appeared to be following the liquor into the drinker's mouth as the last drops were drained. In the 18th century frog mugs were made of red burning clay covered with white **slip**. Later they were made of white **earthenware** at **Sunderland, Newcastle, Leeds** and **Nottingham:** production continued until the 1870s at St. Brede's Pottery, Sunderland. In some of these the frogs were hollow and so arranged that they would spurt a stream of liquor into the face of the drinker.

FRYE, THOMAS

An Irish mezzotint engraver who settled in West Ham in 1738. His experiments in **porcelain** manufacture resulted in the establishment of the New Canton Porcelain Manufactory at **Bow**, of which he was works manager and patentee of the formulae and processes used.

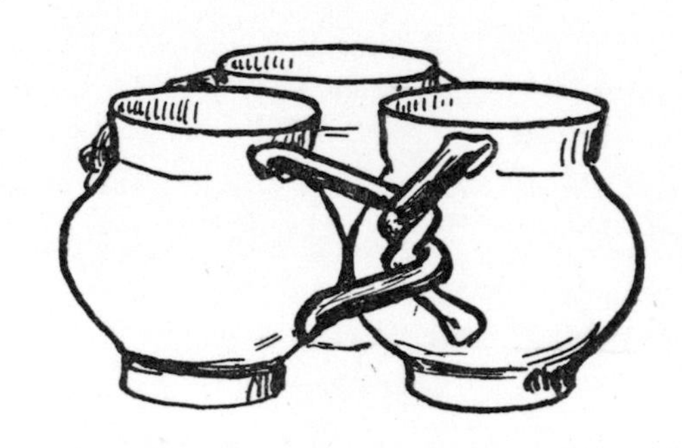

FUDDLING CUP

A vessel composed of three to six conjoined cups with internal communication through bodies or handles so that to empty one the entire set must be emptied. Made of coarse **earthenware** and **slip**-decorated.

FULHAM STONEWARE

A brown **salt-glazed stoneware** first made by **John Dwight** in 1671 and continued until the present day.

GALENA

Natural sulphide of lead from which was prepared the oldest form of **lead glaze** used in England on **slip**-decorated ware and early **cream-coloured earthenware**. The galena was powdered, then dusted over the unfired clay, body and galena being fired in one operation.

GALLIPOT

Defined by the *Oxford English Dictionary* as "a small earthern pot, especially one used by apothecaries for ointments and medicines." The earliest reference given is taken from some domestic expenses of 1465: "Item, the same day my mastire paid for a galy pot, III^d." A potter's advertisement in the *Bristol Gazette* 1773, refers to "Gally pots for Apothecaries".

Lady Fermanagh, writing to her husband in 1721 (*Verney Letters*) refers to a consignment of anchovies which she had "ordered in stone potts, and hath sent them in pittiful galley pots". Gallipots are here differentiated from the much stronger stoneware impervious to liquids. Earthenware was glazed with *galena*: liquid **lead glaze** was introduced in the early 1750s. Gallipots were, then, earthenware vessels covered with galena glaze. It is possible that gallipot is a corruption of galenapot.

GARNITURE

The Georgian term for a set of five **porcelain** or **earthenware** vases, usually a pair of trumpet-shaped beakers and three covered vases of baluster shape.

G. H. & Co. MARK

The mark of G. Haynes. *See* **Cambrian Pottery**.

GILDING

This method of ornamenting English ceramics was little used until early Georgian days as it could be fired only at a low temperature, and consequently was very impermanent. Unglazed red ware of the late 17th century might be enriched with gilding, relief work standing out against a brilliant gilded ground. The **relief** work on drab-coloured **salt-glazed** ware dating from the 1730s might also be gilded. The gold leaf used throughout the 18th century was beaten from ingots of 23½ carat gold: a book of fifty leaves cost sixpence in 1750. In times of gold scarcity the gold-beaters might hammer their leaves from golden guineas. The progressive changes in gilding methods make it possible for collectors to group specimens into well-defined classes.

Oil gilding: a method of "gilding china" described by Blancourt in 1699. The gold was fixed to the ware by means of a linseed oil preparation containing gum arabic and mastic. This was painted upon the ware in the desired patterns and dried for two days. Then by breathing upon this the gilder made the surface slightly tacky. A special thick gold leaf cut to shape with a graver was blown upon it and pressed down with a pad of cotton wool. The ware was then placed for two or three hours in an oven of "a Heat no greater than one's Hand may Endure, or the Vessels will crack". This method of oil gilding was practised in Staffordshire as late as 1800. Such gilding could not be burnished.

Underglaze gilding: unfired oil gilding, when dry, could be made permanent by covering with a film of transparent **glaze**. This, however, considerably dulled the lustre of the gold. The gilding was washed with borax water, coated with crystalline powder, and fired at a temperature sufficient to melt this.

Japanned gilding: in this method of gilding the gold leaf was fixed to the ware by means of japanner's size or varnish, and fired in a reverberatory furnace at a low heat. It was possible to burnish such gilding, but direct application of the burnisher tended to tear the gold from the varnish. Instead, the burnisher was applied over a piece of thin calendered paper laid over the glaze.

Honey gilding: dates from about 1755 when **Chelsea** introduced this more permanent method of gilding from France. Gold leaf was ground with one-third of its weight in honey or other flux and tempered with oil of lavender. This was painted upon the ware to which it could be applied in considerable thickness if required, raising it appreciably above the surface of the ware. It was then fixed by low temperature firing.

The presence of the honey destroyed the rich brilliance of the gold, resulting in a slightly dull appearance. Honey gilding is less lustrous than japanned gilding, but much harder, even to the extent of withstanding scraping. The porcelain makers such as Chelsea and **Worcester** might apply such gilding thickly for enrichment by chasing.

Amber gilding: this was an improvement on japanned gilding dating from the early 1760s. The fixing medium was varnish prepared from crushed amber of fine quality. Immediately before use the gilder ground a little white lead into the amber varnish, painted a thin film on the ware, and applied the gold leaf. Where time was of no consequence the gilded ware was stored in a warm room for several months until the gilding had hardened: more usually, however, it was fired in a reverberatory furnace. If overfired the gold peeled away from the glaze. The gilding was scoured with a brush dipped in fine wet sand as a test for permanency: it was then burnished by direct application.

Mercury gilding: this was a cheaper method dating from the late 1780s, although the basic processes had long been well-known. This produced a harder film of gold than did former methods, distinguished by its rather brassy appearance. The gilder prepared an amalgam of grain gold, less pure than that obtained by using gold leaf. This was well rubbed together with some alcohol and a little bismuth subnitrate, and dried at a temperature of about one hundred degrees centigrade. The amalgam was then rubbed to a smooth soft paste with fat oil and applied to the ware with a pencil brush and fired. This drove off the mercury in vapour form leaving a film of dull gold attached firmly to the surface of the glaze. This was given a brilliant lustre by burnishing.

Raised gilding: a type of decoration in which enamel modelled in relief was brush-applied to the ware. After firing the enamel was gilded and refired, the effect suggesting solid gold.

Brown gold: invented by William Cornelius in 1853 but little used until the late 1860s. A thin paste made of gold chloride, bismuth oxide, borax and gum water was applied by pencil brush. After firing the surface was dull, but after burnishing and cleaning with vinegar the resulting gold had a rich brilliance not produced by any other method.

Liquid gold: although extremely brilliant this gold is not wear-resistant. Although in use at **Dresden** by 1830 it was little employed in England until 1855 when it decorated cheap bone china and earthenware. Most of the formulae are secret, but are based on the power of various oils containing sulphur to dissolve gold or retain it in suspension.

Acid gilding: an early Victorian innovation. The ware was printed with an acid-resist and then immersed in hydrofluoric acid which ate through exposed glaze. The ware was then gilded, fired and burnished. The raised pattern, where the glaze had been retained under the gilding, came into contact with the burnisher while the gilding remained matt on the parts where the acid had removed the glaze.

GILES, JAMES

A well-known outside decorator of **porcelain**, first established in the early 1750s at Kentish Town: stock and premises were acquired by **Duesbury** in 1777. Decorations from his workshops were never signed, but examples of enamelling attributed to him have been recorded on **Bow**, **Chelsea**, and **Derby** porcelains.

GLAMORGAN POTTERY (Swansea, Wales)

Established 1813 or 1814 by Baker, Bevan and Irwin, making **earthenware** products similar to those of the **Cambrian Pottery** until 1839. This printed mark was in use during all that period.

GLASGOW POTTERY. *See* **Bell, J. and M. P.**

GLAZE

An impervious, usually glassy, material applied to ceramics to make them impervious to liquids; to give them a brilliant surface; and to act as a foundation or protection for painted ornament. Early lead glazes were soft and were easily marked by cutting with a knife or stirring with a spoon: hence the preference for wood or metal plates and bowls until the introduction of "Greatbach's china glaze" in about 1764.

Lead glaze (dusted): until the introduction of liquid lead glaze in about 1750, lead glaze was applied to ceramic surfaces in the form of finely powdered and sifted natural sulphide of lead, known to contemporary potters as smithum and to collectors as galena. The shaped and decorated ware, sprinkled with smithum, was fired only once at a moderate temperature, baking the clay and melting the lead in one operation. The smithum spread into a film covering the surface of the ware with a rich yellowish or brownish glaze, caused by the presence of iron in either the clay or the smithum. A colourless glaze of higher gloss was more expensively secured by using calcined lead ground to a flour-like powder. This glaze penetrated further into the body than did that prepared from smithum. A range of purples and browns was obtained by blending the colourless glaze with manganese—known to contemporary potters as magnus—and greens by adding copper oxide.

Salt glaze: a hard translucent non-porous glaze on **stoneware** produced by the action of sodium chloride (common salt) upon the red-hot surface of the clay. The shaped ware was enclosed in **saggars** perforated with large holes, piled one above the other in a specially designed furnace. Salt was introduced into the kiln at the moment of peak temperature, immediately before full vitrification occurred, being shovelled in through apertures made for the purpose. The perforations permitted the fumes from the volatilized salt to reach the ware, when chemical changes occurred, causing a fine coating of silicate of soda and alumina to be deposited over the surface of the ware. When cold this appeared as a thin, intensely hard film of transparent soda glass. Brilliant and of long durability, salt glaze was characterized by tiny pin-holes or granulations giving a roughness unsuited to the everyday use of plates and dishes.

Lead glaze (liquid): the invention of firing ware to a **biscuit**, dipping it into a liquid glaze and re-firing, is usually credited to Enoch Booth in the early 1750s. Liquid glaze had been used earlier, however, and is fully specified in **Thomas Frye's** patent of 1748. The combination of fluid glaze and double firing was of the highest importance in the history of commercial ceramics. Calcined lead was ground with calcined **flint** clay and water. The biscuit was dipped into this and subjected to a second firing. This gave a highly lustrous and uniform surface to the ware, and for the first time every piece in a matching service could be glazed exactly alike. Early liquid glazes were not resistant to abrasion nor to the impure atmospheric conditions of industrial centres. Long periods of exposure to corrosive vapours dulled the glaze and made it iridescent.

An improved liquid lead glaze was introduced by the **Wedgwood and Bentley** firm in about 1764 by John Greatbach. This glaze produced a smoother, harder surface better suited to use with foodstuffs than any earlier glaze on soft **porcelain** or **earthenware.** The glaze was prepared from a **frit** and other fusible materials ground to a creamy consistency in water. The coated **biscuit** was dried in a heated room, then fired, emerging from the oven with a clear brilliant surface. Perfect results depended so largely upon securing exact harmony between composition of body and glaze, the exact temperatures of firing in biscuit and glost ovens, and the subsequent decoration that few potters other than the celebrated masters achieved such success until the 19th century.

Felspathic glaze: this was used on the **hard porcelains** made at **Plymouth, Bristol** and **New Hall**, as lead glaze fails to adhere firmly to the surface of such porcelain. Felspathic glaze consisted of the same constituents as the body, but in different proportions, containing more felspar and less kaolin than the body. Calcareous glazes of similar constituents with the addition of a limestone flux were also used on hard porcelain, these being more transparent than the felspathic glaze and penetrating further into the body. Felspathic glazes, more viscous and slightly milky, were applied more thickly and have a more velvety, richer appearance than calcareous glaze.

Leadless glaze: a hard, white, highly lustrous glaze evolved in 1820 by John Rose of **Coalport** in an effort to avoid the health hazards associated with glaze containing lead. Glaze dippers had invariably died at an early age. Although glaze made from fritted lead was virtually innocuous, so exact was the firing needed to produce a good glaze that it was never used. The

Society of Arts reported Rose's glaze to be the finest that had come under their observation and awarded him the Isis gold medal.

Rose's leadless glaze had the advantage of fusing at a lower temperature without producing specks or flaws. Enamelled decoration incorporated solidly with it, brilliance and tint being unaffected. Lead glaze adversely affected delicately-tinted enamels, and those containing gold or chrome. Nevertheless, because borax, one of the ingredients, then cost about five shillings a pound, this leadless glaze was used only on costly services until the early 1830s. Its principal ingredient was felspar ground to a fine powder. The published recipe, which was not patented and remained free to all, was "27 felspar, 18 borax, 4 Lynn sand, 3 nitre, 3 soda, 3 Cornwall china clay. This was melted to a **frit**, ground to a fine powder with 3 parts of calcined borax added before grinding." In expensive and elaborate decorations, requiring repeated firings, the absence of lead in the glaze resulted in more radiant colours.

Smear glaze: an almost invisible glaze with the suggestion of a dull polish, as in domestic **parian ware**. This glaze was not applied directly to the **biscuit** as a coating, but was introduced into the **saggar** containing it in the firing kiln. Whether placed in a small cup or thickly painted over the walls of the tightly-sealed saggar, the glaze melted as the temperature increased, its vapour settling as a fine mist on the ware. Hollow-ware intended to contain liquids might be liquid glazed within, and the exterior smear-glazed.

GOAT-AND-BEE JUGS

Made at **Chelsea**, moulded in relief with two reclining goats lying head to tail supporting the body of the jug,

which was decorated with raised flowers and a bee, which might be ascending or descending. The handle was shaped as a twig. Sometimes these jugs were in white, on others the raised flowers were touched with colour. They are known with considerable variations suggesting the use of several moulds. The design was adapted from a silver jug by Edward Wood, bearing the London hall-mark 1737. The earliest authenticated piece of English porcelain is a goat-and-bee jug, incised with the name Chelsea, a triangle, and the date 1743. They are found marked with the triangle alone; with the triangle and the name Chelsea; with these and the year 1745; unmarked; as 19th and 20th-century reproductions.

GOSS, W. H. (Stoke-upon-Trent).

Celebrated for its miniature china decorated with coats of arms in full colour, the firm was founded in 1858. The delicate ivory-tinted porcelain has a seemingly waxen surface and is really **parian ware** of high quality. This heraldic china is stamped with the firm's name: German copies are obviously of poorer material. Every place in England possessing a coat of arms was represented in Goss china.

During the 19th century Goss produced other ware far above the average. This included jewelled porcelain in the styles of **Sèvres** but of finer quality: the Goss jewels never fall away, having been set in specially prepared hollows. Parian ware vases and tazzas were magnificently decorated with classical figures, landscapes and flowers. Many parian ware busts were made modelled by Gallimore who, according to Blacker, had previously worked at **Belleek.** The parian ware was marked with a rising falcon. Brooches, ear-rings, charms and the like were not made in the celebrated ivory porcelain, but in a **biscuit** resembling that of 18th century **Derby**, with hand-modelled flowers, sometimes painted in colours. Fine quality **terra cotta** was made in highly original styles, characteristic being the use of leaves in relief.

GR (monarch's cypher) MARK. *See* **Excise mark.**

GRAINGER, LEE & COMPANY (Worcester)

Porcelain factory established in 1801 by Thomas Grainger, nephew of Humphrey Chamberlain and a former decorator with the Chamberlain firm. At first he decorated **bone china** tableware bought from **Coalport** in a style resembling that used by the Chamberlain firm. In 1812 he was joined by a Mr. Lee and the firm styled Grainger, Lee & Company, their address being the Royal China Works, Worcester. By 1815 they were making a fine **soft-paste porcelain**, but by 1820 had abandoned this in favour of **bone china.** Their early tableware was embossed with sprays of wild roses and leaves, birds and other flowers enriched with polychrome enamelling. An intensely deep opaque *gros bleu* was also used in sprays and stripes. From about 1830 until absorbed by the **Worcester Royal Porcelain Company Ltd.** in 1889 the firm made **lithophanes** and inexpensive bone china for everyday use.

GRANITE WARE

A cream-coloured earthenware with a greyish or bluish mottled **glaze** made by **Wedgwood**, not to be confused with the industrial granite ware evolved from **Mason's** ironstone china in the mid-19th century.

GREATBACH, WILLIAM

A former apprentice of **Whieldon's** who started on his own in 1762 at Lower Lane, Staffordshire, working under an agreement by which **Wedgwood** paid him fixed prices for his entire output. He modelled and made relief designs of landscapes found on **green-glazed ware**. By 1770 he had removed to Lane Delph where he produced black **transfer-printed** ware overpainted with colours, specializing in tea-pots banded with low relief work above the transfer work. These sometimes bear the inscription "published as the Act directs, Jany 4, 1778". This date is not necessarily the year the ware was made, but the date of the Act protecting the design.

GREEN, CHROMIUM

This colour was prepared from chromium oxide, discovered in 1749, but not until the early years of the 19th century was it brought into use for decorating English ceramics. Formerly copper oxide was used in preparing green enamels which could only be used overglaze. The chromium greens are less transparent than the copper greens and are slightly yellowish in tone. From the early 1820s they could be used underglaze on **bone china**, displaying a faintly greyish hue. Chrome greens were never used on **soft porcelains** of the 18th century.

GREEN-GLAZED WARE

This was the medieval potter's standby so far as decoration was concerned, copper oxide producing in **lead glaze** various leaf-green and speckled green effects, on a buff body. Collectors sometimes term such pottery Tudor ware because of its great popularity during the 16th century. In 1759 **Josiah Wedgwood** developed a clear liquid green glaze, fired in the glost oven. This, his first considerable success as a potter, enabled him to produce a new species of coloured ware, notably his cauliflower and pineapple series. The glaze was soon copied by other potters, and has in fact been in continual production ever since.

GREEN WARE

Unfinished clayware which has not been fired. This term has no reference to colour, and is probably comparable with the application of the term green to unseasoned wood.

GREENS BINGLEY & CO. MARK.

See **Smith, William.**

GREYBEARDS. *See* **Bellarmines.**

GROG

Finely ground **porcelain** or **earthenware** incorporated among the materials of a recipe to lessen shrinkage of the body in firing. Also used in various **glazes,** particularly on **soapstone porcelain.**

HACKWOOD, WILLIAM

Chief modeller of **bas-reliefs** for **Josiah Wedgwood** whom he joined in 1769. He was mainly employed in adapting busts and reliefs from the antique, but much of his original work was equal in every way to that of more celebrated artists of the period. In January 1776 Wedgwood recorded

that *The Birth of Bacchus*, modelled by Hackwood from Michaelangelo's seal, was then the largest **jasper** plaque to have been produced. It measured twenty-seven inches across by twelve inches high and sold for thirty shillings. *The Triumph of Bacchus* made immediately afterwards was larger. Hackwood's excellent profile portraits included those of George III, Queen Charlotte, Josiah Wedgwood, David Garrick, all modelled in 1777, Admiral Keppel, Dr. Priestley, Louis XVI, and an old bricklayer, Edward Bourne, employed on the Wedgwood pottery kilns. This and the profile of Wedgwood are signed W H in script, the only instances of a modeller's mark on the surface of any jasper bas-relief.

A descendant, William Hackwood, trading as William Hackwood and Sons, made **transfer-printed** wares at New Hall, 1846–50. One of the firm's marks is reproduced on this page.

HALL, JOHN and RALPH (Tunstall, Staffordshire)

Makers of **transfer-printed earthenware** and **figures** from about 1805 to 1822. After 1822 John Hall and his sons were at Burslem until 1833, while Ralph Hall was at Tunstall until 1846. The mark HALL may be found impressed.

HERCULANEUM. *See* **Liverpool.**

HICKS, MEIGH and JOHNSON (Shelton, Staffordshire)

Minor potters, established 1806, making **transfer-printed** wares and **lustres** until absorbed by the Ridgway firm.

HIGH TEMPERATURE COLOURS. *See* **Colours.**

HILDITCH AND SONS (Longton, Staffordshire)

Makers of **earthenware** and **bone china**, some well potted but in no way outstanding, with **transfer-printed** ornament. This might be marked as shown, printed in red. The firm was active 1795 to 1830.

HOLLINS, SAMUEL

Established as a potter of highly-finished red-ware tea-pots at Shelton, Staffordshire, in 1774 using the seam of clay worked by the **Elers** at Bradwell. From 1790 he also made excellent imitations of **Wedgwood's jasper ware** in red, blue, green, and other colours. Until 1802 the mark was S. HOLLINS impressed. He was then joined by his sons and the mark became T & J HOLLINS impressed. Samuel Hollins was also a partner in the **New Hall** company. *See* **Toby jugs**.

HYLTON MARK. *See* **Sunderland**.

H. M. & Co. MARK. *See* **Minton**.

H. P. MARK. *See* **Palmer**.

IMARI (Japan)

Hard porcelain made in the province of Hizen and shipped from the port of Imari. Decoration was mainly floral in underglaze blue on white. Brocaded Imari in underglaze blue, red and green, with **gilding**, was a style introduced by the Dutch East India Company early in the 18th century: they commissioned the merchants of Imari to obtain porcelain with decorative themes taken directly from native brocades. These designs were adapted and copied by the English makers of finer **porcelain** and **bone china**. *See* **Japan patterns**.

INCISED DECORATION

Designs scratched into the unfired clay without variation of colour. *See* **Scratch blue**.

IRONSTONE CHINA. *See* **Stone china** *and* **Mason ware**.

ISLEWORTH (Middlesex)

Established by Joseph Shore of **Worcester** in 1760 making **pottery** in a small way and specializing in domestic **Welsh ware** such as meat dishes, in production until the factory was closed in 1820. When Richard Goulding joined the firm as partner in 1795 tea-pots, **figures** and vases were made in a waxy red or chocolate coloured **terra-cotta**, with designs in relief in an adapted **Japanese** style. Some authorities consider the colour of red Isleworth to be the nearest English equivalent to old Samian ware. These bear the impressed mark S & G or S & G ISLEWORTH. Similar wares with marks FG and W S & S are reported by W. B. Honey to be of German origin.

In the early 19th century Isleworth made hound jugs in brown **stoneware** decorated with sporting subjects in high relief and with greyhound handles. These were marked S & G ISLEWORTH or S & G. It has been stated, wrongly, that **soft-paste porcelain** decorated in underglaze blue was made here until 1787.

J.A. Sc. MARK. *See* **Pot-lid pictures**.

JACKFIELD (Shropshire)

Potters are known to have been active here in the reign of Henry VIII, but the name is usually considered as the generic term for black glazed **earthenware** made during the second half of the 18th century. Original Jackfield earthenware has a red body, a brilliant black **glaze**, ornamented with scrollwork and flowers in relief, and frequently with oil **gilding** and unfired painting (*see* **Colours**). This was made from 1751 to 1772 by Maurice Thursfield, and known as "black decanters". The base was generally unglazed, displaying the red body. Teapot lids were surmounted by birds with outspread wings. Similar ware was produced by John Thursfield at Benthall, Salop, from 1772 to 1818. Contemporary Staffordshire potters, including **Astbury** and **Whieldon**, also issued such ware.

JACKSON, J. *See* **Transfer-printing**.

JACKSON, T. *See* **Pot-lid pictures**.

JAPAN PATTERNS

A term indiscriminately used for both Chinese and Japanese designs copied by the English decorators and including **famille rose, famille verte,** brocaded **Imari**, and **Kakiemon**. **Chelsea** during the gold anchor period copied brocaded Imari in colours far superior in brilliance to the original Japanese. **Worcester** delighted in Japan patterns from about 1760. In the Worcester sale catalogue of 1769 reference is made to "old mosaick japan pattern" and to "fine old japan fan pattern". Japan patterns were used to a lesser extent at **Derby** and other contemporary factories. They appeared on **bone china** from about 1800 and continued until the 1830s, first on **Spode** and soon afterwards on Chamberlain's Worcester, and in the following decade on Derby ware, the proprietor advertising in 1817 for "painters of japan patterns". **Minton, Coalport, Rockingham** and several Staffordshire makes of bone china from 1817 decorated in such styles. *See* **Imari** and **Kakiemon**.

JASPER WARE

A dense white vitrified **stoneware** of nearly the same properties as **porcelain**, developed in 1774 by **Josiah Wedgwood** and in production to the present day. Its finely-grained surface was never **glazed**, and when thin in section is translucent. The extremely hard body contained carbonate or sulphate of baryta, and could be coloured throughout its texture by the addition of metallic oxides. When stained throughout with colour it was called solid jasper: when a white piece was dipped in a solution of liquid tinted jasper it was known as jasper dip. Early examples had a creamy hue. From about 1780 until 1820 texture was fine and uniform of grain, and never chalky in appearance. Jasper made by Wedgwood between 1780 and 1795 feels almost like satin to the touch. This is known to collectors as waxen jasper.

Josiah Wedgwood appears to have used seven ground colours: dark blue, lavender, a bluish pink known to collectors as lilac, sage-green, olive-green, an intense black, and, rarely, an attractive yellow. These hues varied in tone for technical reasons not then overcome. They formed the backgrounds against which classical reliefs and other motifs were applied, usually in white jasper. From wax originals moulds were made in plaster-of-paris or fired clay. The moist white jasper was pressed by the potter's thumb into such a "pitcher" or intaglio mould until every line and dot was filled. The superfluous clay was then scraped off level with the face of the mould with a modelling tool. After drying for a few minutes the white jasper relief was skilfully extracted from the mould, wetted with water, and applied by hand to the coloured panel, a process known as **sprigging**. While the clay was still soft the modeller tooled the reliefs, undercutting the edges to give sharpness to shadows and perfecting the surface. The subsequent firing was a skilled operation. The long slabs of jasper to which the reliefs were applied were perfectly flat, while seldom exceeding a quarter-of-an-inch in thickness.

Other firms making jasper ware in close imitation of Wedgwood productions included **William Adams**, Greengates, who gave a violet hue to his jasper by adding gold filings to the sulphate of baryta; **John Turner**, a greenish-toned jasper; **S. Hollins**; **Palmer, Neale and Wilson**.

J. AUSTIN Sc. MARK. *See* **Pot-lid pictures.**

J R F S Co. MARK. *See* **Coalport.**

JUGS. *See* **Bear, Double-walled, Lustre, Mason, Puzzle, Toby**.

JWR MARK. *See* **Ridgway and Sons.**

KAKIEMON

Seventeenth-century Japanese potter who worked at Arita, for which Imari was the export centre—hence the association of these names. True Kakiemon designs must be distinguished from the later intricate brocaded mosaic patterns, and the Kakiemon palette of bluish green, soft Indian red, pale blue, pale yellow and gold distinguished from the coarse, muddy colours of much later exported Japanese and pseudo-Japanese ware. *See* **Japan.**

KEYS and MOUNTFORD. *See* **Parian ware.**

KISHERE. *See* **Mortlake.**

LACEWORK, PERFORATED

Finely perforated net lacework or embroidery decorating the flower-decked dresses of **bone china figures** made at **Derby** from about 1830, often enriched with hand-modelled flowers. Such figures are often assumed to be of **Dresden** origin, but were, in fact, copies of Berlin porcelain, although the technique was first introduced at Rouen. They were made from about 1840 by Alfred Singer & Sons, Vauxhall Potteries, fine pieces being marked with the monogram A S in crimson.

The fragile bone china lace was made by soaking machine-made lace in bone china slip, made to the consistency of cream, and filtered through fine lawn. The lace held the particles of the slip until the latter became vitrified in the kiln, the heat of which destroyed the threads of textile, leaving only the china.

LAKIN AND POOLE (Hanley, Staffordshire)

According to Wedgwood and Ormsbee this firm was established in 1770 by John Lakin to make **cream-coloured earthenware** and black **basalt.** By 1780 he had been joined by Richard Poole, when they specialized in cream-coloured useful wares decorated with blue **transfer prints** of landscapes. They also achieved a reputation for the excellence of their **figures** and groups, including **toby jugs.** Their marks impressed were: LAKIN; LAKIN & POOLE; R POOLE. The firm closed down in 1794.

LAMBETH (London)

The **delft-ware** potteries that flourished along the banks of the Thames extending from Vauxhall to Clerkenwell are usually classified as Lambeth. A wide variety of ware was produced, including serving bottles; **puzzle-jugs** with narrow in-curved necks; porringers with oval handles, each with an oval or heart-shaped **piercing**; candlesticks in the style of contemporary pewter; **fuddling cups**; posset pots; **tygs, mugs.** Some of this was painted in blue, a small amount in high temperature **colours.** *See* **Doulton, Dwight, Spirit flasks, Stoneware.**

LEAD GLAZE. *See* **Glaze.**

LEEDS (Yorkshire)

This was chief among the potteries that made **cream-coloured earthenware.** The pottery is believed to have been founded in 1760 by the brothers Green. In 1774 they were joined by a partner named Humble and seven years later by William Hartley who saw a great future for the factory, which by 1790 had branch establishments at **Swinton** and **Don**. A pattern book was issued as early as 1783, described on the title page as: "Designs of Sundry Articles of Queen's, or Cream-colour'd Earthenware, manufactured by Hartley, Green, and Co., at Leeds-Pottery: with a Great Variety of other Articles. The same Enamel'd, Printed, or Ornamented with Gold to any Pattern; also with Coats of Arms, Cyphers, Landscapes, &c. &c." The yearly turnover for 1790 exceeded £50,000 with an export trade extending into Holland, Germany and the Baltic. Hartley died in 1821 and the firm gradually declined in importance until it closed in 1878.

Leeds' celebrated cream-coloured earthenware was of a fine light clay, yellowish in tone, covered with a rich glassy **glaze** that had a tendency to run into a faint green tinge when full. The best Leeds glaze has the appearance of having been floated on and spread without bubbling or **crazing**; it scratched less easily than most contemporary creamware. Being lighter than the ware of its rivals it was admitted to continental countries at a cheaper rate of import tax. In comparison with the cream-coloured earthenware of the **Wedgwood** firm at this period it was warmer and brighter in tone. The ware of **Mayer**, which it most nearly resembled, was yellower and less even of surface: that of **Herculaneum** was greyer.

Leeds drew upon three main styles of ornament: Chinese, **rococo**, and classic. The debt to Chinese porcelains is important: they made gourd and melon-shaped sugar-boxes and sauce boats derived from naturalistic Chinese design. From China, too, came the typical handle for tea- and coffee-pots, two intertwined strips ending in leaves and berries. The Staffordshire potters had used such handles much earlier, but the design became established as a distinctive Leeds attribute, and one seldom lacking on the squat low tea-pots with their curved spouts and flower finials.

Pierced decoration was characteristic, patterns being cut with hand

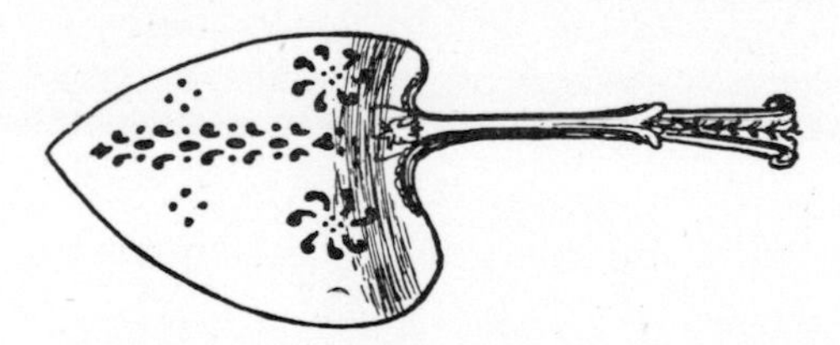

punches, hole by hole. Diamonds, hearts, circles and other motifs were so cleverly combined as to suggest a pattern of lace. This form of decoration was used to edge tea and dessert plates; it was the basis of the intricate pierced baskets, shell dishes, and candlesticks: in some of the elaborate centrepieces and urns it took on the quality of fine silverwork. The server shown here is taken from an 1815 Leeds catalogue. **Basket-work** was also made, built up from extruded strips of clay.

The majority of cream-ware was

issued undecorated, but fine, black **transfer-printing** was produced and in the 19th century blue-printed ware. Other pieces might be painted with overglaze enamels, in shades of red, violet and green, but no high artistic level was reached.

Leeds also made other types of pottery, including fine-grained **agate, pearl** and **tortoiseshell** pottery as well as **lustre wares**. A thriving business was carried out in **engine-turned basalts**, red **stoneware**, and small **figures** in the **Ralph Wood** style.

The marks changed very little over a long period. The first mark of importance, dating from 1783, was LEEDS★POTTERY, sometimes impressed twice and crossed on blue-printed ware of the early 19th century. Instead of an asterisk a dot or hyphen might be used, and all are sometimes found following the Y instead of being centrally placed. Another mark is HARTLEY · GREENS & CO/LEEDS POTTERY sometimes impressed in the form of a double horse-shoe. Rarely, and very small, the mark L P is found.

W. B. Honey has pointed out that in the genuine, rarely marked, old Leeds the letters composing the mark were usually somewhat irregularly set. Marked black basalt medallions and cream-ware with silver lustred reliefs are modern. Much of the ware was unmarked, however, and from 1888 some notable pierced work was made for Slee of Leeds by Senior, impressed with the old marks.

Hunslett Hall Pottery, Leeds, was founded before 1792 by Petty and Rainforth to compete in the cream-ware trade. Their products might be impressed RAINFORTH & CO.

LIMEHOUSE (London)

A **porcelain** factory established in 1746 near Dick's Shore, Limehouse. The *Daily Advertiser* January 1, 1747 announced "that the new-invented blue-and-white Limehouse ware" was on sale. Closed 1748. Its productions remain unidentified.

LINDSAY POWELL & CO. *See* **Parian ware.**

LITHOGRAPHY. *See* **Transfer-printing.**

LITHOPHANES

Transparencies made from a thin, glassy, **hard porcelain**, giving the effect of detailed mezzotint engravings by precise variations in the thickness and consequent opacity of the material. The process was invented in 1827 by Baron de Bourgoing, who sold the English rights to R. G. Jones, Brewer Street, London, who in his turn disposed of the manufacturing rights in 1828 to the firm of **Grainger, Lee & Company**, Worcester. Known at the time as "Jones's method of ornamenting china", the ornament was used on various articles in which there would be the essential light behind it, such as lantern panels, lampshades, night-lights, and hand fire-screens. Teacups were given the normal painted decoration on their sides and surprised their users with lithophane decoration in their bases, which became visible only as the cups were tilted against the light.

After 1842 a number of other potters made lithophanes, including **Minton, Worcester**, and the Kennedy Porcelain Manufactory, Burslem.

LIVERPOOL

Earthenware was being made here by 1660 in considerable quantity. So prosperous became the trade that during the second half of the 18th century more than eighty master potters were established in the town.

Earthenware and delft-ware: mugs and jugs were made for export in ordinary earthenware. By 1710 **English delft ware**, made from a light buff clay, was in production, *The Post Boy* referring to "fine white and painted pots and other vessels and tiles". Liverpool became celebrated for delft ware blue painted punch bowls, giant examples being a speciality. The principal makers were Seth and John Pennington, Richard Chaffers, Zachariah Barnes and S. and T. Shaw. A considerable trade was carried out in **tile**-making. **Cream-coloured earthenware,** noticeably light in weight, displaced delft ware in the 1780s, being decorated in **cobalt blue**, in polychrome enamels, or in blue or black **transfer-printing.**

Porcelain and bone china: characteristics of the different Liverpool porcelains varied, making it impossible to give hard and fast rules regarding classification, for rarely indeed are 18th-century marks to be found. There are, however, a few guides to assist the collector. Compared with other soft-paste porcelains the Liverpool productions have a distinctly greyish hue. The basic clay of local origin appears to have contained impurities which the primitive methods of refining failed to remove.

Soapstone porcelain is known to have been manufactured in Liverpool in 1756. Already, four years earlier, Richard Chaffers had established a pottery on Shaw's Brow for the manufacture of delft-ware painted blue. In December 1756 he was advertising that his "Porcelain or China Ware . . . is proved with boiling water before it is exposed for sale." This heat-resistant soapstone porcelain had a clean, hard-looking, very slightly grey body with a faintly bluish milky **glaze**. When held to the light a greenish translucency showed, varying in intensity according to thickness of section. The glaze, which was marred by tiny bubbles, was brush-applied, leaving bare patches on the foot-rim; a **thundercloud** effect was often present.

Some of Chaffers' porcelain was decorated with moulding in low relief,

9. Staffordshire figures: (*Top left*) salt-glazed white stoneware figure of Shakespeare, after the statue in Westminster Abbey made by Peter Scheemakers. About 1780. Height 18 inches. (*Top centre*) Black basalt figure "Mercury on the Rock", marked "Wedgwood". 1786. (*Top right*) Earthenware painted with enamels, made by Enoch Wood, Burslem, about 1790. 18½ inches. (*Centre left*) Earthenware with patches of coloured glaze, 1770s. 7½ inches. (*Above*) Salt-glazed white stoneware figures of Turk and lady copied from J. J. Kaendler's porcelain figures of about 1745. About 1760. 7¾ inches. (*Centre right*) Chung-li Ch'van, one of the Taoist Eight Immortals, in salt-glazed white stoneware, about 1750. 7¼ inches. (*Left*) Astbury figure in earthenware, 1730s. (*Right*) An Astbury Grenadier, about 1740.

10. (*Top left*) Wedgwood queen's ware painted with the grape and vine border in purple and green. 1773. Length 17½ inches. (*Top centre*) Caughley porcelain painted in underglaze blue. Mark "Salopian" impressed. About 1780. (*Top right*) Wedgwood queen's ware with open trellis-work rim, and black printed decoration. Mark "Wedgwood" impressed. Made at Etruria, printed in Liverpool. About 1780. Length 11¾ inches. (*Lower left*) Spode sauce tureen, stand, and plate in bone china, trial pieces for a complete service made for the Prince Regent in 1811. (*Lower centre*) Staffordshire salt-glazed white stoneware dish moulded and

forming reserves for decoration in cobalt blue under the glaze, or in enamels over the glaze. High lights in the relief work might be accentuated with colour. Chaffers' blue-and-white was cleanly painted, the blue itself inclining towards a slaty tinge. Designs were copied and adapted from Chinese importations.

Enamels were also applied in the Chinese style, motifs including rocks, flowering plants, birds, and robed figures, and the most frequent colours being pale yellow, brick red, emerald green and blue. A red border around the rim of a piece of hollow-ware was characteristic, as were also several simple diaper borders. Chaffers was also responsible for the **Liverpool bird**. Some black and red transfer prints were used, the majority of lines being coarse and blurred because of some defect in the glaze.

The bases of Chaffers' hollow-ware were invariably glazed, and handles shaped in the **Worcester** style but thinner. His jugs were the first in which the lip was raised slightly above the level of the rim, a style continued by later potters. He also began the vogue for barrel-shaped mugs with everted rims and grooved base rings. Foot-rings were triangular in section and slightly undercut.

Following the death of Chaffers in 1765 the firm came under the control of Philip Christian, a delft-ware potter who continued the soapstone formula until the early 1770s. In 1774 he sold the lease of his soapstone quarries in Cornwall to Thomas Turner of **Caughley**. He then made some excellent table-ware and vases of highly translucent, finely glazed porcelain. The quality of his enamelled decoration surpassed that of any other Liverpool potter.

Seth Pennington, established in the early 1780s, was outstanding among Liverpool potters for the consistent high quality of his productions. These, when held to the light, show a green translucency. There is a distinct tinge of colour in the glaze, resulting in a duck-egg green appearance. Table-ware was exceptionally heavy and thick, particularly at the base, and might be decorated with relief ornament beneath the rim—blue flowers and designs of a mythological or symbolical character. His blue enamel was of an exceptionally light hue. A letter P, as a capital or in script has been noted as a Pennington mark.

James Pennington, brother of Seth, established as a potter in about 1768, became a specialist in porcelain punch bowls decorated with a brilliant blue applied so lavishly that it stood out from the surface. He also advertised "elegant, cheap and serviceable china ware which for brilliancy of colour is equal to any made in Great Britain."

Zachariah Barnes, a master tile-maker, began the manufacture of underglaze **blue-printed** porcelain early in the 1780s. The paste of his table-ware was so thick as somewhat to resemble earthenware. Variations

Liverpool marks. *Top line from left,* Herculaneum 1790–1822 impressed or blue printed; Herculaneum 1822–33 impressed; Herculaneum 1822–41 generally impressed. *Middle line from left,* Reid and Company 1756–60; Philip Christian of Shaw's Brow 1760–75; impressed mark found occasionally. *Bottom line, left and centre,* Case, Mort and Company, 1822–41 (from Liverpool crest); *right,* Richard Chaffers.

in the paste were made from time to time, but the majority of pieces show a cloudy yellow in the thinnest parts if held to the light. Some thin pieces are known, and these display a faintly brown or blue translucency. The glassy glaze appears starchy blue and faulty firing caused the surface to be flawed with specks of black and blue. The thick, blurred lines of the transfer-printing in dark **cobalt blue** suggest that the transfer process had not been thoroughly mastered.

Bone china: Richard Abbey in 1793 established a factory specializing in finely **transfer-printed** pottery jugs, but without commercial success. Premises and plant were acquired in 1796 by the firm of Worthington, Humble & Holland, who abandoned the traditional methods of Liverpool and introduced modern methods, including forty experienced hands from Staffordshire. They named the works Herculaneum, and produced cream-coloured earthenware. By 1800 they were making **bone china** of heavy, almost opaque paste: glaze and potting were excellent. All kinds of table-ware were made, **bat-printed** tea- and coffe-services being a feature, decoration in various colours showing views of country seats and spas, or stippled figures of men and women. These were sometimes overpainted in coloured enamels. Urn-shaped vases in sets of three were enamelled in brilliant colours, the body usually being in a red, blue or orange ground colour: handles were in the form of conventionalized dolphins, birds, winged heads, and so on. Herculaneum closed in 1841.

LIVERPOOL BIRD

A bird vaguely resembling the partridge-type of **Chelsea** and **Worcester**, but more speedily painted. Evolved by Richard Chaffers (*see* preceding entry) in 1757 and copied by many succeeding **Liverpool** potters during the next half century, the bird had a red head and neck, a breast speckled with red dots, the upper wing blue and the flight feathers outlined in black.

The yellow body was speckled with red dots and ended in a patch of red before a purplish tail.

LL (crossed) MARK. *See* **Longton Hall** *and* **Sèvres.**

LLOYD, JOHN and REBECCA (Hanley, Staffordshire)

Makers of "toys" and chimney ornaments, 1834–50, and continued after John Lloyd's death by his widow. The mark LLOYD, SHELTON may be noted impressed.

LOCKER AND CO. (Derby)

This firm made **bone china** from 1848 to 1851. *See* **Derby.**

LONGPORT MARK. *See* **Davenport.**

LONGTON HALL (near Newcastle-under-Lyme)

Until the recent discovery by Dr. Bernard Watney concerning this factory, it had been thought that William Littler, a successful **salt-glaze** potter, established Staffordshire's first **porcelain** factory in 1750. *The Times* October 4, 1955, referred to Dr. Watney's discovery of original agreements showing that "William Jenkinson had started the factory on his own account, having 'obtained the art, secret or mystery of making a certain porcelain ware in imitation of china ware'. The earliest agreement discovered is dated August 25th 1753, and refers to an even earlier one dated October 7th 1751 in which Jenkinson decides to take two other partners into the business, one of these being William Littler, who then became the manager of the factory." Soft-paste porcelains of two major types were made here, variations occurring in each. Early productions were in a soft, creamy-white, glassy paste, very translucent, with a small amount of bone ash in its composition. It resembled **Chelsea** in its first period but was of inferior quality. Later the paste became noticeably heavier owing to the introduction of lead oxide, a result of using flint-glass in preparing the frit. This paste was rather grey in colour with a greenish cream translucency displaying **moons** when held to the light. Surface specks were usual. A distinctly uneven surface characterized Longton Hall porcelain.

Glaze at first was thinly applied and is recognized by its cold, glittering surface. Although faintly tinged with **cobalt** it was whiter than **Bow** or Chelsea. A glaze slightly greyish in tint was used on the later, heavier paste, and gave the surface a look of having been dipped in candlegrease. This ended usually a fraction of an inch above the base. The exposed **biscuit** has absorbed two centuries of dust and now appears as a dark line.

The first productions, according to Dr. Pococke, were "statues of elephants, lyons, and birds . . . the percentage of wasters being high". These were in the white, and so thickly covered with greenish-hued glaze that modelling details were obscured. Longton Hall early made small hollow-ware such as sauce-boats, decorated with wide uneven borders or with solid grounds, in which reserves enclosed simple oriental motifs, the intention being to emulate the *gros bleu* developed at Vincennes in 1749. This underglaze blue ground, characteristic of Longton Hall and lavishly used on decorative porcelain, had little richness or depth. It always had a streaky appearance as though sponge-applied to the biscuit by an amateur, and the glaze was thin. Longton Hall blue was often ornamented with cartouches outlined in raised white enamel scrollwork. This feature is not found on other English porcelain, although it had been used on Littler's salt-glaze ware. Longton Hall blue was lighter than that used at Chelsea and was brighter than the blue grounds of **Derby** and **Worcester**. From 1753 the blue reserves might contain ornament in polychrome enamels: flowers, exotic birds and figure paintings.

Polychrome decoration was used throughout the period. At first **unfired colours** were used, which have tended to flake away with the passing of years. **Dresden** flower motifs were painted from 1753 by a single artist whose style is unmistakable, his petals being irregularly outlined. Longton Hall landscapes with buildings and exotic birds were characterized by peculiar-hued brown and yellow enamels; a feature of the foreground was a tuft of rushes with the tips of some leaves turned over. **Gilding** was always sparse and was never burnt into the glaze: it was applied in the form of thick gold leaf fixed with size, and in consequence is dull of surface.

Figures, made of a heavy grey paste, tended to lack skill in modelling and artistry in enamelling. They were supported by **rococo** scrollwork bases unskilfully moulded and decorated with a few lines of enamel applied to the edges of the scrolls. Costumes were decorated with star or diaper patterns, never with flower motifs. Characteristic colours were a harsh crimson, an uneven yellow, a dry yellowish green and a poor red. Heads were carefully modelled and the faces enlivened with a distinctive red marking the features.

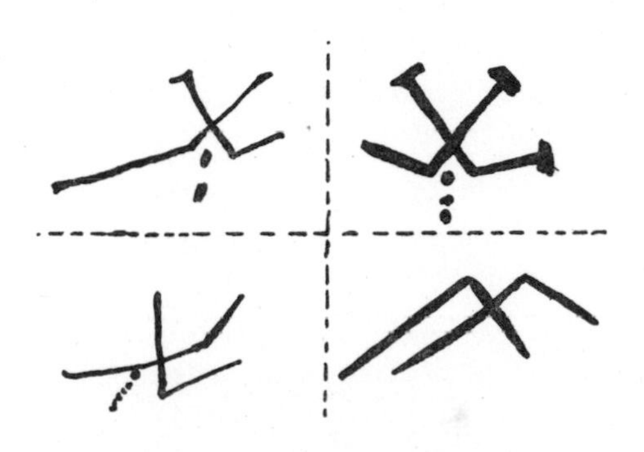

The Longton Hall mark, rare, and found only on early pieces, consists of a monogram of two L's crossed, with a string of three dots placed vertically below, in underglaze blue. The monogram is reasonably assumed to mean Littler, Longton, but some authorities have suggested that it is an adaptation of the crossed L's of Vincennes (later **Sèvres**). The marks illustrated are all in blue; that on the bottom right, in the field of the decorations.

LOWDIN'S BRISTOL. *See* **Bristol soft-paste porcelain.**

LOWESBY (Leicestershire)

Established in 1835 by Sir Frederick Fowke to make small ware of **terra cotta** ornamented in black, in imitation of **Wedgwood's rosso antico**. Other work produced here was enriched with brilliant enamel designs over a surface coated in dull black. **Tortoise-shell ware** was also produced. The mark was an impressed fleur-de-lis from the Fowke arms with the name LOWESBY in an arc below.

LOWESTOFT (Suffolk)

Established 1757 by Robert Browne, a practical potter experienced at **Bow**. Early productions were intended to supply only the needs of East Anglia, and such **porcelain** was always the factory's main concern. The existence of a London warehouse in 1769, however, suggests that, for a time, porcelain of finer quality was made to meet the competition of **Bow**, **Chelsea**, **Derby** and **Worcester**. It appears that there was never more than a single kiln in use and the firm was also engaged in the seasonal occupation of herring curing. The great loss sustained when the French seized several thousand pounds' worth of its porcelain at Rotterdam, with the competition of **bone china**, was responsible for closing the works in 1802.

Lowestoft porcelain was generally

poorly potted and inexpensively decorated. Its paste, chemically approximating that of **Bow**, was less skilfully manipulated during manufacture. It was a soft-paste porcelain of the bone ash type and was fairly opaque and of uniform transparency.

At least three distinct varieties of paste appear to have been made. The first had a bluish **glaze** and was decorated in blue designs. In this the blue and white of **Worcester** was extensively imitated. The second and most characteristic paste was of a deep creamy white tint, showing a yellowish tinge if held to the light. The thin glaze, almost invariably tinged with blue, tended to disguise the creamy whiteness of the paste. While wet the glaze had a tendency to settle more thickly in crevices of relief moulding and within the inside edge of rims and handle joints, displaying a decidedly bluish hue in such places. The surface was usually marred by innumerable microscopic black and blue specks, fine sand and tiny bubbles. Sometimes age has caused it to become slightly discoloured towards the foot of a vessel.

A third variety was evidently intended to imitate superficially Chinese hard paste, as the glaze was green-tinted to correspond with Oriental productions of the same character. This had a peculiar duck-egg tint: placed side by side with characteristic Lowestoft porcelain the green is pronounced. Chinese decorations and colours were copied on such ware.

Much of the old tea ware was decorated in underglaze blue, but the colour has run in most existing examples. This early blue-and-white was generally associated with moulding in relief. A **powdered blue** ground was also used with white reserves painted in underglaze blue. Blue and white patterns included the Oriental pine cone, flowers, foliage, feathery scrolls and a wide variety of designs copied or adapted from the pattern book *The Ladies Amusement*. Some **transfer-printing** in underglaze blue was used from about 1765; the copper plates were unskilfully engraved and the hatching amateurish. Between 1770 and 1785 table-ware might be printed with a pagoda pattern accompanied by coarse dark flowers and fruits.

Coloured enamels applied overglaze were first used in association with underglaze blue and appeared shortly after 1765. Chinese mandarin figures were painted in light reds, verging on brown, with additional motifs in strong pink, light turquoise blue and green. The horizontal brush lines painted below these figures were in reddish brown. These decorations closely resembled Worcester decoration of the same type, the Worcester enamel being richer in colour and more thickly applied. Sprays and borders of simple flowers in polychrome enamels, with green leaves, were used in several more or less standard patterns together with feathery **rococo** scrolls. Painted diapers were popular on hollow-ware, the trellis diaper being a favourite. Some Lowestoft diapers are not met with elsewhere, such as trellis in red or pink applied with equidistantly spaced darker spots. Hexagonal and other cell diapers in blue were frequent, and might also be in red and blue. Pink scale borders were also used. The finest flower painting was done between 1773 and 1780. Among the most frequent of the Lowestoft motifs was the rose. (The full rose is part of the arms of the old borough.)

Moulding in low relief was characteristic and often enclosed panels of painted decoration. Delicate scroll-work, wreaths of floral ornament, and beaded borders might be accentuated with touches of opaque white enamel. Wickerwork decorations in relief and ropework with rosettes at intersections were widely used.

No standard trade mark was used at Lowestoft. A poorly shaped number, between 1 and 60, was generally inscribed in underglaze blue on the inner side of the foot rim. So frequently are they found in this position that they might almost be considered as factory marks: they are not found on porcelain made elsewhere. The letters H, S, R, Z, W, and R.P., found in the same position, are workmen's marks. The Lowestoft firm was also a prolific imitator of marks belonging to other factories, the most favoured being the Worcester crescent. The crossed swords of **Dresden** were also copied.

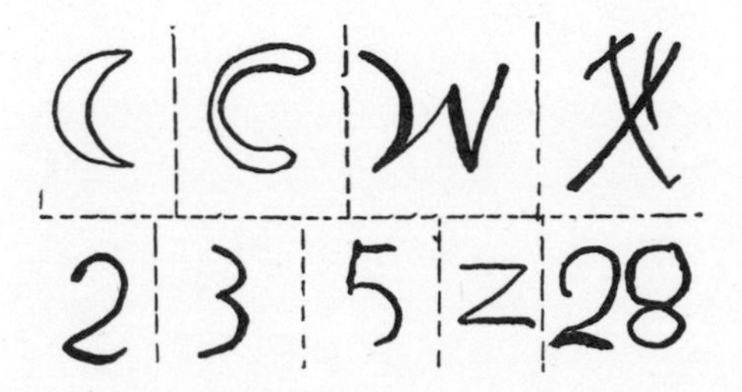

LP MARK. *See* **Leeds**.

LUSTRE

An English commercial adaptation of Hispano-Moresque pottery, not manufactured successfully until the early years of the 19th century. Diffracting effects were produced on a film of lustre by firing in a reducing atmosphere for eight to twelve hours. The basic metallic oxides were mixed with balsam of sulphur and oil of turpentine thinned to the required consistency with oil of lavender. This liquid, with the metal held in suspension, was brush-applied to the ware which was then fired in a muffle. Heat dissipated the oxygen and destroyed organic matter in the metallic coating, leaving a hard, fast film of lustrous metal. Lustre was applied to **cream-ware**, **earthenware**, and **bone china**. Decoration was restricted to unlustred reserves with white or coloured grounds. These might display: blue **transfer-printed** designs; paintings in sepia or purple lustre or polychrome enamels; black transfer-printed work often over-painted with colours or thin purple lustre. **Sprigged** ornament in relief came into use on lustre about 1820, at first meticulously modelled in continuous scenic bands with such themes as huntsmen, hounds and fox. It was enriched by colouring with purple lustre and enamels, and usually broadly banded with plain lustre. Although the list of makers is extensive little lustre ware seems to have been marked. One firm established in 1831 to make silver resist lustre ware has continued its manufacture ever since, using original formula, processes and shapes. Other potters are now making gold and copper lustres.

Copper: prepared from copper oxide, dated from 1840 and was often disfigured with specks, pin-holes, pimples and bubbles. The earthenware was distinctly heavier than lustred creamware.

Gold: varied in colour from yellow guinea gold to reddish gold and the not very durable ruby. It was produced from gold oxides, widely different hues resulting from gold of different carats. The more copper in the gold alloy the more suggestive of bronze was the lustre. First reference yet noted to such lustre appears in an advertisement issued 1807 by the Cambrian Pottery warehouse describing it as "Ware ornamented with an entirely New Golden Lustre". This was a superior earthenware made at **Swansea** under the name of **opaque china**. Until 1823 gold lustre was applied to glazed ware: later often directly to a specially prepared reddish-brown clay finished with a smooth mirror-like surface that gave consistent depth and richness of tone to nine carat gold lustre—then termed copper lustre. In high quality work the **biscuit** was covered with a **glaze** stained purplish pink with purple of cassius: this made the lustre sparkle like shot silk. In other ware a first coating of purple lustre might be given for the purpose of increasing brilliance.

Marbled or Moonlight: effects introduced by the **Wedgwood** firm, 1810, under the name of moonlight lustre. Evolved by mingling various tints of purple lustre. Immediately copied by other potters.

Purple: produced from purple of cassius—a mixture of gold chloride and tin chloride—suspended in an oily fluid prepared by dissolving sulphur and venetian turpentine in ordinary turpentine. This was thinly brush-painted over the glaze, oil of lavender being added to make it the required consistency, and fired in a muffle. The tint varied with the gold-tin ratio, one to four producing light purple, one to five a rose shade. It was used chiefly for ornamental banding, conventional motifs and painted scenic pictures. This lustre was greatly used by the **Sunderland** potters.

Resist: dates from 1810, the stencil process (see below) being used in reverse. The white glaze, or a ground colour, was used for the intricate, detailed pattern, brilliantly displayed by the setting of metallic lustre. The pattern was painted over the glaze with a resist material such as china clay mixed with honey or glycerine. This resisted the metallic oxide solution, with which the ware was then painted, so that the solution did not adhere to the protected area. The resist was later washed away, leaving the metal on the glaze ready for firing in a muffle. Designs appeared almost invariably in white or cream glaze until about 1831, exceptions being hand-painted grounds, which included the colours buff, pink, apricot, blue, rose, and canary yellow. Patterns included all-over grape and vine-leaf designs—adapted from Hispano-Moresque lustre—formalistic scroll patterns, and the purely English inspirations featuring song-birds, roses, strawberries, thistles, ivy, fuchsias (late), sporting scenes, and many others.

Silver: obtained from platinum oxide. The Wedgwood firm began manufacture in 1805, introducing narrow bandings encircling the ware, often in association with coloured enamels. Manganese oxide added to the platinum produced polished steel lustre. All-over silver lustre in forms resembling sterling silver plate was seldom made before 1823. Earlier silver lustre now tends to display a greyish black hue. White, yellow, or light grey clay mixtures were then used, two coats of platinum solutions in different qualities being applied to the biscuit. Three-piece tea-sets of teapot, sugar-bowl and cream jug, rectangular on plan, were popular and a wide variety of domestic ware was issued during the following forty years. Early productions were of good quality and were without relief work, apart from fluting and beaded edges. After about 1845 interiors might be lined with a white glaze and exteriors painted with gaudy flowers or banded in horizontal rings of blue, cream or pink. Electro-metallurgy produced a less costly silver lustre, invented in 1852 by **John Ridgway & Co.,** Cauldon Place, Staffordshire. The film of platinum was applied by a chemical process, but was so thin that it failed to stand up to wear, and production was abandoned in the early 1860s.

Splashed or Mottled: purple lustre applied over glaze and sprayed with oil blown through a tube in which the end near the lustre was covered with fine muslin. The oil expanded in the muffle, forming tiny bubbles which burst and produced irregular spots, waves and splashes. In most instances panels were reserved for printed or painted decoration over the glaze. The ware is associated chiefly with **Sunderland**, but Staffordshire, **Liverpool** and **Bristol** used the same process.

Stencilled: evolved 1806 by **John Davenport** of Longport. Cut-out paper patterns were pasted upon glazed ware and the entire surface waxed. When the wax-coated patterns were removed the design remained exposed on the glaze. This was coated with lustre. When dry the rest of the wax was removed with benzine and the ware fired. Silhouettists were employed as paper pattern makers, cutting so skilfully that hair-line details were of pen-and-ink fineness.

Transferred: gold and platinum transfer-printing was patented in 1810 by Peter Warburton of **New Hall**. An impression was taken in oil from a copper plate by means of a glue and isinglass **bat**. The oil impression was transferred to the ware and sprinkled with the powdered preparation of gold or platinum and then fired.

M & B MARK. *See* **Minton**.

M & N MARK. *See* Mayer & Newbold.

MADELEY (Shropshire)

Established in 1825 by Thomas Randall, who was a gilder at **Coalport** until 1803, then a decorator at **Derby** until 1808. He then moved to **Pinxton** where the manufacture of **soft-paste porcelain** was being attempted based on a formula used by **William Billingsley** during his partnership there. In 1812 Randall established himself as a decorator in London and within three years was employing more than forty decorators.

George IV as regent and as king was an avid collector of **Sèvres** porcelain: the resulting nation-wide collecting vogue for this ware caused examples to fetch fabulous prices. Dealers searched in vain for a potter willing to make a soft-paste porcelain of the Sèvres type, and capable of decorating it in the early style. Randall was the man who most nearly met their requirements, but he would never give his expensive copies of early Sèvres the double-L mark.

Characteristic Madeley porcelain was of the **Nantgarw** type, but much thicker of section and only dimly translucent, easily abraded with a file, and possessing a **glaze** tinged faintly green. Moulding in relief was sometimes used. By 1828 the paste had a mellow, creamy hue closely resembling that of old Sèvres, with a thin, hard glaze. Much Madeley porcelain was decorated with ground colours having the slightly granular appearance of powdered enamel applied over the glaze. Flaws in the body, and there were many, such as fine hair cracks, were concealed beneath this ground colour, which might be in dark blue, light blue, turquoise, apple green, or soft pink. *Bleu de roi* was seldom used without a delicate covering of gold tracery in patterns of network, vermicelli, or **œil de perdrix**.

In the late 1830s the demand for old Sèvres reproductions ceased and Randall produced **bone china**, decorating it in the Coalport style. Most of this was purely domestic ware. In 1840 he abandoned manufacture and set up as a decorator at Shelton, near Hanley. No porcelain or bone china made by Randall is known to have been marked.

MALING. *See* **Sunderland.**

MANSFIELD (Nottingham)

William Billingsley established himself in Belvedere Street as an independent decorator a few months after leaving **Pinxton** in 1799. He bought **bone china** in the white from **Spode**, and from Rose of **Coalport**, and **hard-paste porcelain** from France. No distinguished work was issued, although Billingsley's hand is recognized in fine groups of garden flowers painted against canary yellow grounds enriched with heavy **gilding**. Few authenticated pieces are known and these are signed "Billingsley Mansfield" in script, on the base in gold or puce. The ware itself sometimes bore the maker's mark.

MANSION HOUSE DWARFS. *See* **Callot dwarfs.**

MARBLED WARE

Surface ornament on English **earthenware**, classed in three groups: slip marbling, granite marbling, and underglaze painted marbling.

Slip Marbling is thought to date from the 16th century: its manufacture was recorded at Burslem in 1677. This marbling was carried out on the modelled earthenware by thinly applying lines or splashes of light coloured **slips** in two or more shades, such as red and white, buff and brown, light red and buff, dark red and brown. While fairly moist these slips were worked singly or mingled together

over the surface of the ware with a wire, leather or horn comb and a sponge, using the same technique as the paper marbler, for the combed marbling in book end-papers. Great skill was eventually acquired, as is demonstrated in the collection of early 18th-century owl jugs in the British Museum. Slip marbling continued almost until the end of the 18th century and is found on mugs, jugs, posset cups, loving cups, piggin plates and other ware.

Granite marbling: decorated **creamware** during the fourth quarter of the 18th century, and was made by **Josiah Wedgwood**, Neale & Co., and **Enoch Wood**. The effect was achieved by spraying.

Painted marbling: decorated cream or white earthenware from about 1815 until 1835. **Leeds** issued a series of tankards and mugs, often with sharply fluted moulding at neck and foot, thinly coated with bright green glaze. The marbling, which resembled the freer type of paper marbling, covered the body in streaks of yellow, reddish brown, and chocolate colour and was made at the **Don Pottery**, **Swansea**, and elsewhere.

MASON WARE (Lane Delph, Staffordshire)

Made at a pottery established in 1797 by Miles Mason for the manufacture of **cream-coloured earthenware** decorated with enamels on relief patterns. This was styled "Cambrian Argil" because Welsh clay was used in its composition. Table services were made in imitation of old Nankin. This ware was impressed with an imitation oriental square seal with MILES above and MASON below.

By 1804 Mason was making **stone china**, which he advertised in that year as "more beautiful and more durable than Indian Nankin china, and not so liable to snip at the edges, and more difficult to break". It was **transfer-printed** in blue or red with landscapes, figures and Oriental patterns and enriched with **gilding**.

In 1813 his son Charles J. Mason was granted a patent to make ironstone china, the term "ironstone" being used on account of its extreme hardness and clear ring. Ordinary stone china reached its peak of popularity during the 1820s, but Mason's patent ironstone china continued a favourite until the mid-century. The Mason firm became celebrated for colourful jugs, octagonal on plan with snake handles, the head being turned to the left. The colours were hand-applied in flat washes over printed outlines, and consisted chiefly of vermilion reds, brilliant deep blues and apple greens. Pink, puce and pale green sometimes appeared, and occasional patches of black and brown. Many types of colour-decoration were used in quaint, jumbled designs, the motifs including combinations of the following: large flowers resembling

a peony and a full-blown rose, sprigs of hawthorn, and daisies, all with appropriate foliage, and with birds of paradise, water-fowl, butterflies, dragon-flies, gnats or other flying insects on the reverse.

Mason's blue-ground stone china dated from 1825. White reserves were filled with landscapes, flowers, birds and other motifs in enamel colours. The blue ground was left plain, en-

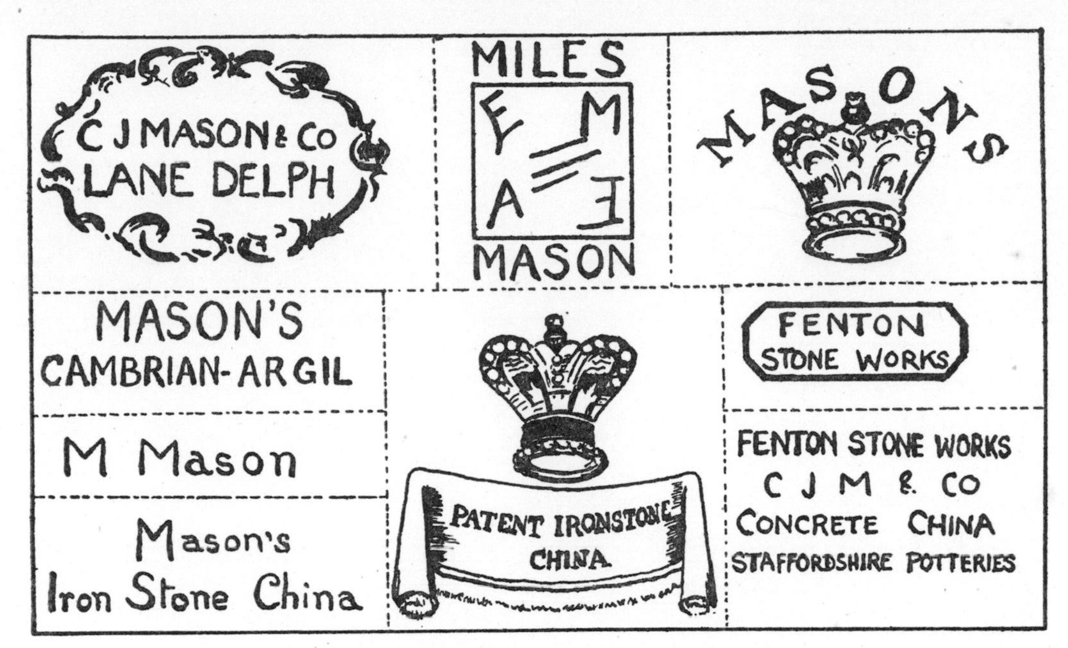

Some of the principal marks used by the Mason firm

riched with gilding, or decorated in colours with raised enamels. Blue and white transfer-printed ware with gilt borders dated from this period. The Masons disposed of their business in 1851, the original Mason marks continuing to be used by their successors.

MAYER, ELIJAH (Hanley, Staffordshire)

Established in 1770 as an enameller to the trade until about 1790 when he became a manufacturer, operating until 1830. He was celebrated for the excellence of his enamelled **cream-coloured earthenware**, black **basalt**, and **bamboo wares** decorated with lines and foliage in blue and green enamel. Simeon Shaw in *History of the Staffordshire Potteries*, 1829, recorded that Mayer and a potter named Moss produced more ware than any others in the Potteries. The basalts were noted for their fine texture and blue-black colour, the relief decoration being **sprigged** and hand finished. Many commemorative pieces were issued in this ware, such as jugs embossed with a portrait of the Prince of Wales when he became Regent in 1811, and coronation pieces made ten years later. Wellington, Nelson and other portraits have been noted. Until 1813 the name E MAYER was impressed, afterwards E MAYER & SON.

MAYER, THOMAS (Longport, Staffordshire)

In 1829 Thomas Mayer acquired **Joseph Stubbs'** pottery where he continued **transfer-printing** in a more attractive blue. Vine leaves and trumpet flowers composed a typical border pattern and a fine lace edge might be printed around each central picture. The rims of table-ware carried a narrow edge decoration of overlapping scale motifs interrupted at regular intervals by spoked wheels. Mayer's views appear to have been issued singly, not in unified series. He was responsible for a very elaborate, now extremely valuable, series of dishes printed with the arms of the various States of America. Mayer's impressed mark resembled that of Enoch Wood, with the inscription surrounding the eagle altered to T MAYER STOKE STAFFORDSHIRE WARRANTED. His printed mark, the largest found in English ceramics, consisted of an American eagle with a scroll flowing from its beak bearing the words E PLURIBUS UNUM. *See* page 149.

MAYER & NEWBOLD (Lane End, Staffordshire)

This firm was active in the first half of the 19th century, making a wide range of **bone china** wares.

MAZARINE BLUE

Chelsea, **Derby** and **Worcester** imitations on soft **porcelain** of the *gros bleu* of Vincennes, but less brilliant and of a deeper hue: also found on good quality **bone china** from about 1825. The smalt or zaffre was applied direct to the soft porcelain **biscuit** in wet washes: the brush-work resulted in subtle gradations of tone which saved such ware from monotony, particularly when the colour was laid on thickly. *See* **Cobalt blue**.

MEIGH, JOB, and HIS SUCCESSORS (Hanley)

Established at the Old Hall in 1770 to make **cream-coloured earthenware** and red pottery. By the end of the century blue-printed ware was made and by 1810 the **transfer-printing** had reached a high standard, being clear and bright. Black ware was made decorated with matt and burnished **gilding** and coloured enamelling. By 1816 the firm was styled Job Meigh and Son, and in 1823 Job Meigh was awarded the Society of Arts gold medal for a leadless **glaze** suitable for use on a coarse red pottery. In the late 1830s the son, Charles, operating as Charles Meigh and Sons, began to make a **stone china** which was sold under the name of white enamel ware, although it was given the semi-matt finish of **smear-glazing**, and, with its vitrified texture, bore some resemblance to the later marble-imitation known as **parian ware.** Appreciating the classic restraint of its marble whiteness, Meigh introduced the ware in neo-Gothic designs and a considerable range was evolved. By the mid-1840s more than seven hundred workers were employed. The firm became the Old Hall Earthenware Company in 1861, succeeded by the Old Hall Porcelain Company. Marks included the initials J. M. & S. on blue-printed ware, the name MEIGH, and, from the 1830s, ENAMEL PORCELAIN, OPAQUE PORCELAIN, INDIAN STONE

CHINA. On the bottom left of those shown is the mark of the Old Hall Earthenware Company Limited.

MEISSEN. *See* **Dresden.**

MEXBOROUGH (Yorkshire) POTTERY

Cream-coloured and other earthenware following the Staffordshire trend was made here from 1790, by Sowter and Bromley.

MIDDLESBRO' POTTERY COMPANY (Yorkshire)

Established in 1834 mainly to make **cream-coloured** domestic ware, much of it **transfer-printed.** In 1844 the mark became I. W. & CO., MIDDLESBRO. The firm closed in 1887.

MINTON, THOMAS

Established at Stoke in 1789 as a master engraver of copper plates for ceramic **transfer-printing** and a supplier of stock transfers to small potters. In 1793 he began to manufacture blue-printed **cream-coloured earthenware** on a small scale, and in 1796 began the production of **bone china.** In 1798 he secured the financial assistance of William Pownall, and the technical knowledge of Joseph Poulson, making them partners and trading as Minton, Poulson & Pownall. By 1808, however, he was once again sole proprietor trading under his own name and employing about fifty workers. His son, Herbert Minton, succeeded to the works in 1836.

Early Minton bone china had a faintly greyish tint and was inclined to be flawed with black specks. When John Turner joined the firm in 1803 and became managing potter he made remarkable improvements in paste and **glaze.** By 1815 Minton ware equalled that of any competitor. Decoration until 1820 was simple. In addition to blue-printed underglaze transfers in the Nankin style, there were transfer-printed shell and seaweed designs in dark brown. Some excellent **bat-printed** work belongs to the Regency years. Enamel decoration consisted chiefly of painted flower motifs. Slight landscapes painted in black, red or blue monochrome were also issued. Decorations in the style of **Derby,** but painted with greater clarity, came into use from about 1820, and ten years later ground colours of exceptional purity began to be produced, including carmine, purple, *bleu turquoise, rose du Barry, gros bleu*, and apple green.

After M. Leon Arnoux was appointed chief designer in 1848, Minton decoration followed the style of old Sèvres, and the production of cabinet pieces never intended for utilitarian service became important.

Herbert Minton, by effectively modernizing various processes without affecting appearance, converted formerly expensive table services into everyday commercial wares, and he issued blue-printed ware of greatly improved technique at a period when that of other potters declined in quality.

The firm became renowned during the third quarter of the century for the now scarce reproductions of French **faience**, Palissy ware, Della Robbia ware, and maiolica. The faience gave an effect of intricate inlay, its pure white clay body being covered by interlacing arabesques with spaces filled with vari-coloured slips. Palissy, maiolica, and Della Robbia ware displayed very distinct characteristics, but all were made from a calcareous clay body covered with opaque white enamel, painted with coloured enamels. The exquisite *pâte-sur-pâte* decoration developed at Sèvres was made from about 1870. This took the form of ornamental motifs and figure subjects on a bone china ground coloured green, blue, dark grey, or black. A thin wash of the slip appeared as a translucent film over the ground colour so that, by washing on successive layers where required, gradations of tint were produced.

The early mark consisted of the crossed L's of Sèvres somewhat modified, with the addition of the letter M, usually in blue enamel, and sometimes also a pattern number. A Roman M belonged to the same period. Between 1836 and 1841, when John Boyle was in partnership with Herbert Minton, the mark was an elaborate blue-printed cartouche containing the name of the pattern and the initials M & B. From 1842 symbols were used to indicate the year of manufacture. From 1851 a filled-in trefoil or an ermine mark with three dots above might be impressed or printed. The name MINTON impressed dated from 1865 and the globe with the name Minton inscribed across it first appeared in 1865.

MOCHA WARE

This style of inexpensive decoration on **earthenware** was originated early in the 19th century by **William Adams** of Cobridge, and named because of its resemblance to the quartz known as mocha-stone. Early mocha decoration had a **cream-ware** body, but from

11. (*Top*) Wedgwood vases: left, surface marbling, mark "Wedgwood & Bentley", 1772; centre, jasper, white on blue, about 1785; right, white on black, mark: "Wedgwood", 1790. (*Below*) Leeds cream-coloured earthenware: left, cistern and basin, mark "Leeds . Pottery 19"; centre, stand for branched candlesticks; right, centre-piece.

12. (*Top*) Part of a Derby (*Bloor*) dessert service painted with views "In Great Britain, Germany and Italy"; painted borders. (*Centre*) Wedgwood queen's ware trial dishes for the Empress Catherine's dinner and dessert service. 1773. (*Below*) Derby (*Bloor*) bone china with views in colour.

13. (*Top*) Nantgarw dessert plates and tazza: impressed "Nantgarw C.W". (*Centre*) Swansea, pair of square bulb pots marked "Swansea" in red. (*Below*) Derby, a pair of two-handled campana-shape vases.

(*Left*) Earthenware jug transfer-printed and hand-coloured with stage coach scene and with silver lustre ornament, dated 1810. (*Centre*) Delftware puzzle jug with pierced neck, inscribed and dated 1721 in cobalt blue. (*Right*) Staffordshire grey stoneware puzzle jug with incised decoration coloured blue, dated 1764. Height 7¾ inches.

(*Left*) Cream-coloured earthenware barrel-shaped jug transfer-printed with a farming scene and, on reverse, a pseudo coat-of-arms; silver resist lustre borders. (*Centre*) Ralph Wood toby jug with pale brown coat, yellow breeches, dark brown hat and shoes. 1780s. (*Right*) Martha Gunn toby jug by John Davenport, adapted from the Ralph Wood original and decorated with pink lustre. 1820s.

14. (*Left*) Cream-coloured earthenware jug with blue transfer-printed shooting scene against a silver lustre ground. (*Centre*) "Fair Hebe" jug decorated with coloured glazes, original modelled by John Voyez in 1778 and made by several potters during the 1790s. (*Right*) Earthenware wine jug by Ralph Wood II, with a relief figure of a seated Bacchus.

the 1830s white earthenware or a hard cane-coloured **stoneware** was used. A ground colour covered the shaped clay, various shades of brown, green or yellow being usual: chestnut brown is invariably found on early cream-coloured ware. Over this was applied a pigment—usually brown, but blue, green and black were also used—mixed with tobacco and hop. This spread into the markings, suggesting trees, feathers, or moss.

Mugs and jugs for public-house service, decorated in this way from 1824, bear the **excise mark** applied by the Weights and Measures office. Mocha ware was widely made in Staffordshire and North East England from about 1810 to mid-Victorian days.

MONKEY BAND

A set of about twenty figures of monkeys dressed as musicians, designed to ridicule the Saxon Court Orchestra, evolved by **Dresden** in about 1750 and in continued production ever since. They were copied in **soft-paste porcelain** by **Chelsea** from 1756 and by **Derby** during the 1760s. In the 19th century copies and adaptations were made in **bone china** by **Spode's** successors, Copeland and Garrett (1833–47). These were brilliantly decorated in enamel colours, red, blue, orange and green. Groups of monkeys on rectangular bases were also made. These were marked COPELAND & GARRETT surmounted by a crown in green.

MONOCHROME PRINTING

A decorative effect obtained by utilizing various shades of a single colour, such as blue on a white ground, after the Chinese.

Until 1828 all **transfer-printed** ornament was in monochrome, although subsequent over-painting by hand might be in polychrome.

MOON BROTHERS. *See* **Parian ware.**

MOONS

Disc-shaped spots of higher translucency than the main body of the paste observable by transmitted light in some **soft-paste porcelains.**

MORTLAKE (Surrey)

Earthenware was made here from the mid-18th century by William Sanders. In 1827 the firm was transferred to Vauxhall Potteries, Lambeth, and operated by Alfred Singer until 1846. Singer specialized in **bone china figures** decorated with **lace work.**

Joseph Kishere, from about 1800 to the early 1840s, made ordinary drab brown **stoneware spirit flasks,** jugs and mugs ornamented in low relief with the usual sporting and drinking scenes. These were impressed KISHERE MORTLAKE; KISHERE; or KISHERE'S POTTERY, MORTLAKE, SURREY.

MORTLOCK. *See* Cadogan tea-pot.

MOUNTFORD, JOHN (Stoke)

Parian ware maker around 1851. His name, incised, as John Monford, has been noted.

MUGS.

This term at first included all **earthenware** vessels, bowls, jugs, ewers and so on: potters specializing in these were known as mug-potters. A mugger was a hawker of such earthenware. Since the mid-17th century the term has been in common use for a cylindrical drinking vessel with a handle. The original meaning continued into early Georgian times.

N MARK. *See* **New Hall** *and* **Derby**.

NANTGARW and SWANSEA PORCELAIN (Glamorgan, Wales)

Founded by **William Billingsley** and Samuel Walker in 1813 to make **soft-paste porcelain**, reported in 1814 as displaying "a combination of the Qualities of the best French Porcelain, Whiteness and Transparency, with the firmness and closeness of Grain peculiar to the Saxon or Dresden porcelain". Unfortunately distortions and cracks in the **biscuit** oven were extensive, the venture proving unprofitable. Lacking capital, they joined L. W. Dillwyn at Swansea in October 1814, faced with the task of strengthening the body of their porcelain while retaining the wonderful translucency and chalky whiteness. Experimental work continued until the autumn of 1816, when they produced a porcelain more tractable in the kilns: this had a greenish translucency causing it to be known to collectors as **duck egg porcelain**. This was a commercial failure, however, and production ceased six months later. **Soapstone** was then added to the paste for strengthening purposes, and in the spring of 1817 the new porcelain was ready for marketing. This, however, lacked the notable quality expected from Billingsley by the London dealers, and their rejection of it caused the project to cease in September 1817.

Billingsley and Walker then returned to Nantgarw and, financed by friends with £1,100, were producing before the end of the year a porcelain that the dealers regarded as the finest made in Britain to that date: they contracted to take the firm's entire output glazed in the white. Because of its delicacy only symmetrical shapes could be made, flat ware constituting about 80 per cent of production. Unfortunately fire-cracked and distorted pieces continued on too great a scale and early in 1820 the factory ceased production. Billingsley and Walker then joined John Rose at **Coalport**. A considerable accumulation of seconds porcelain was decorated at Nantgarw during the next three years on behalf of the financiers. In a total of ten years fewer than four were occupied in production.

There was little variation in the Nantgarw paste. It was always soft

NANT-GARW
C.W

and very white, a notable feature being its high translucency, slightly cloudy and with a distinct yellow tone when held against the light. It broke with a granular-looking fracture. The thickly applied **glaze** was soft, pure white, smooth and glassy with a brilliantly lustrous surface seldom disfigured by **crazing**. The Swansea paste continually varied, the final soapstone type lacking translucency and when held against the light revealing a smoky yellow cloudiness. Its thin, dull glaze was disfigured with pigskin pitting. Such porcelain was marked with a trident. A variant of this paste containing about half the amount of soapstone was very hard, extremely glassy, with a dull white surface. Its appearance when held against the light was likened by Turner to sodden snow.

The paste made at Nantgarw from late 1817 was even more highly translucent than the earlier ware, with finer potting and a greater range of shapes. The original glaze was used. Considerable stocks of biscuit were left at Nantgarw: the glaze on these was more creamy in tone and lacked high surface brilliance, and being applied very thinly, it left the texture of the biscuit clearly visible.

Typical decoration on a piece of flat-ware consisted chiefly of conventional flower sprays painted between border motifs in relief, and a central expansive floral bouquet. These were sometimes exact copies of early **Sèvres** plates. Others were decorated in the life-size naturalistic style then fashionable. Yet other plates were ornate cabinet pieces meticulously painted with flowers, birds, landscapes, elaborate figure and classical decoration covering the entire field. Grounds and borders were coloured in the fashionable deep green, turquoise, claret, and *bleu de roi* enamels, and the **gilding**, lavishly applied, was highly burnished.

Swansea shapes included a consider-

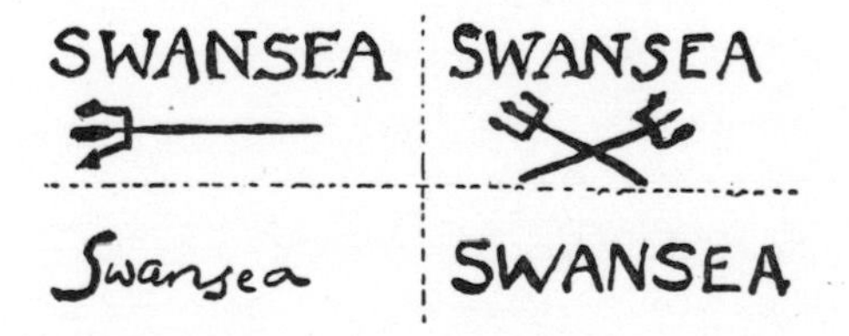

able amount of small hollow-ware adapted from the fashionable and costly French porcelain. Insects, landscapes with floral borders, scattered sprays of flowers, as well as flowers and scrolls in low relief decorated Swansea porcelain. A dark green enamel of peculiar tint was a Swansea characteristic.

Most of the decoration between 1821 and 1822 was carried out by Thomas Pardoe at his enamelling workshop, 28 Bath Street, Bristol. His decoration is recognized by the gritty textures of reds, greens, yellows and blues. All kinds of patterns came easily from his brush, lightly painted sprays of garden flowers, sprigs of foliage, birds, fruit, animals, butterflies, shells, oriental motifs, and landscapes of local interest. He used a fine underglaze blue for borders and his gilding was lavish and in intricate designs.

Of the marks illustrated, the Nantgarw is impressed, sometimes not hyphenated. The top left and right Swansea marks are impressed; the bottom left is in red or, occasionally, another colour; the bottom right is in red or another colour.

NEALE, I., or NEALE & WILSON MARK. *See* **Palmer, Humphrey**.

NEWCASTLE-ON-TYNE (Northumberland)

White **earthenware** is recorded as being made by Warburton of Gateshead from about 1740 to 1816. St. Anthony's Pottery, established in 1780, was taken over by the firm of Sewell & Company in 1804; later the firm was Sewells & Donkin. These names are found impressed. St. Peter's Pottery founded in 1817 by Thomas Fell made **cream-coloured** ware, found with the following impressed marks: F with an anchor; FELL; and FELL NEWCASTLE.

Newcastle productions closely resembled those of **Sunderland** and included **cream-coloured earthenware** decorated by speedily applied enamel **colours, transfers**, and **lustre. Pierced** and embossed work resembling that of **Leeds** was also made. Jewitt has recorded that printing on pottery from wood engraving was practised at Sewell's and that some of Bewick's original blocks were used for the purpose. This is most improbable, but copper-plate transfer-prints of designs obviously taken from Bewick have been noted.

NEW CHELSEA PORCELAIN CO. LTD. (Longton, Staffordshire)

A nineteenth and twentieth-century firm making a speciality of reproducing **Bristol, Plymouth, Bow, Lowestoft, Swansea**, Chinese (Kang H'si period), St. Cloud, **Sèvres, Dresden**, and other porcelains, but in **bone china.**

NEW HALL CHINA MANUFACTORY (Shelton, Staffordshire)

The Cookworthy-**Champion** patent for the **hard-paste porcelain** made at **Plymouth** and **Bristol**, and the exclusive rights to use **china stone** in the manufacture of translucent ware were acquired in 1781 by a group of six Staffordshire potters: **Samuel Hollins** of Shelton; **Jacob Warburton** of Hot Lane; **John Turner** of Lane End; Charles Bagnall of Shelton; William Clowes of Pit Lane, and Anthony Keeling of Tunstall, with Richard Champion of Bristol as the managing partner. The group established themselves at Tunstall. A few months later Champion resigned, having been made Deputy Paymaster-General. The business was then transferred to Shelton where the company converted a mansion known as New Hall into a pottery styled on their bill heads as "Hollins, Warburton, Daniel and Company, manufacturers of real porcelain".

Searle confirms that "the earliest New Hall ware was precisely similar in body and glaze to that of Bristol to which it bears a marked resemblance in ornamentation". This hard-paste porcelain, greyish white in hue, was free from pinholes, with a thin transparent **glaze**, clear and brilliant although tinged faintly blue and green. It continued in production until about 1810, almost the entire output being confined to tea-sets, tea-pots, and dessert services. The well-known "silver-shape tea-pot" associated with New Hall was the most popular of its period. The sides of the oval body, rising vertically from a broad flat base, were widely fluted on each side of the spout and handle. Lacking a foot ring such a tea-pot was necessarily accompanied by a low stand of similar outline, with four rosette or ball feet beneath. As with contemporaneous silver tea-pots, from about 1800 the stand was discarded and four flat feet applied direct to the flat base of the tea-pot itself. Some early cups were without handles, and saucers were made without wells for the cups until about 1810.

Decoration in the 18th century was entirely by hand and included simple flower motifs, often in claret-red, festoon borders, and small baskets of flowers as central motifs. Landscapes and classic figures were painted until 1790; after this the colours tended to be gaudy, their enamels inexpensive. A feature of New Hall decoration was a pair of back-to-back stalkless roses, one pink and the other mauve. **Transfer-printed** outlines for decorations were first used in about 1800: earlier, hand-applied outlines in black had been filled in with coloured enamels.

New Hall abandoned hard-paste porcelain in favour of **bone china** in about 1810, the new paste being more translucent, pure white with a glittering glaze noticeably increasing the brilliance of the enamel decoration. Many of the thousand patterns already applied to the hard-paste continued in use with the addition of a further 629 designs more in harmony with Regency and George IV styles. Bone china continued in production until 1830 when the pottery ceased production.

New Hall hard-paste porcelain was in the main unmarked until 1790 except for the pattern number painted usually in pink, occasionally in mauve

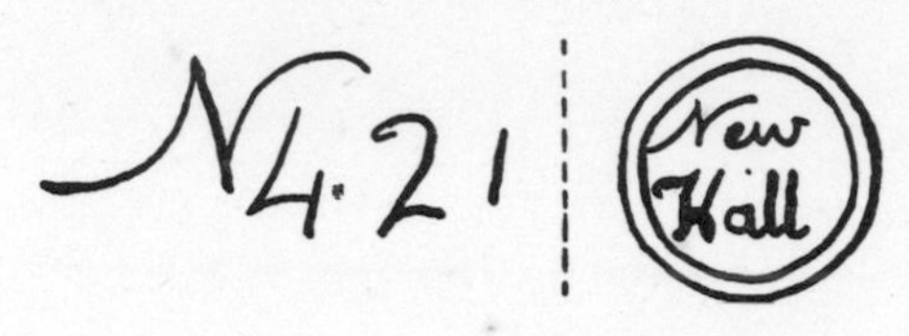

or blue, over the glaze of some large pieces. From 1790 an incised cursive N might precede the painted number, which might then be applied to small pieces. At first bone china was printed over the glaze with NEW HALL in script within a pair of concentric circles. In late examples this mark was applied under the glaze.

NOTTINGHAM

An important centre of fine **salt-glazed stoneware** during the first half of the 18th century. In the late 1680s James Morley established the trade in Nottingham, thereby infringing the **Dwight** patent of 1684 by making "brown mugs of stoneware salt-glazed". Nottingham salt-glazed stoneware had a drab body, was skilfully potted and was light in weight. The body was coated with a film of reddish-brown **slip** in various tones, and the glaze, which had a subdued metallic lustre, was usually much smoother than salt-glaze made elsewhere. Hollow-ware was usually ornamented with double or triple incised bands, or with outlines of stalks and flowers, especially pinks. Large bowls, decorated mugs, tobacco jars, **puzzle** and **bear jugs** were made in quantity and also **double-walled jugs** with floral **piercings**. Less skilfully produced salt-glazed stoneware was made during the second half of the 18th century.

ŒIL DE PERDRIX DECORATION

A ground of circular sea-green or bright blue spots centred with points of black. The background was white, and gilded moulding in relief separated the design from reserves of more important decoration. Alternatively little rosettes surrounded by blue and gold circles might be scattered over the surface. This decoration was

greatly used at **Madeley** and to a lesser extent by **Minton**.

O'NEALE, JEFFREY HAMET

Decorator whose work appears on **Worcester** and **Chelsea** porcelain: his

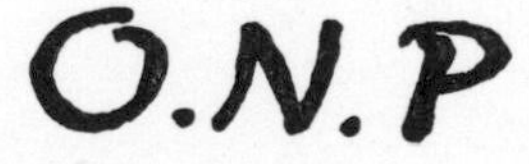

signature is familiar on Worcester wares, painted with naïve but attractive figures in landscapes, huntsmen, classical scenes, and so on.

P MARK. *See* **Pinxton.**

PALMER, HUMPHREY (Hanley, Staffordshire)

Established as an **earthenware** potter in 1760, but by 1770 was recognized as a rival and imitator of **Wedgwood's** decorative wares, particularly **basalt** and porphyry ware. On account of financial trouble in 1776 the business was acquired by his brother-in-law James Neale, who was joined in the 1780s by Robert Wilson. **Cream-coloured table-ware, blue-printed** and later **lustred**, became the chief output. The firm became celebrated for the excellent quality of its **figures** from 1788 when chalk was incorporated into a body specially produced for the purpose, giving them a creamy hue throughout their texture. These were sparsely coloured in clear enamels, the turquoise blue being especially brilliant and characteristic. They usually had foliated scroll pedestals standing on rectangular plinths. All marks were impressed: until 1776 H PALMER HANLEY in a double circle; I. NEALE or NEALE & CO in a double circle, and from 1786 NEALE & WILSON in a single line.

When Wilson died in 1801 David Wilson continued the firm as D. Wilson and Sons. He died in 1816 and the firm went bankrupt in 1817. The name WILSON impressed, or a crowned C or crowned G, impressed, was used as a mark.

PARIAN WARE

A highly vitrified translucent **frit porcelain** invented by the firm of **W. T. Copeland,** 1842, for the purpose of making statuary **figures.** This resulted in an altogether new clarity and delicacy of detail for ceramic figure work executed on a commercial scale. Like the parian marble after which it was named, parian ware was slightly off-white, the ivory tint being due to traces of iron silicate in felspar and clay.

Until 1852 the models from which parian statuary were patterned were always carved by professional sculptors. The firms of **Copeland, Minton** and **Wedgwood** commissioned hundreds of original statuettes from established sculptors, including the most celebrated of the period. After 1852, however, when original statues were required for reproduction in parian ware, reduced copies might be produced by the Cheverton mechanical process. This accounts for the inscription "Cheverton Sc" found impressed on the bases of some parian figures. An early example was "Ino and Bacchus" after the original by J. R. Foley, R.A.

Copeland produced parian ware of the finest craftsmanship and design. One model which sold by the thousand, yet is now strangely rare, was "The Greek Slave" by Hiram Power. "Narcissus" by John Gibson, R.A., and "Innocence" by J. R. Foley, R.A., were other outstanding Copeland figures, which included at least six representations of Venus: Venus de Milo; Venus de Medici; Venus of the Capitol, and others by Canova, Gibson and Thorvaldson. Herbert Minton produced some excellent parian figures including Carrier's equestrian statue of Theseus; Amazon by Veuchere; Pandora opening the fatal box; Psyche and Prometheus. The Wedgwood firm gave the name of carrara to their equivalent of parian ware, after the white statuary marble of Tuscany. They issued numerous models of Venus, nymphs and cupids, and many copies of ancient statues. The name **Charles Meigh** & Sons, Hanley, is often found impressed upon pairs of parian figures including bathers, dancers, templars, and falconers. Pountney and Goldney of Bristol made some handsome parian ware, notably flowers in relief by Edward Raby.

By 1845 a formula had been devised for parian ware which required no frit in its composition, the result proving capable of surviving even boiling water. This body was found ideal for producing elaborately moulded tableware possessing a delicate surface texture comparable with that of the statuary, but in a composition lacking frit this was not acquired automatically in the firing process. **Glazing** was necessary. The glazes applied to other domestic ware, however, were obviously too thick: they would obscure the sharp details and collect heavily in the deep crevices which were an important feature of this handsome ware. All that was required was the faintest trace of glaze and to achieve this a process known as **smear glazing** was used.

The superficial resemblance of this parian ware to the very different **jasper** ware was first noticed by the firm of T. J. & J. Mayer, Dale Hall, Burslem, who evolved a method of applying a rich bright blue to parts of the background to set off deeply moulded white decoration. The colour was restricted to flat areas in which the surface was stippled like the skin of an orange. Cameo parian ware was launched and continued popular until about 1880.

The coloured background consisted of a film of **slip** tinted to the desired shade. It was carefully applied by brush to the parts of the mould where it would be required. The slip for the body was then poured into the mould, and the two materials immediately united by adhesion and without intermingling. Firing completed the union. Colours used were blue, brown and sage green, and occasionally a light green ornament on a dark green ground. In some instances the coloured ground was **lead glazed**, the unglazed relief work standing out as if carved in marble.

Copeland made some elaborate jugs in this medium: Minton tended to apply traces of **gilding**; **Coalport** was renowned for fine tea-pots, tea-services, vases and wall brackets; T. & R. Boote, Burslem, made tall vases in blue cameo parian, decorated with grapes and vine leaves, and flowers in high relief. All this ware was marked. Other makers of cameo parian were Lindsay, Powell & Co., Hanley; Moon Brothers, Longton; Keys & Mountford, Newcastle-under-Lyme; S. Alcock & Company, Burslem; G. **Grainger, Lee & Co., Worcester**

PASTE. *See* **Body.**

PÂTE-SUR-PÂTE. *See* **Minton**

PEARL WARE

Made first by **Josiah Wedgwood** in 1779 and in the early 19th century by many imitators. It was a white **earthenware** body containing more calcined **flint** and **china clay** than **cream-coloured earthenware**. A still whiter effect was secured by adding a trace of **cobalt**. It was coated with a colourless **glaze** and used chiefly for table services with painted or **transfer-printed** decoration.

PENNINGTON, SETH and JAMES. *See* **Liverpool.**

PEW GROUPS

Groups of two or three figures seated on high-backed settees, to which no religious significance was attached. They may be considered in three classes: **salt-glazed**; **liquid lead glazed**; and reproductions. From technical factors it has been deduced that the salt-glazed pew groups were made in the early 1740s. They were hand-modelled in white **earthenware** containing calcined and ground **flint** instead of sand, introduced in about 1740 by **John Astbury**.

So many reproductions have been made that the collector should be familiar with the constructional technique of the pew-group potter of more than two centuries ago. The rigidly posed figures were modelled by rolling, cutting and pinching, their clothing being fitted over skeleton cores. A female figure, from the waist up, consisted of an almost plain solid cylinder, the upper end shaped as a neck. A small sphere was modelled into a head; arms of rolled clay were attached to the body, their flattened ends being tooled to represent hands and fingers. The figure was then dressed with paste rolled flat to one-sixteenth of an inch in thickness. No legs were concealed beneath the widely billowing skirt, composed of alternating strips of black and white clay, the surfaces of the white stripes being decorated with milled lines. Over this was placed a long white apron. A tight bodice and ruffled cap were added and eyes, necklace and other embellishments applied in black slip. The men were more completely modelled than the women, their dress less thoroughly disguising their figures. Their clothing fitted over skeleton cores in the same way, with skirted coats over frogged and buttoned waistcoats. Their heads were bewigged with tightly twisted roll curls. Dark clay was used for hat, neck ribbons, cuffs and shoes. The men were often supplied with musical instruments such as fiddle or bagpipes.

A series of **lead glazed** pew groups in which two crudely modelled figures are seated on a circular bench, and coloured with touches of manganese purple and brown, are impressed on the base with the name WEDGWOOD. This is not the mark of **Josiah Wedgwood** but of one of his several relatives engaged in the pottery trade. An example in the British Museum shows two youths, one reading a book, the other holding a scroll.

PHILLIPS and CO. *See* **Sunderland.**

PIERCING

A type of decoration derived from the Chinese and found in much **earthenware** of the late 18th and early 19th centuries. While the clay was still unfired and in a leather-hard condition the pattern was punched out hole by hole with a hand punch. **Wedgwood** used a set punch, as did the Staffordshire potters who made border piercing to plates and dishes.

See **Leeds, Newcastle-on-Tyne** *and* **Lacework.**

PINXTON (Derbyshire)

Made a **soft-paste porcelain** from 1796 to April 1799 and **bone china** from 1799 to 1813. This was the first of **William Billingsley's** unsuccessful ventures into porcelain making. Financed by John Coke and trading as Coke and Billingsley, the firm employed about thirty operatives and decorators. A fine glassy porcelain was made, equal to that of **Derby** but rather more translucent: it had a slightly undulating surface and when viewed against the light showed faintly green. The **glaze** had a cold, greyish tone.

Elaborate decoration on Pinxton porcelain was rare. The majority of pieces were painted with landscapes or country house scenes in the style of Zachariah Boreham. (*See* **Derby**). Some Pinxton landscape decoration was in monochrome in a russet-red colour. The so-called Tournay sprig and the Paris cornflower were used almost to the exclusion of other flowers. Little of Billingsley's Pinxton porcelain appears to have been marked apart from a series of upper case letters impressed.

Following Billingsley's departure from Pinxton in 1799 the factory made bone china, until 1803 under the direction of John Coke, and from 1803 to

1813 under the proprietorship of John Cutts, a well-known decorator. This ware was of poor quality and almost opaque, decoration following con-

temporary **Derby** styles. Canary yellow, the only background colour used, was characteristic. The mark during Coke's period was an open crescent with a star between the horns, adapted from his coat of arms. Later a script P was painted overglaze in various colours but usually in red; also various arrow forms in red. The name **Pinxton** is sometimes found in gold.

PLYMOUTH (Devonshire)

The first **hard-paste porcelain** factory in England was pioneered here in 1768 by William Cookworthy. He spent about twenty years in prospecting the West Country for deposits of **china clay** and **china stone** which he finally discovered on the Cornish estates of Thomas Pitt, later created Lord Camelford, and in the development of manufacturing technique from the initial preparation of the materials to the final firing of the decorated ware. He was then granted a patent on July 14, 1768. Cookworthy styled his firm The Plymouth New Invented Porcelain Company, and before long he was employing between fifty and sixty operatives.

Existing examples show that at first the body was white with a slight tendency towards grey and a translucency also faintly grey. Fractures had a granular appearance, and fire-cracks, warping, pinholes, and other flaws were frequent. Upon a change being made in the formula the porcelain became milky white with a surface suggesting polished ivory. Translucency varied from a faintly yellowish green to a cold white-grey tone. Fractures were smooth. There were seldom any surface defects apart from occasional dark brown spots with black centres, brought about by the presence of iron particles in the clay: such defects were rare in **soft-paste porcelain**. Fire cracks were frequent. A characteristic of Plymouth porcelain was **wreathing**. Imperfect **wedging** caused minute depressions on the surface, known as "pig-skin pitting". Technical knowledge of kiln construction was insufficient to prevent what Cookworthy referred to as "those tinging vapours" during firing. Consequently most Plymouth porcelain had a faintly brown or smoky appearance.

Plymouth at first followed the

Chinese method of drying the modelled clay to leather consistency, dipping it into **glaze** and then firing it. Uneven patches brought about by imperfect fusion caused this to be abandoned in favour of a glaze separately

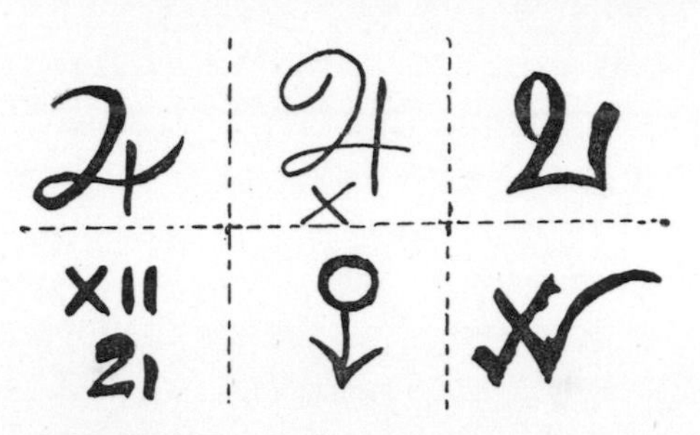

Marks used by Plymouth and (top centre) Bristol, in blue, brown, red or gold.

fired in the soft porcelain manner, consisting almost entirely of china stone. This glaze, brilliant, thin, and transparent, incorporated with the body, causing the porcelain to appear dense and semi-opaque. Where this smooth glaze collected in crevices it displayed tints varying from a pale greenish yellow to a faint cobalt blue.

Blue painted underglaze was the sole decoration on early Plymouth. The colour was dull and often over-fired to a brownish-black. Eventually this was improved and the result was a deep blue-black, so thickly applied that it was inclined to run with streaky effect. Naïve oriental flowers were the usual motifs. Decorations in bright coloured enamels were in the form of Chinese figures, birds, butterflies, foliage and floral sprays. These stood out sharply against the brilliant glaze. Enamels were difficult to fix to the thin, hard glaze, however, and might display a dry effect when some of the flux was lost to the glaze without softening into it. This sometimes caused the colour to flake away, leaving merely a rough surface to the glaze. Unfortunately many colours were ruined by over-firing.

Vase decorations superficially resembled those of **Chelsea**, particularly in brilliantly plumaged exotic birds. Rich coloured grounds might be used and **gilding** was frequent. Cookworthy issued many **figures**, most of them clumsily executed, their clothing decorated with widely spaced motifs and their bases touched with red or brownish crimson.

The chemist's symbol for tin was the mark used at Plymouth and has been noted in five colours: blue underglaze on blue and white porcelain; gold; red; reddish brown; and blue enamels. It was occasionally incised.

POOLE, JOHN ELLISON (Burslem, Staffordshire)

Born 1766, and known to have been in partnership with Lakin (1791–95) and Shrigley, making a wide range of **figures.** He died 1829. The mark POOLE may be found impressed.

PORCELAIN

A translucent vitrified ware which has been fired at a high temperature.

Hard-paste: made of white **china**

clay or kaolin (the plastic infusible ingredient) and fusible felspathic stone or **Cornish stone,** which gave translucence. When blended together and fired at a great heat these produced a vitreous white substance of extreme hardness, ringing with a sonorous metallic note when lightly struck and breaking with a clean smooth fracture, disclosing a fine sparkling grain of compact texture. Strength and whiteness were increased by ageing the paste. The Chinese stored theirs for decades before use: in England at **Plymouth, Bristol**, and **New Hall** seven to eight months was considered sufficient. The unfired clay was difficult to mould, and since it softened at one period during firing, tended to collapse beneath its own weight, hence a considerable percentage of wasters. In an effort to prevent this the ware was made of varying thickness by a process known as **wreathing**. The **paste** and **glaze** of hard porcelain were fired in one operation, making it difficult to tell in a fractured section where the glaze ended and the paste began. *See* **Felspar porcelain.**

Soft paste: is a relative term when applied to porcelain, the standard of hardness being the hardness of Chinese porcelain. Nearly all porcelains of the 18th century were imitations, so far as their composition was concerned, containing a vitreous **frit**—a mixture of white sand, gypsum, soda, alum, salt and nitre melted together in a mass, then broken and pulverized.

This frit porcelain was a thoroughly vitrified substance, displaying at its best a creamy or ivory white tint to which glazing gave a waxy surface.

Soft-paste porcelain was first fired at a temperature higher than that required for glazing, but not by any means so high as that for hard-paste porcelain or porosity would have been lessened, making the ware incapable of retaining the glaze. **Colours** applied underglaze slightly sank into the soft **biscuit** which was then glazed and refired. In overglaze decoration the colours were fixed by refiring again at a still lower heat than the glazing temperature. These artificial or soft-paste porcelains were incapable of withstanding the great heat required in the production of hard porcelain: consequently they emerged from the kiln appreciably softer in texture and were sensitive to sudden changes of temperature.

Test to distinguish hard from soft porcelain: hold the porcelain at a slant to the light. On hard porcelain the glaze is rather dull and light is not reflected: on soft-paste the glaze and colour gleam together. In soft-paste porcelain the paste, colours and glaze blend into a tender brightness. So soft was the glaze on early soft-paste porcelains that cups were scratched inside merely by the stirring of spoons. Where chipped, soft-paste porcelain will feel roughish and granular. On perfect pieces—usually beneath the base—will be found a small unglazed area. If the paste is marked when scratched by the finger nail or with a penknife blade, it is soft porcelain. While scraping with the nail it is almost possible to feel the paste crumbling away. If the paste is hard, scratching will roughen the finger nail. *See* **Soapstone porcelain, Felspar porcelain, Bone china.**

PORTOBELLO (Edinburgh)

Made **cream-coloured earthenware** from about 1770 under the proprietorship of Scott Brothers. In addition to domestic ware they made **figures** and other ornamental pieces. **Transfer-printed ware** was issued and figures of shepherds in tartan. Marks were impressed: SCOTT BROS and SCOTT P B followed by a pattern number. This must not be confused with Porto Bello ware. *See* **Astbury.**

POT-LID PICTURES

Lids from white glazed **earthenware** containers of bear's grease, pomade, macassar oil, fish pastes and potted shrimps, decorated with printed pictures in multi-colour, the majority being made by F. and R. Pratt, Fenton, Staffordshire, between 1846 and 1880. Until early in 1849 lids were flat-topped, uneven of surface and printed in two colours. Afterwards they were slightly domed, smooth of surface and decorated with four- or five-coloured pictures. At first such pots were used as containers for the hair oil sold as bear's grease, and a series of twelve was issued ornamented with bears, especially performing bears, as the dominant motif.

The first firms to realize the value of these colourful lids for pots of fish paste were Tatnell & Son, and S. Banger, both of Pegwell Bay, near Ramsgate: about eighteen lids are known displaying picturesque scenes in the Pegwell Bay district.

Multi-colour printing on pottery was developed by Jesse Austin, chief engraver with the firm of F. and R. Pratt, and about fifty of the five hundred colour prints issued from this factory are signed "J. Austin Sc" or "J A Sc". Four specimens of Pratt lids have been found with the signature of T. Jackson.

Mr. H. G. Clarke, the leading authority on the subject of pot lids, has divided the pictures into ten main groups: bear motifs; views of the Great Exhibition; military subjects; Shakespearean; portraits of celebrities; nautical scenes; London views; topographical scenes; sports and pastimes; landscape and general pictures.

The Pratts' successors discovered the original copper plates of some two-hundred pot-lid pictures engraved under Austin's supervision. These have been extensively re-issued on a harder earthenware than that used for the originals. It is not difficult to distinguish between the old and the new. Colours on original lids have brilliancy and depth of body, particularly in reds and blues. They are also covered with fine **crazing**. A pot-lid can always be tested by allowing it to hang from the finger and tapping it with another lid. If it sounds dull, as if it were cracked, the lid is likely to be genuine; if it emits a clear ringing note it is of recent manufacture, although artificial crazing tends to dull the clear ring. *See* **Printing, multi-colour**.

POTTERY

Soft, lightly fired, opaque **earthenware**.

POWDER BLUE. *See* **Cobalt blue**.

PRATT WARE

The name given to a type of **cream-coloured earthenware** decorated in underglaze high temperature **colours** irrespective of its maker. Potters in **Staffordshire, Liverpool, Newcastle** and Scotland made such ware between about 1790 and the 1830s. The colourless **glaze** has a characteristic faintly bluish tint, and the colour range is distinctive—thick orange ochre, pale yellow, dull blue, olive green, greyish brown, purple brown, often with a mottled or stippled effect. Wares include rustic jugs with ornament in relief, tea-pots, busts, and primitive **figures**. Felix Pratt (1760–1859) was the best considerable maker, establishing a factory at Fenton, Staffordshire, in about 1803. His impressed name was found on some examples, and as a result collectors have classed the entire group as Pratt ware.

PRINTING, MULTI-COLOUR

Perfected in 1848 by Jesse Austin, head engraver of F. and R. Pratt & Company, Fenton, Staffordshire, and developed on **earthenware pot-lids**. The process used was underglaze **transfer-printing** by a method in which five transfers were superimposed one upon the other in different colours. Stippled transfers were used for the first three or four colours—buff, blue, pink, and red were usual—with a final transfer in brown from a line-and-stipple engraving, the flesh portions only being stippled. Green was occasionally used. The colours were applied as for ordinary transfer-printing and were prevented from blurring by accurate registration, tiny circles on each side of the transfer being used for this purpose. Slightly raised patches of colour sometimes found on completed pictures are the result of finishing by hand-painting.

Multi-colour printing was applied to a wide variety of work in addition to **pot-lids** of earthenware such as dessert services, cups, saucers, plates, **mugs**, jugs, vases, boxes and bottles for the toilet table, all in **bone china**. Most of these were printed with copies of pictures by celebrated painters such as Gainsborough, Landseer, Wilkie and Mulready. This new method of ceramic decoration, when displayed at the Great Exhibition 1851, attracted the attention of the Prince Consort. Subsequently a royal crown was added to the firm's mark, followed by the inscription "Manufacturers to H.R.H. Prince Albert".

PUZZLE JUGS

These decorative **earthenware** jugs for use on convivial occasions have been made in England since medieval times. The majority, however, were made during the late 17th and early 18th centuries to the order of tavern keepers, of whom there were more than 60,000 in the 1690s. Although these jugs varied greatly in form, the principle was identical in nearly all. In the majority the vertical neck was ornamented with openwork **piercing,** thus making the jug unsuitable for normal use. Around the rim were a number of nozzles, sometimes as many as eight, all entering a tube encircling the rim and leading into a hollow handle which extended to the base and opened into the interior of the jug. By covering all but one of the nozzles it should be possible to drink from such a jug. There was, however, one single inconspicuous hole which had to be located and covered if the liquor was to be secured. Such jugs in **slip-ware** are relatively common, but the collector must remember that 20th-century firms have issued such jugs in numbers. They were also made in **English delft**, **stoneware**, and **cream-coloured earthenware**, and some excellent examples have been noted in **bone china**.

QUEEN'S WARE

An **earthenware** of ivory or **cream-colour** developed by **Josiah Wedgwood**. The name was later adopted at **Leeds** and by other potters for similar material. In 1767 Wedgwood wrote of "cream-coloured, alias Queen's ware".

R. MARK. *See* **Bow** *and* **Chelsea.**

R&L MARK impressed

Robinson and Leadbeater, of Stoke were makers of statuary **parian ware,** from about 1865 to 1908.

RAINFORTH and COMPANY. *See* **Leeds.**

REGENT CHINA. *See* **Worcester.**

RELIEF DECORATION

Produced by modelling, moulding, **turning**, **pâte-sur-pâte**, **sprigged work**, **slip**.

RIDGWAYS

Established in 1794 by Job Ridgway who built Cauldon Place Works in Shelton, Staffordshire, in 1802 when he produced **bone china** and **earthenware.** He was the father of the celebrated

A collection of bone china cottages, castles, toll houses, etc., used as pastille burners, night-light holders and chimney ornaments.

Earthenware dishes transfer-printed in blue: (*Left*) showing the vivid three-dimensional effect obtainable with a single colour transfer-print. "Triumphal Arch" from the Spode Caramania series. (*Right*) Spode's Gothic pattern: the border is in a Chinese mood, but its medallions include a strange assortment of animals.

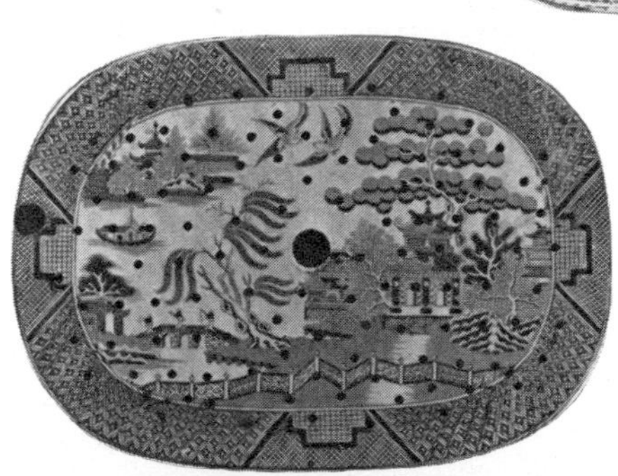

16. (*Above*) Wedgwood cream-coloured earthenware with blue transfer-printed view. Mark "Wedgwood" impressed. About 1830. (*Left*) Willow pattern earthenware: fish strainer by J. and E. Baddeley, Shelton, about 1810; and (*below*) Caughley pudding dish with two figures on the bridge. Mark "C" in blue underglaze. About 1790. (*Right*) The interior and lid of a Spode covered dish, showing "Hog Hunters Meeting by Surprise a Tigress", taken from *British Field Sports* by Samuel Howitt, 1807.

REGISTRY OF DESIGNS

Index to the letters for each year and month from 1842 to 1883

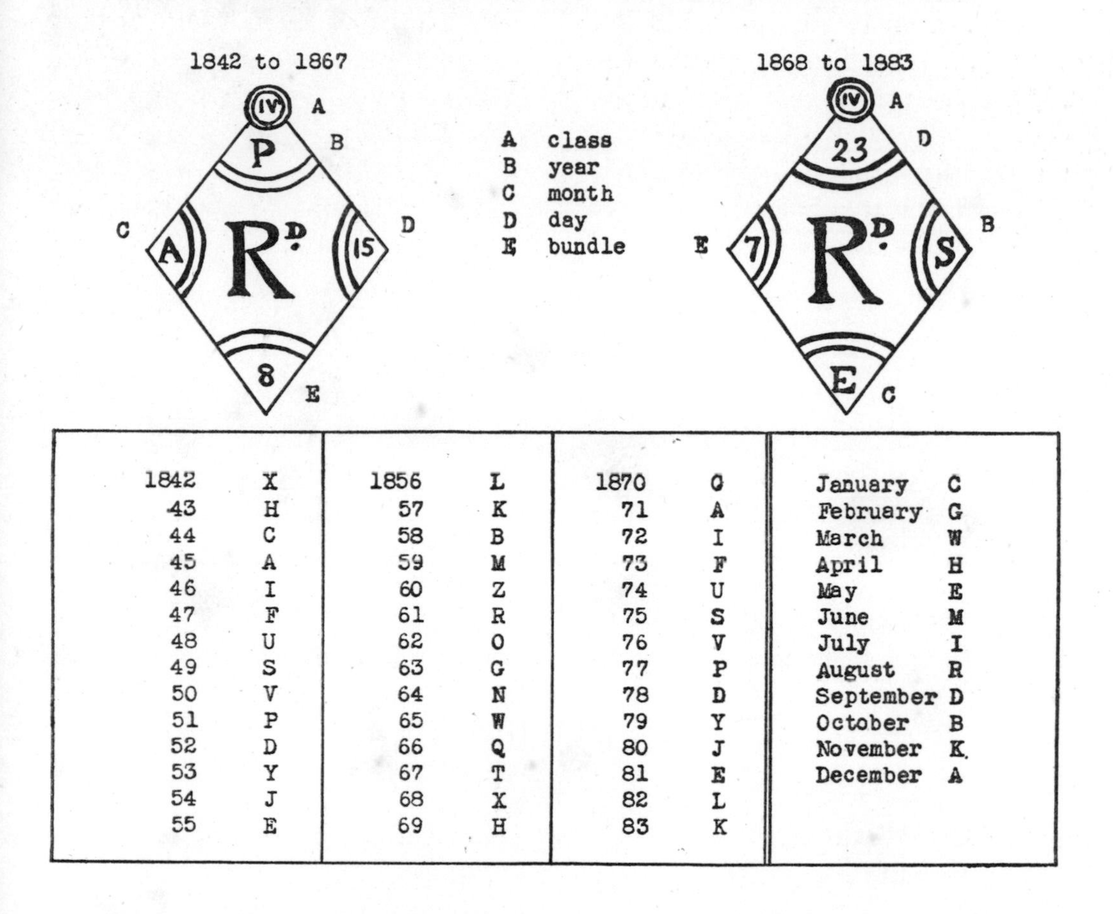

Year	Letter	Year	Letter	Year	Letter	Month	Letter
1842	X	1856	L	1870	C	January	C
43	H	57	K	71	A	February	G
44	C	58	B	72	I	March	W
45	A	59	M	73	F	April	H
46	I	60	Z	74	U	May	E
47	F	61	R	75	S	June	M
48	U	62	O	76	V	July	I
49	S	63	G	77	P	August	R
50	V	64	N	78	D	September	D
51	P	65	W	79	Y	October	B
52	D	66	Q	80	J	November	K
53	Y	67	T	81	E	December	A
54	J	68	X	82	L		
55	E	69	H	83	K		

For September 1857 ?R used from September 1st to September 19th.

For December 1860 ?K used.

For March 1st to March 6th 1878 the following mark was issued:

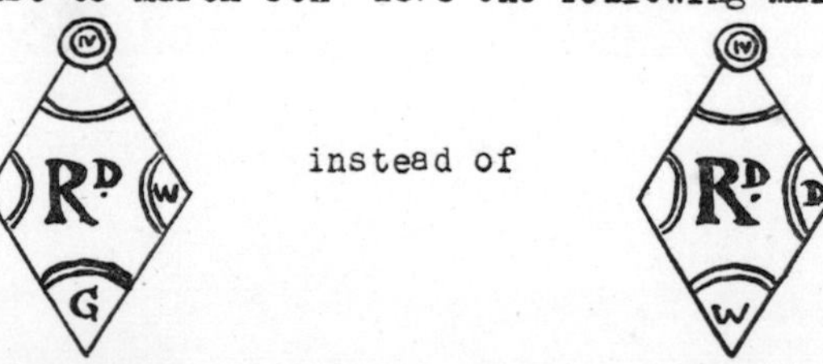

Much ware between 1842 and 1883 bore a registration mark to prevent design piracy and the corner letters and figures are here explained. Class IV covered all ceramic wares. The "bundle" contained the original design filed at the Patent Office and the date was that of the design's introduction and not necessarily that of the ceramic so marked.

potters John and William who traded after his death in 1814 as J. and W. Ridgway. This firm eventually became an enormous organization producing every kind of **porcelain** and pottery. At Cauldon Place excellent bone china was made until 1859 as well as parian ware and fine earthenware. Some of the Ridgway ceramics are equal in every way to the contemporary productions of **Copeland** and **Minton**. They received continental orders over a long period from royal and noble houses thus showing their ability to compete with the state subsidized factories of the continent. Ground colours are of remarkable purity and evenness and **gilding,** both burnished and matt, has the appearance of solid metal. Characteristic during the mid-century were dessert services with outer rims formed of loops of ribbon standing clear from the beaded edge of the plate.

Marks included I. RIDGWAY; RIDGWAY & SONS; J.W.R. in a shield; JOHN

RIDGWAY & CO., CAULDON PLACE, POTTERS TO HER MAJESTY, with the royal arms above and BY ROYAL APPOINTMENT beneath. *See* page 149.

RMA MARK

Initials of Richard Meir Astbury (1765–1834) have been noted incised. Astbury made Voyez's well-known "Fair Hebe" jug.

ROCKINGHAM (Yorkshire)

Established 1745 at Swinton, near Rotherham, after Edward Butler had discovered a bed of fine clay near Swinton common. He made nothing more than a common brown domestic **stoneware**, and upon his death in 1765 the factory continued uneventfully under Thomas Malpass. None of their ware has been identified.

Earthenware: in 1778 the factory was acquired by Thomas Bingley in association with John and William Brameld. They modernized and enlarged the plant and premises, increasing the range of productions to include white earthenware painted and **transfer-printed** in blue. Bingley won repute for his firm by originating the well-known Swinton tea and coffee services, brown, chocolate-coloured, and mottled, and often richly **gilded** with oriental and floral designs. Jugs in brown-glazed earthenware were also issued in tens of thousands. From 1787 to 1806 the firm was in partnership with **Leeds**, trading as Greens, Bingley and Company. The Bramelds became sole proprietors in 1807, and the wares, which had previously been unmarked, began to bear their name.

From about 1790 the firm had produced a type of glazed white or cream-coloured earthenware known as "brown china". The **lead glaze** was heavily stained with pure oxide of manganese, producing a purple-brown, lighter on the neck of a piece and darker at the foot through running during firing. Fine examples display a beautiful "bloom". This coloured glaze was at once christened "Rockingham glaze" because the pottery premises were built on land owned by the Marquess of Rockingham. A wide range of tint is to be found in this ware, which included tea-, coffee- and dessert-services. The Bramelds also made a lustrous blackware, resembling that of **Jackfield** but decorated with **water gilding**. Fine **creamware** and open **basket ware** were made from 1807, superficially resembling that made at Leeds. In 1813 the works passed into the possession of William Brameld's three sons, Thomas, George Frederick, and John Wager Brameld.

Bone china: the brothers Brameld were soon engaged in experiments which resulted in their setting up as manufacturers of fine bone china. In 1820 there appeared a small amount of the ornamental ware which for more than two decades was to give Rockingham the reputation for lavish splendour. While other potters were governed by production costs the Bramelds entirely ignored such consideration in their determination to achieve technical perfection. The resulting china in its more luxurious forms displayed more advanced potting technique and more beautiful decoration than any comparable contemporary work. Despite a continuation of the profitable earthenware manufacture, however, the Bramelds' bone china products were so costly that their financial resources proved unequal to the strain. But, instead of bankruptcy, they attracted the interest of their landlord, Earl Fitzwilliam, who came to their aid in 1826, when the Fitzwilliam crest, a griffin passant, was introduced as the factory trade mark.

The **colours** used at Rockingham were unrivalled during the 1830s: particularly gorgeous were the ground colours, perhaps the most perfect of their period. Among these the thick, smooth opaque apple green is the most celebrated and was peculiar to Rockingham: the somewhat harder shade of green sometimes noted resulted from the use of an impure metallic oxide. Rockingham blue grounds, which include a deep *gros bleu* verging on violet, were notable for their rich shadings and variations of tone, the mazarine and *bleu de ciel* being particularly soft and attractive. Reds varied from a deep pink to a maroon closely resembling that used by **Chelsea** more than half a century earlier. **Derby's** canary yellow was copied, but the Rockingham version was considerably darker. The delicate peach tint of Rockingham is very rare. A pink ground enriched with a gilded diaper pattern was a favourite decoration.

In an effort to outshine their rivals the Brameld brothers turned to the lavish application of **gilding**, often in delicate lace patterns never made elsewhere, but usually in highly burnished areas of solid gold. Wide gilt borders with heavy gilt knobs and gilt animals for handles and cover finials were characteristic. With the passing of years Rockingham gilding has tended to acquire a faint coppery tinge.

Dessert-services were characterized by relief-moulded edges, usually enriched with delicate gilt scrollwork and handles in the form of moulded leaves in which the veins were picked out in gold. Dinner-services adapted from late Georgian silver and enriched with delicate sprays of flowers in natural colours, often against a yellowish background, were issued in considerable numbers, as was a wide variety of ornamental ware encrusted with exquisitely modelled flowers in high relief. (*See* **Flower-encrusted bone china.**) **Baskets** constructed of bone china straws were handsomely enriched with such flowers.

Among table-ware decorations, teacup interiors might be painted with well-composed views, the outsides ornamented with patterns of gilding. Rockingham originated the resplendent style of painting a tray or dish centre in a gilded cartouche that contained a skilfully executed miniature in each corner. Rockingham vases, although excellently modelled, display little originality in form or decoration, many of them obviously inspired by **Derby** and **Worcester.**

Rockingham **figures** and statuettes are sometimes as gracefully elegant as anything comparable in English ceramics. Unfortunately, however, they were coarsely enamelled with broad washes of semi-translucent colour. A Rockingham figure may usually be identified by a gold-inscribed title on the plinth. Small shepherdesses, dancers, and similar minor figures were made in a rather chalky **biscuit** and may easily be mistaken for unmarked Derby.

Rockingham animals are world-famed, but none surpassed the fine craftsmanship of the poodle series. These were exquisitely modelled, with curly hair on neck and head composed of fine china threads. Although they were widely copied elsewhere no other firm succeeded in producing more than a matted effect.

After the death of William IV the patronage of the peerage was transferred to potters favoured by the new monarch. The Bramelds refused to lower the high standard of their decorations, a policy which quickly resulted in financial disaster and closure of the works in 1842. It must be emphasized, however, that the manufacture of Rockingham ware was continued at Coburg Place, Bayswater, London, from 1844 to 1854, by John Wager Brameld, who used the original paste and glaze. He specialized in finely decorated cabinet ware as splendidly enamelled and as lavishly gilded as before. There was, too, a considerable output of domestic ware, and among Brameld's display at the Great Exhibition 1851 was table-ware ornamented with flowers, rose, shamrock, and thistle in brilliantly coloured enamels.

The Bramelds did not consistently mark their bone china: the majority was issued unmarked. Until 1826 an applied medallion might be used bearing the word "Brameld" in relief surrounded by a wreath of national floral emblems. On less costly ware the name only was impressed, or printed in red or purple.

Marks were always printed after 1826 when the griffin passant was placed above the inscription "Rockingham Works Brameld" in copperplate script. This was printed in red, brown, or purple. In 1830 the griffin was surmounted by a royal crown and the inscription "Manufacturers to the King" was added below the factory name. After 1837 the word "King" was changed to "Queen". The royal crown surmounting the script legend "Royal Rock^m^ Works Brameld"—without the griffin—is sometimes noted on bone china made during the period 1830–40. There is no record that the firm actually made any ware to the commission of Queen Victoria, and late in 1840 marks bearing royal references were discontinued, the firm reverting to the mark used between 1826 and 1830. John Wager Brameld printed the griffin with the name "Brameld" on his London-made china, 1844–54. *See* **Cadogan tea-pot**.

ROCOCO or ROCAILLE

A style of light, inconsequent decoration associated with France and fashionable in England during the second quarter of the 18th century. It was distinguished by a profusion of flamboyant ornament, especially the shells and rockwork from which it derived its name, but also including all manner of scrolls, foliage and so on, tending to obscure the basic forms it was designed to ornament. This was made the more conspicuous by the fact that the whole design was frequently asymmetrical. English work was more moderate than the Continental, and current tastes were often met by surrounding a cartouche decoration with light, irregular scrolls.

ROGERS, JOHN and JAMES, (Dale Hall, Burslem, Staffordshire)

Makers of domestic **earthenware**, 1786 to 1842, specializing in **transfer-printed** ware from about 1802 to 1830, and issuing many American scenes. Traded as John Rogers & Sons from about 1810. Mark, ROGERS impressed.

ROSE-ENGINE-TURNING. *See* **Engine-turned decoration.**

ROSSO ANTICO

A hard, fine red **stoneware** made by **Josiah Wedgwood**: a refinement of an earlier red stoneware made by the **Elers** brothers.

RSW MARK. *See* **Stevenson, Ralph.**

S MARK. *See* **Caughley, Coalport** *and* **Shorthose.**

SA & Co. MARK. *See* **Samuel Alcock.**

SADLER and GREEN (Liverpool)

John Sadler and Guy Green established themselves as transfer printers on tiles in 1756, and later printed on **earthenware** and **porcelain** sent to them for this purpose by other potters. They were for long believed to have been the inventors of **transfer-printing.**

SAGGAR

A closed fireclay box in which ceramic ware is placed for firing to protect it from direct contact with the flame. The pieces of ware, shaped and air-dried, are placed on a foundation of powdered alumina.

SALOPIAN WARE

Soft-paste porcelain and **earthenware** made at **Caughley.**

SALT, RALPH (Hanley) 1782–1846

Maker of **figures** which may be impressed on the back with his name. These were in the **Walton** style with similar **bocage** backgrounds, though the oak sprays tended to be less exactly modelled, a trend that became more pronounced in other imitations. Some figures were decorated with **lustre.**

SALT GLAZE. *See* **Glaze** *and* **Stoneware.**

S and G MARK. *See* **Isleworth.**

S B & Co. MARK. *See* **Sunderland.**

SCALE PATTERN

A blue or pink diaper resembling overlapping fish-scales made at **Worcester** and copied on 19th century **bone china** from about 1820.

SCALLOP

Ornament derived from the shape of the scallop shell, and consisting essentially in the repetition of an arc in series.

SCENT BOTTLES

Known at the time as smelling-bottles, these were made at **Chelsea** in considerable numbers and were listed in auctions of Chelsea wares in 1754 and 1755, "mounted in Gold and ornamented with stones of several sorts, as rubies, diamonds etc". Early Chelsea bottles had deep hollows or kick-ups in their bases, their designs were simple and colours subdued. Models of monks and nuns, birds with their heads forming the stoppers, and plain pear shapes painted with flowers and river scenes were typical. Later, in the gold anchor period, came brilliant colours, touches of **gilding** and an immense range of designs, from the familiar boy with a goat beside a stump bearing grapes and vine leaves to the simplest bottle, shaped and coloured as a stick of asparagus. Lively birds, elaborate dovecotes, bouquets of rosebuds, groups including the harlequins copied from **Dresden**, were issued, but it must be stressed that a marked example is most unlikely to be genuine.

Worcester and **Derby** also made fine scent bottles, and poorly finished examples were made elsewhere. In **bone china** they were made by Derby and some of the Staffordshire potters.

SCOTT BROS., SCOTT, P. B., AND SIMILAR MARKS. *See* **Portobello** *and* **Sunderland.**

SCRATCH BLUE

Patterns incised into the surface of Staffordshire **salt-glaze** ware with a sharp tool before firing and emphasized by the application of powdered zaffre into the lines (*see* **Cobalt blue**). After firing the line decoration appeared in dark blue where the zaffre had stained out. *See* **Sgraffiato.**

SÈVRES (France)

Like **Dresden**, this was one of the most important Continental sources of style and decoration, and any English

collector requires some knowledge of its products. Sèvres **porcelain** for the first ten years was in soft paste, then, from 1768, in hard paste. The factory produced the finest of all French porcelain. Even to list all the decorations that appeared on Sèvres porcelain would be impossible. They were enclosed in radiant ground **colours**, dark and light blue, turquoise, canary, apple green, soft pink, and lavish **gilding.** All these were copied by **Chelsea, Derby** and other English potters, some of whom might include one of the marks used by Sèvres until 1790—a double L in the form of a cypher—and a fictitious date letter. Some of the later typical Sèvres marks illustrated here were adapted by some English **bone china** makers.

The marks shown are: *top*, from 1753, with crown for hard-paste porcelain, including date letter. *Middle*, for République Française (1792–1800) and for Charles X (1824–28). *Bottom*, for Charles X (1829–30) and for Louis Philippe (1835–48).

SEWELL & COMPANY, SEWELLS & DONKIN MARKS. *See* **Newcastle-on-Tyne.**

SGRAFFIATO

A type of scratched decoration in which **slip** ware displayed a design in two contrasting colours. Body and slip materials were of almost the same quality: the lighter coloured slip was spread over the darker body, or, less frequently, *vice versa*. The ornament was obtained by scratching away the upper stratum with a sharp point so as to disclose the lower in the desired pattern. In 1832 **Ralph Wood** introduced the method of dipping coloured ware into white clay slip, scratching a design through the coating to display a design in dark colour.

SHARPE, WM. and CO. *See* **Torksey.**

SHORTHOSE and Co. (Hanley)

Minor potters who produced **transfer-printed ware** in various colours, 1783–1826. The mark Shorthose & Co has been noted, impressed or

blue-printed; also Shorthose & Heath. Arrows, impressed or in brown, are conjecturally ascribed to this firm.

SLIP

Potter's clay in a liquid state of about the consistency of cream used for **slip decoration** and **casting**, and for attaching handles and spouts.

SLIPWARE

Coarse reddish-burning clay which after shaping was decorated with **slip.** This was applied to its surface by means of a quill through which it trickled to make lines and dots forming figures, borders, medallions, conventional designs and so on. A **lead**

glaze, often mixed with manganese oxide, was applied before firing. This gave to the body and to the slip, whatever its colour, a rich yellow transparency. **Tygs**, posset pots, jugs, dishes, plates and candlesticks were made in this medium until a century ago. The principal areas in which slipware potters operated were London, North Staffordshire, Kent, Derbyshire, Sussex, Cheshire and Devonshire, each producing a distinct local type.

SM & CO., S. MOORE & CO. and similar marks. *See* **Sunderland**.

SMALT. *See* **Cobalt**.

SMEAR GLAZING. *See* **Glaze**.

SMITH, SAMPSON (Longton, 1813–78)

Makers of useful wares, **lustre wares** and **earthenware figures** around 1850.

SMITH, WILLIAM & COMPANY (Stockton-on-Tees)

Established the Stafford Pottery in 1825 and made **cream-coloured earthenware** until 1870. The marks, which might be impressed or printed, were W. S. AND CO. QUEEN'S WARE STOCKTON. W. S. AND CO.S WEDGWOOD, and W. S. & CO. STAFFORD POTTERY. During 1848 a perpetual injunction was granted to **Josiah Wedgwood and Sons** restraining this firm from marking its wares WEDGEWOOD (note spelling) or WEDGWOOD & CO. Large quantities of **queen's ware** bearing this mark had been issued before Wedgwood's attention was drawn to the imitation.

See **Ferrybridge**.

SOAPSTONE PORCELAIN

A **soft-paste porcelain** containing 35 to 45 per cent of finely pulverized steatite (hydrated silicate of magnesium) from Cornwall, in place of china clay. Very soft and slightly plastic, it vitrified at a comparatively low temperature, producing a porcelain denser and harder in texture than other soft porcelains, considerably heavier, and with a less undulating surface. It could withstand contact with boiling water without cracking, and it seldom **crazed**, as expansion and contraction of the glaze and paste were fairly well matched. Soapstone porcelains were used at **Bristol** (soft paste) 1748–52; **Worcester** 1751–1820s; **Liverpool**, Chaffers and Christian until the early 1770s; **Caughley** 1775–99; **Swansea** 1817 (*see* **Nantgarw**).

SPIRIT FLASKS

In **stoneware**, were first made by Joseph Bourne, **Denby**, in the 1820s and continued to the late 1840s. These flat-faced brown-and-buff bottles, varying in height between seven and eleven inches, were surmounted by highly individualistic bust and figure portraits in full relief, including royalty and political celebrities. Early in

William IV's reign the long series of reform flasks were issued, culminating in an issue of many thousands when the Reform Bill became law in 1832.

In view of the popularity of these flasks other potters also developed them, retaining the basic simplicity, cheapness of material, and limited range of colours. Each manufacturer issued his own version of a jolly sailor seated on a barrel, impressed with the name of the liquor concerned, such as "Old Tom" found on Oldfield flasks. Figures representing "Smoking" and "Snuffing" came from the **Vauxhall Pottery**; mermaid-shaped flasks were made by Stephen Green of **Lambeth**, whose marine subjects also included large fish. Green also made flasks in designs ranging from pistols, pocket-books, and powder horns to pigs and grandfather clocks as well as the series in the form of tipstaffs during the early 1840s.

SPODE-COPELAND (Stoke-upon-Trent)

Josiah Spode (1733–97), the founder of this organization, was among the several celebrated master potters apprenticed with **Whieldon**. At the age of twenty-nine he was appointed manager to the firm of Turner and Banks, and upon the death of Turner, in 1770, he acquired the business on mortgage, continuing to make inexpensive domestic **earthenware** and sporting jugs with decoration in relief. By 1776 he was sole proprietor of a pottery trading under his own name and working on the development of **cream-coloured earthenware** decorated with blue **transfer-printing** under the **glaze**. This was brought to perfection in the early 1780s, and so successful was the new decoration that he established a London warehouse under the management of William Copeland.

Spode then turned his attention to the production of domestic ware in a stronger, whiter, more translucent porcelain. He achieved this by evolving a method of dispensing with the **frit** and using bone ash in its composition. In 1796 he was issuing **bone china** in vast quantity, having installed new ovens and other plant for the purpose. The profit for the first year exceeded £15,000, of which William Copeland received £1,000 as a gift, at the same time becoming a partner in the firm which was now styled Spode, Son and Copeland. Upon the death of the founder in 1797 the pottery came under the direction of his son, Josiah Spode II, with William Copeland responsible for sales. Copeland died in 1826 and Josiah Spode II a year later. Both were succeeded by their sons, W. T. Copeland and Josiah Spode III. Within two years the latter had died, and Copeland became sole proprietor. Under his progressive guidance output rose to immense proportions and in 1833 he took Thomas Garrett into partnership, the firm trading as Copeland and Garrett until 1847. Since then the name of Copeland has stood alone, the firm being controlled by direct descendants to the present day.

Spode's designers in the early days profited largely by decorations used by the established makers of soft-paste porcelain. They fully realized the inherent fitness of Chinese decoration on bone china and expressed the spirit of oriental designs. Blue printed transfer designs comprised the major part of this decoration and included a **willow pattern** adapted for Spode by **Thomas Minton** from the original **Caughley** version. Spode bone china was fortunate in escaping the crowded design which too often disfigured other and later "well-covered" Staffordshire china. *See* page 149.

New patterns were continually produced. "A very pretty gallery they make", wrote Arthur Hayden, "with a wide range of subjects and rich enamel **colours** and subtle **gilding.** Because of their affinity with Chinese prototypes they stand rather aloof throughout a period of ceramic art not especially noteworthy for the excellence of its designs. Simplicity is their outstanding note and the touches of Spode's *naivité* have endeared a whole series of well-known designs to collectors." The Shanghai pattern was a decoration of Chinese inspiration. But Spode modified it for western tastes by changing the colour of the blossoms in the floral pattern and using those familiar in England.

Regarding the Spode **Japanese** designs, the evidence of the old pattern books proves that such decorations in deep velvety blues, bold patches of scarlet, and rich gilding were superior to the flood of Japanese designs from **Derby** commonly termed Crown Derby Japan patterns. Spode productions in the Imari manner were superior to those of Derby. Less numerous, but equally characteristic of Spode's Japanese vein, were the highly successful decoration of the **Kakiemon** type.

The second Josiah Spode was the finest imitator of his day and copied **Chelsea** with great success. His most ambitious attempt was the claret ground with bird decoration in gold: the ground colour, however, was not quite perfect. Spode's copies of **Dresden** ware would have been difficult to distinguish from the genuine ware if it were not for the quality of his paste: the same was true of his numerous French imitations. It was in his efforts to copy **Worcester**, however, that Spode was most successful. The blue in his salmon-scale decoration was livelier than that of the Wall period. His *gros bleu* was a perfect copy.

Marks on Spode bone china were plain and unmistakable. Although frequently altered they were never cryptic, or contrived in any way to resemble the marks of another pottery.

Felspar porcelain was introduced in 1800, being extensively used for table services until 1833. This was remarkably translucent, a factor greatly enhancing the beauty of enamel decoration. It was marked SPODE FELSPAR PORCELAIN printed in puce and surrounded by a wreath of roses, thistles and shamrocks, or else the inscription only was printed in blue.

Josiah Spode II in 1805 invented a **felspathic earthenware** known as "stone china". This was opaque, extremely hard, and had a delicate blue-grey tinted body of finer texture than ordinary earthenware. It immediately captured public favour. The pleasant Chinese decorations it displayed were derived chiefly from **famille rose** porcelain.

Marks on stone china consisted of a pseudo-Chinese seal with the name SPODE overprinted in a rectangular panel and STONE CHINA beneath, printed in blue.

SPRIGGED WORK

Relief decoration shaped in a separate mould, removed and immediately applied or "sprigged" on to the body of the ware before firing.

SPUR MARKS

When ware was dipped in light **slip** or **glaze** and fired in saggars, three bit-stones separated each piece to prevent them from sticking together. These were later replaced by three spurs or stilts, triangular pieces of **earthenware** or **stoneware**. The points of the bit-stones or spurs left the three rough spots on the underside of the ware now known to collectors as spur marks.

STEATITIC. *See* **Soapstone.**

STEVENSON, ANDREW (Cobridge, Staffordshire)

Made dark blue **transfer-printed earthenware,** in which the decoration displayed high technical ability, from 1810 to 1818. More than thirty English

scenes are known, but most of his productions were intended for the American market, and he even sent a young artist named W. G. Wall to sketch views on the spot. Borders were handsomely designed with large flowers, roses and foliage. Andrew Stevenson impressed his ware with a crown surmounted by A. STEVENSON WARRANTED STAFFORDSHIRE, or imprinted in blue with the name of the scene accompanied by an eagle or a draped urn. A three-masted ship was often included in his mark. *See* page 149.

STEVENSON, RALPH (Cobridge, Staffordshire)

A specialist in finely **transfer-printed** Staffordshire blue from 1815 to 1840. His "English Views" were enclosed in handsome acorn and oak leaf borders and in some instances rim edges might be in white relief. "British Lakes" were enclosed in ornate flower and scroll borders; American views were in other leaf borders. Little of his ware was marked and then only with his name STEVENSON impressed. During the late 1820s he was joined by W. Williams, and the impressed marks R S W, or R STEVENSON & WILLIAMS were subsequently used. *See* page 149.

STIRRUP CUPS

Date from about 1770 in the shape of fox-masks, first made in **earthenware** by **Whieldon**, boldly modelled and splashed with green. Later Whieldon cups were less deeply moulded and were enamelled in naturalistic colours with green collars encircling the neck rims. Whieldon designs included the earless fox-head of creamy-white pottery with olive-green markings. A wide variety of fox-head stirrup-cups was made by Staffordshire potters during the next seventy or eighty years, but rarely is an example marked, and it is impossible to attribute specimens to individual factories. Until 1825 earthenware stirrup-cups were skilfully modelled and coloured naturalistically.

Fox-head and other stirrup-cups were made in **soft-paste porcelain** during the last quarter of the 18th century. The Chelsea-Derby sale catalogue of 1780 showed them to have been sold in pairs, large-size fox-heads at 8*s*. 6*d*. the pair; "one pair foxes heads for drinking cups 6*s*.", and "one pair hare's heads enamelled and gilt". **Derby** fox-heads in porcelain were skilfully modelled, sometimes enamelled in tawny-red tones with gilt collars. In **bone china** they frequently had yellow ears and pink collars; others were glazed in a pearly white; others again were in a single colour throughout, such as brown or yellow, matt on the exterior and glazed within. Later Derby fox-heads were less efficiently modelled, without collars, and highly glazed, the **glaze** now displaying hair-vein **crazing**.

Hound-heads ran a close favourite to fox-heads. **Ralph Wood** II, Burslem, made them in earthenware with a light olive-green translucent glaze. John Turner of Green Dock modelled some very life-like examples in earthenware, including the unglazed cane-coloured series with glazed interiors. At least thirty Staffordshire potters made hound-heads. Until 1820 they were well-modelled with ears laid flat, and with delicately tinted muzzles. Tones of reddish-brown and black, with gold and black collars, are found, brown markings being a common variant.

Derby, **Rockingham**, **Coalport** and some two dozen Staffordshire potters specializing in bone china issued hound-heads in natural colourings. Lavender-tinted examples came from Rockingham as did some vigorously modelled in plain white, their necks encircled with collars of highly lustrous gilding. From Staffordshire came the bone-china hound-heads in a dull, white **biscuit**, and a well-modelled series coloured in tones of black and grey, reddish-brown, or grey-brown. Black ears and a light maroon muzzle distinguished another extensive series.

Other stirrup-cups were in the form of a deer- or stag-head without antlers; a trout-head; a hare-head; a cock's-head; a bear's-head; a clenched fist; and the heads of such other dogs as bull-dog, bull-terrier, setter, and dalmatian.

STONE CHINA

A **felspathic earthenware** developed by **Josiah Spode II** in 1805. It is opaque, but of far finer texture than earthenware, extremely hard, emitting a clear ring when lightly tapped. So fine is its dense body that it closely approximates **porcelain**. The body of Spode's original version has a delicate blue-grey tint. *See* **Mason ware.**

STONEWARE, BROWN

Halfway between **hard porcelain** and white **earthenware**, and considerably stronger than either. Opaque, intensely hard and non-porous, this clay ware displayed a glassy texture when fractured. It was generally made from a single plastic clay with the addition of **felspar**, and quartz in the form of sand or crushed calcined **flint.** When fired at a high temperature the clay became wholly vitrified, ensuring a closeness of texture which made it as hard as stone—hence its name—and impervious to fluids. The colours to which good quality clays usually burn range from a yellowish-buff to a dark brown. Stoneware until about 1840 was usually **glazed** by introducing **salt** into the kiln. This resulted in a durable, inexpensive, non-poisonous glaze which gave the surface an attractive sheen. Variation in tint was obtained by **slip-glazing** parts of the surface before firing. The heat of the kiln combined with the salt glaze to colour this a rich brown.

STONEWARE, WHITE, SALT-GLAZED

This was developed from a drab-coloured material under the guidance of **John Astbury** who was the first Staffordshire potter to incorporate crushed calcined **flint** into his formula, producing at first a dull cream body, and eventually one white enough to show off the transparent **salt-glaze** to its best advantage. This was also the first step towards **cream-coloured earthenware.** By the 1740s white salt-glazed stoneware was competing with Chinese porcelain, being made as thin and light and transparent as possible. It might be **cast** or moulded. By 1750 more than fifty Staffordshire potteries were making white salt-glazed stoneware. Contemporary advertisements refer to this as flint-ware to distinguish it from brown stoneware. *See* **Glaze.**

STUBBS, JOSEPH (Longport, Staffordshire)

A specialist in old Staffordshire blue, established as a maker of **cream-coloured earthenware.** Between 1810 and 1829 he issued **transfer-printed** English scenes bordered with a design of foliage and pointed scrolls, and American views enclosed in borders consisting of an eagle, flower and scroll design. Some attractive milkmaid pieces which occasionally come to light were a Stubbs product. Most of his work is unmarked, but some early pieces have the name STUBBS impressed. From 1816 the mark was JOSEPH STUBBS LONGPORT encircling a star. The impress STUBBS & KENT is evidence of a partnership before 1829. *See* page 149.

SUNDERLAND (Co. Durham)

Made inexpensive white **earthenware** from 1740 and **cream-coloured earthenware** from 1780. Decorations were mainly **transfer-printing** and **lustre.** The vast quantity of earthenware made can be visualized when it is realized that one only of the several flint-crushing mills operated with a weekly output of twenty tons early in the 19th century. Collectors look for lustre wares; **frog mugs;** chimney ornaments; ware decorated with transfer prints of Wearmouth Bridge, opened in 1796, and known in twenty-two versions, fourteen of them rare, (this is often wrongly termed Sunderland Bridge, 14 miles distant); Sunderland lions; sets of matching ewers and jugs from cream-jug size to two-and-a-half gallon capacity; **mugs** decorated with portraits of Jack Crawford, a local hero of the battle of Camperdown in 1797; and a wide range of gift china.

Deptford, or Ball's Pottery: established by William Ball in 1857. His purple lustre was notable for its distinct orange tinge. Ball later acquired the original moulds for the Sunderland lions: in his productions the vicious-looking fangs of the originals were replaced by a row of even teeth. Occasionally the impressed mark BALL BROTHERS SUNDERLAND is found, dating after 1884.

Low Ford, or Dawson's Pottery: founded in 1800, and remained under the ownership of John Dawson until his death in 1848. From about 1840 output exceeded that of any other Sunderland pottery, but the firm closed in 1864. Productions included *tiles* with landscape views in colour or sepia; lustre wares; round table tops to fit into cabinet work; canary yellow mugs with the bridge transfer-printed in black; inkpots shaped as birds' nests. Marks include: FORD POTTERY SOUTH HYLTON 1800; DAWSON; J DAWSON LOW FORD; FORD; DAWSON & CO; DAWSON & CO LOW FORD; J. DAWSON & CO LOW FORD POTTERY.

North Hylton Pottery: established 1762 and continued until 1867. During the first half of the 19th century the firm was celebrated for domestic and ornamental ware painted with purple lustre. The following impressed marks are known: until 1815 MALING; HYLTON POT WORKS; and PHILLIPS & MALING; then JOHN PHILLIPS HYLTON POTTERY; J PHILLIPS HYLTON POTTERY.

Southwick Pottery: established in 1788 by Anthony Scott and continued until 1897, making ware of higher quality than was usual among the Sunderland potters. This firm produced some of the most clear-cut of the Sunderland lions and mosaic ware in olive grey or brown made by mechanical process devised in about 1830 by Thomas P. Scott. **Jasper** ware in the **Wedgwood** style was made in the mid-19th century. A wide range of transferred work was issued on white earthenware, and enamelled designs on cream-coloured earthenware. Marks were usually impressed and include: SCOTT; ED. ATKINSON; ANTHONY SCOTT & SONS; S. & SONS SOUTHWICK; SCOTT BROS; SCOTT BROTHERS & CO; S B & CO.

Sunderland, or "Garrison" Pottery: it is thought that John Phillips became owner in 1807. From 1813 to 1819 the firm was styled Phillips & Co., and/or Dixon & Co.; 1820–26, Dixon, Austin & Co.; 1827–40, Dixon, Austin, Phillips & Co.; 1840–67, Dixon, Phillips & Co. These firms were also proprietors of the Hylton Pottery. The range of productions included pink lustre, sponged, printed, and painted copper and silver lustre, lively **figures**, tobacco jars, stands for clocks and watches, and so on. Marks were impressed and included: J PHILLIPS SUNDERLAND POTTERY; PHILLIPS & CO; PHILLIPS & CO SUNDERLAND POTTERY; PHILLIPS & CO SUNDERLAND 1813; DIXON & CO SUNDERLAND 1813; DIXON & CO; DIXON & CO SUNDERLAND POTTERY; DIXON & AUSTIN'S SUNDERLAND POTTERY; DIXON AUSTIN PHILLIPS & CO; DIXON PHILLIPS & CO (enclosing an anchor).

The Wear Pottery: established in 1786 by John Brunton and the name changed to S. Moore & Company in 1861 until the firm closed in 1883. Productions of interest to the collector included the lustre wares, and chintz pattern jugs in addition to the usual Sunderland wares. No marks were used until 1861 after which the following appeared: S. MOORE & CO; S M & CO; MOORE and CO; MOORE & CO SOUTHWICK.

SUSSEX POTTERY. *See* **Cadborough ware.**

SWANSEA PORCELAIN. *See* **Cambrian Pottery** *and* **Nantgarw.**

SWANSEA POTTERY

Established in 1769 and continued for a century. At first **delft ware** was made. From the late 1770s until 1801 under George Haynes some fine **cream-coloured ware** was made, also blue **transfer-printed** table ware, many of the designs being from copper

17. Sunderland pottery: (*Top*) transfer-printed jugs; (*Centre*) copper lustre ware; (*Below*) cups, saucers and mug hand-painted in pink lustre, the plate in speckled lustre.

(*Left*) Unglazed red ware with unfired gilding, probably by J. P. Elers. Late 17th century. Height 3½ inches. (*Centre*) Red ware with applied white clay reliefs and yellowish glaze. Staffordshire, about 1740. 6 inches. (*Right*) Salt-glazed white stoneware with unfired gilding, about 1740. 5¼ inches.

(*Left*) Salt-glazed white stoneware in the form of a kneeling camel, handle as a scaly dolphin. About 1745. 4½ inches. (*Centre*) Marbled in blue, white and brown clays, with lid knob in form of a Chinese lion. About 1745. 4¾ inches. (*Right*) Salt-glazed white stoneware with reliefs painted in pink, yellow, green and red. About 1760. 4¼ inches.

(*Left*) Chelsea porcelain painted in colours and gold, with dark blue ground. 1760s. 5 inches. (*Centre*) Longton Hall porcelain painted with Italian landscapes; handle in form of vine stem and grapes. About 1755. 4½ inches. (*Right*) Staffordshire salt-glazed white stoneware painted in the style of Chinese *famille rose* porcelain. About 1765. 5 inches.

18. (*Left*) Small Spode earthenware teapot printed in blue with the Milkmaid pattern introduced 1814. 4 inches. (*Centre*) Rockingham bone china painted in colours and gold. About 1840. 7 inches. (*Right*) Spode felspar porcelain decorated with bands of pink, flowers in colour, scrolls and wreaths in gold. About 1820.

Salt-glazed white stoneware: (*Left*) in the form of a three-storied house, moulded in low relief, about 1745. 5½ inches. (*Centre*) With incised decoration coloured blue, about 1740. 5½ inches. (*Right*) Heart-shaped on plan with relief decoration of fruiting vine and traces of oil gilding. About 1745. 5 inches.

(*Left*) Cadogan teapot with no lid opening and filled from the base by means of an interior spiralling tube. Impressed "Copeland and Garrett". About 1840. (*Centre*) Engine-turned teapot in red marl; late 18th century. (*Right*) Cane-ware hand-painted in blue, glazed only on the interior; made by Josiah Spode about 1790.

(*Left*) Worcester porcelain, with stand, painted in enamel colours and gold. Barrel-shaped body with nearly flat cover. About 1775. 4⅞ inches. (*Centre*) Bristol hard paste porcelain painted in colours and gold with highly domed cover. Mark, the sign for tin, in gold. About 1770. 9¾ inches. (*Right*) Salopian porcelain painted in blue. About 1775.

19. (*Left*) Spode bone china decorated in the Japan style with red, blue, and green enamels, and gilding. Mark "Spode 967" in red. (*Centre*) Spode bone china with blue groundwork printed in gold by the bat-printing process. 1820s. (*Right*) Copeland stoneware with blue ground and white figures applied in relief. About 1850.

20. Sunderland pottery: (*Top*) animals touched with lustre; (*Centre*) silver lustre; (*Below*) figures and carpet bowls.

plates engraved by R. Rothwell. The marks were: the name CAMBRIAN POTTERY in capitals on either one or two lines, or in a cursive script in one line; the word CAMBRIAN alone; and G. H. & Co. in either capitals or lower case letters. Marks might be impressed or painted in red or in gold. The mark shown is a rare early one in purple **lustre.**

The factory was acquired in 1801 by L. W. Dillwyn who, in addition to earthenware, made "opaque china". He employed W. W. Young as chief decorator from 1803 to 1806, and later as a freelance. Young was an outstanding painter of naturalistic birds, butterflies, and shells, favourite motifs being the kestrel, hen-harrier, and merlin, and, among butterflies, the red admiral, peacock, painted lady and speckled wood. Some notable landscape work was produced. After sixteen years the Cambrian Pottery was sold to Haynes, Roby and Bevington who worked it until 1824. It thereupon came into the possession of Dillwyn again. But in 1850 it was acquired by Evans, Glasson and Evans, the firm becoming Evans and Company in 1859, and later D. J. Evans and Company. It closed in 1870.

Black **basalt** was made during the early period and **Etruscan ware** in the 1840s. *See* **Nantgarw.**

SWINTON. *See* **Rockingham and Don Pottery.**

SWWBB MARK. *See* **Torksey.**

SYNTAX DESIGNS

Decorations in blue and white **transfer-printing** adapted from the "Three Tours of Doctor Syntax", three books of verse published by Ackerman between 1815 and 1821. These were written by William Combe, and illustrated by Thomas Rowlandson. Some eighty different Syntax designs taken from Rowlandson have been noted on **earthenware** by **J. & R. Clews** and **William Adams,** and about fifteen on **Derby bone china.**

"T" and "T^{o}" MARKS

Believed by collectors to be the marks of the repairer Thibaud who anglicized his name to Tebo. The marks are found impressed on **figures: Bow** until 1762; **Worcester** 1762–68; **Plymouth** 1768–70; **Bristol** 1770–74. In 1774 he was working for **Josiah Wedgwood.**

TERRA COTTA

Unglazed porous **pottery** varying in colour from yellow to red. It is softer and more porous than **earthenware** and fired at a lower temperature.

THROWING WHEEL

The machine upon which the potter shapes hollow-ware. Until about 1750 this consisted of a vertical shaft beneath a revolving wheel kept in motion by the thrower who operated it with his foot. The effort required to manipulate such a machine was so great that large articles could not be made on it. In about 1750 a potter named Alsager improved the throwing wheel by fitting a rope from a pulley fixed to the vertical shaft, and thus linking it to a large driving wheel a short distance away. This was turned by a boy who could thus rotate the potter's wheel at various speeds dictated by the shape and size of the ware being thrown. Production was vastly increased by this improvement.

THUNDERCLOUD

The dark bluish-grey shading that appeared where **cobalt**-tinted **glaze** collected in crevices.

TIGER WARE

A collector's term for Rhenish **stoneware** of the Elizabethan period, covered with mottled brown glaze. (Illustration in previous column.)

TITTENSOR, CHARLES (Hanley, Staffordshire)

Maker of **figures,** etc., in the **Walton** manner, 1802–25. His mark was TITTENSOR impressed.

TOBY JUGS

Named after Henry Elwes who was nicknamed Toby Fillpot after drinking two thousand gallons of stingo from his favourite silver beaker. The original model presented a short, corpulent, unsmiling old man wearing a full long coat with capacious pockets low in the skirt, a spacious waistcoat with a cravat resembling barristers' bands, knee breeches, stockings, and buckled shoes. On his head was a three-cornered hat over long lank hair, each corner forming a spout. The cup-shaped crown was detachable to serve as a lid. Sitting back in his chair he balanced a brimming jug on his knee, the other hand lifting a foaming glass to his lips. A well-filled churchwarden pipe rested against the side of his chair.

This figure, dating from about 1770, was adhered to for about twenty years, then it began to be accompanied by other eccentric figures. The name toby jug persisted, however, no matter what the subject, of which more than twenty are known to collectors. These include three forms of sailor dating from mid-1794; the drunken parson; the night watchman; the old English gentleman; the squire; the planter; the publican; the convict; the Welsh country gentleman; King Hal; the hearty good fellow; the snuff-taker; the thin man; the postillion; the bargee; the fiddler, usually impressed with the mark T & J HOLLINS; the one-armed toby; and Martha Gunn, made by **Davenport** from about 1821.

Toby jugs may be grouped into seven distinct classes so far as technique in potting and methods of decoration are concerned.

Coloured glaze decoration: 1770–90. Toby jugs in this class were modelled in a buff or whitish body. Several moulds were brought into use to build a complete jug. When the parts were assembled the jug, whilst plastic, was tooled by a skilled hand-modeller whose touches produced the vigorous life-like effect. The range of colours was limited to green, brown, blue, manganese purple, and greyish olive, but there were many colour gradations. **Ralph Wood II** made toby jugs from about 1775, some being standing models.

Overglaze enamel colours: 1790–1820. These were dull, flat and staring in comparison with the earlier group and less carefully modelled. The enamels were brush-applied over the brilliant semi-transparent **glaze** in a far wider range of colours than had formerly appeared on such jugs and were fixed by low temperature firing.

Overglaze enamel colours: 1815–40. Colours were harsh and garish, glaze whiter than formerly, but less smooth. These jugs were less expensively produced by **casting** in a hollow mould of plaster-of-paris.

Brown stoneware: 1820–40. Made in large numbers resembling modern **Lambeth** ware.

Brown glazed earthenware: 1800–38. Known as "**Rockingham** china" and usually in the form of the ordinary sitting toby, and a larger standing version of the snuff-taker, and also various crinolined feminine models towards the end of the period.

Bone china: 1820–30. These were made at Rockingham and depicted a red-haired, white-suited man taking snuff.

Lustre: 1810–40. Toby jugs with purple lustre coats are rare, as are those in silver lustre, although several have been recorded.

Marks: identification marks are rare and when present are found impressed beneath the plinth. Marks noted on toby jugs include: (1) RA WOOD BURSLEM, sometimes with the addition of a mould number; (2) E WOOD 1794; (3) WALTON on a raised ribbon; (4) NEALE & CO; (5) DAVENPORT with a cable anchor and mould number; (6) T & J HOLLINS, until 1820; (7) a crown, impressed by Neale and Wilson, until 1816 (*see* **Palmer, H.**); (8) PRATT; (9) SWANSEA; (10) SHARPE on jugs made by Thomas Sharpe of Swadlincote, 1821–38. Most of these potters are to be found under appropriate headings. Other potters recorded as makers of enamelled toby jugs are Robert Garner, **Lakin & Poole, Wood & Caldwell,** John Turner to 1803, **Ralph Salt** from about 1820, **William Adams** to 1805, and **Josiah Spode II.**

Fakes: the best test is found in the **crazing** of the glaze, the presence of large cracks indicating faking; genuine toby jugs are covered with innumerable tiny crackles. The faker's crazing is seldom small enough.

TORKSEY (Brampton-in-Torksey, Lincolnshire)

William Billingsley was associated with a **porcelain** factory here from 1803 to 1807 in partnership with Samuel Walker and three others. Traces of a kiln have been found and it is known that **bone china** bought in the white from elsewhere was decorated. They traded as William Sharpe & Company, Brampton China Manufactory. Some examples were marked SWWBB representing the initials of Samuel Walker, William Billingsley, and Brampton. Other pieces marked BRAMPTON MANUFACTORY are known.

TORTOISESHELL WARE

Earthenware decorated in imitation of the shell of a tortoise at a period when this was a favourite form of somewhat stylized ornament in various media. Metallic oxides were dusted on the **lead-glazed** surface of the ware before the glaze was fired—manganese to give madder brown, bronze and purple; copper for green; iron for orange and yellow; **cobalt** for blue. When fired the mingling of colours produced markings in a wide range of variegated tints, the more usual combinations being mottled green and brownish grey; brown, green and slate blue; mottled grey, green, slate-blue and yellow. *See* **Whieldon.**

TRANSFER-PRINTING

A process of applying engraved decorative designs to ceramic surfaces. Its earliest use appears to have been at the Battersea, London, enamel works in 1753, the three partners each having made an individual contribution to its success: Stephen Theodore Janssen perfected the strong, hairless, pin-hole-free transfer paper; John Brooks initiated the special technique required for engraving the copper plate; and **Henry Delamain** was responsible for preparing enamels with printer's ink in such a way that firing fused the design to the enamel surface.

Battersea failed in 1756, and it is thought that **Robert Hancock,** experienced in engraving for transfers, carried the process first to **Bow** and later in the same year to **Worcester.** This process of transfer-printing began with engraving the design in such a way as to produce sharp clear lines on

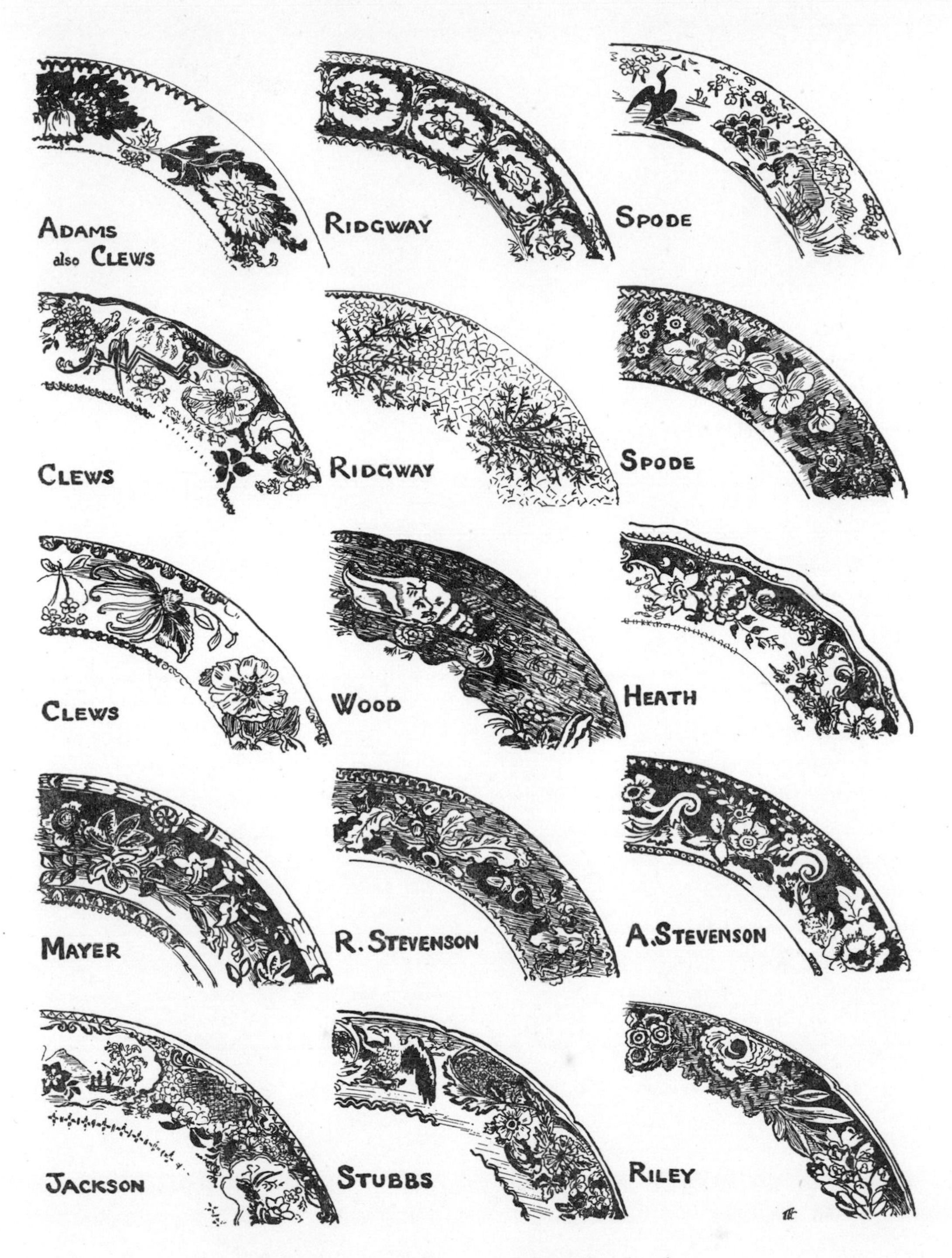

Transfer-printed blue and white plate borders

a thin copper plate, made hard-textured by the battery hammer. The engraved plate was warmed on a stove and coated with prepared colour. This was rubbed into the incised lines with a wooden tool and any excess removed with a flexible steel knife. The plate was then wiped with a beaver pad, leaving colour in the incised lines. A sheet of thin, strong tissue paper was made non-absorbent by brush-coating with printer's size. When dry, this paper was laid upon the prepared copper plate and subjected to pressure so that it received a clear impression of the design. When the paper was peeled from the copper it bore a perfect imprint. This inked impression was laid over the ware and rubbed gently with a flannel.

Overglaze printing: this early form of transfer-printing was applied on the **glaze** of **soft-paste porcelain** and then fired in a low-temperature, hardening-on kiln. It consisted of simple designs in black, brick red, dark purple, and brown, and might be over-painted by hand with washes of near-transparent colour.

Blue underglaze: also black and sepia, was originated by Robert Hancock at Worcester during the early 1760s, developed by Thomas Turner at **Caughley**, and perfected by **Josiah Spode** in about 1781. The transferred design was applied to the **biscuit**, fired, and afterwards glazed, giving the decoration a protective coat with a lifetime of hard wear resistance. The clarity of outline and brilliance of colour on an **earthenware** notably whiter than that of competitors brought Spode immediate popularity. Until 1805 patterns followed the established convention of adaptation from Chinese porcelain. Not until about 1800 was an improvement made in the slightly smudgy effect of cross-hatching associated with 18th-century blue underglaze-printing. In the early 1800s engraved lines were thinner, making possible a variation in tone, thus introducing dark shades and high lights. From 1810 finer tone variations were secured by combining line and stipple engraving on a single copper plate.

The colour particularly associated with underglaze transfer-printing is blue on a white ground. The blue obtained with **cobalt** oxide was, apart from black, the one colour unspoiled by glaze firing and was also capable of producing numerous gradations of tint. In some early 19th-century examples dark and light blue transfers might be used on a single piece of ware. Until 1830 shades of cobalt blue continued under such trade names as canton blue, zaffres, willow blue, flow blue, flower blue and mazarine. Deterioration in quality is observed in blue and white made after about 1830, the blue being lighter and patterns less meticulously engraved.

Among the two hundred or so potters who made Staffordshire blue, probably no more than twenty issued fine quality ware and it is this that the collector seeks, for most of it is impressed or printed with a trade mark. Some firms had their own range of exclusive border designs: typical specimens are shown on page 149.

Enoch Wood and his sons were responsible for some outstanding examples between 1819 and 1840; late printing was, however, in a blue too dark to display perfect clarity. **Andrew Stevenson** of Cobridge printed in dark blue, 1810 to 1818, high technical ability being displayed in his work. **Ralph Stevenson** of Cobridge operated between 1815 and 1840, his views being enclosed in richly printed leaf borders. **James and Ralph Clews** from 1819 until 1834 made some exceptionally picturesque ware in a blue rather less richly deep than that chosen by **Spode** and continued by **Copeland. Joseph Stubbs** of Longport issued admirable blue between 1810 and 1829. **John Ridgway**, Hanley, from 1817 to 1824 printed in a blue paler than that of his contemporaries, but tone differentiations were unblurred: he issued colour transfers from 1830 to 1834. Among other firms who made excellent blue-printed ware were J. & S. Jackson, Burslem, Joseph Heath, Tunstall, using the mark J H & CO.; **Charles Meigh,** Hanley; E. J. Phillips & Co., Longport; Thomas Green, Fenton; **Wedgwood; T. Mayer; J. & R. Riley; Shorthose & Co.; Miles Mason; William Adams**, Stoke.

The collector will distinguish between the soft cobalt blue of early underglaze blue-printed ware and the harsher synthetic blues used from about 1845. Light-weight earthenware usually belongs to the late 18th century. If the glaze of the blue-printed ware is examined with a light falling obliquely upon it, the surface of an old piece appears to be finely dappled, rather resembling the appearance of smooth sea-sand after a shower of rain. Once recognized, dappling is unmistakable, and is a feature that has not been reproduced. It is seldom visible on ware dating from 1800 and never after 1820.

Colour underglaze: in 1828 it was found that by mixing finely powdered green, yellow, red and black enamel with barbadoes tar it was possible to apply transferred designs in various shades of these colours without distortion. Two or more of the colours might be printed on a single piece, a separate firing being required for each transfer. This increased cost and examples are uncommon.

Multi-colour underglaze: in 1848 a process was invented by F. Collins and A. Reynolds, Hanley, by which three colours—blue, red and yellow—could be fixed from a single transfer requiring but one firing. Brown and green were included from 1852. The trade mark F C & A R has been noted impressed beneath some examples, but it is known that complete transfers were also supplied to other potters. The process continued in use until the 1860s. *See* **Pot-lids.**

Gilding: : invented 1835 by Godwin Embrey who sold prepared transfers to leading potters of the day. Examples are uncommon, but they are as brilliant as when made, having withstood burnishing after firing.

Lithography: first used on ceramics in 1839 in light blue carried out with artificial ultramarine under the glaze. From 1845 lithography was carried out in multi-colour, pink, green, purple, grey and black all being used in a single picture. Examples made before the late 1850s are recognized by their dull, uninteresting surface owing to the small amount of colour used. The impression was taken from lithographed stones, but, instead of ink, potter's varnish was used. This was transferred to the paper, and thence to the surface of the glazed ware, and dusted with colour powder.

Bat printing : an overglaze process producing pictures and designs of extreme delicacy, introduced to England in the early 1760s, but little used until the 1780s. The copper plate was stippled with a fine point, short lines also being included, but subsidiary to the stipple dots. The design was printed in oil upon a bat—a flexible composition sheet of glue, treacle and whiting, about one-quarter inch thick. This was transferred to the ware and dusted with the colour required, any surplus being removed with cotton wool. Bat-printing was little used from about 1800 until 1825 when a special transfer paper was evolved for the purpose, results being equally fine.

TRIDENT MARK. *See* **Nantgarw.**

TUNNICLIFFE, MICHAEL (Tunstall, Staffordshire).

Maker of **earthenware figures,** 1828–35. The impressed mark TUNNICLIFF TUNSTALL has been noted.

TURNER, John (Lane End, Staffordshire, 1738–87)

Maker of **figures** and busts in black and cane-coloured **basalt,** marked TURNER impressed.

TURNING

Finishing **cast** or moulded ware on a lathe by cutting and polishing with tools.

TYG

A name formerly given to porringers by Staffordshire potters: now

applied by collectors to drinking cups with three or more handles so that several people might drink, each from a different point on the rim, by using a different handle.

UNFIRED COLOURS. *See* **Colours.**

VARIEGATED WARES
Earthenware made either by the use of different coloured clays extending throughout the body as in **agate ware**, or by the mixture of colours in the **slip glazes** as in mottled, sprinkled, freckled, **marbled** and **tortoiseshell wares.**

VOYEZ, JOHN (Cobridge, Staffordshire, c.1735–1800)
Figure modeller on his own account and for **Wedgwood, Palmer** of Hanley and others. Among his better-known work are jugs with figures in relief, such as one with figures of Bacchus and Pan and with a dolphin spout, and one known as the Fair Hebe jug because this name appears on the tree trunk forming the jug, as does also Voyez's name. Rustic figures are grouped round the jug. This jug has been faked. He also made **Toby jugs.** His mark might be VOYEZ or J. VOYEZ.

VR (Monarch's cypher) MARK. *See* **Excise mark.**

W MARK. *See* **Worcester.**

W & B MARK. *See* **Wedgwood.**

W & C MARK. *See* **Wood.**

W&R MARK
Wayte and Ridge, Longton, Staffordshire, at work in the mid-1860s, made **earthenware, china, parian ware,** and **lustrewares.**

WALKER MINORIES MARK
The impressed mark of a London dealer appearing on **cream-coloured earthenware** of about 1800.

WALL, DR. JOHN (1708–76)
The founder of porcelain manufacture at **Worcester** in 1751. The "Wall period" dated from then until the death in 1783 of William Davis, a shareholder, technical decorator, and works manager.

WALTON, JOHN (Burslem, Staffordshire)
Established in 1806 and became a specialist in small **figures** of a brittle **earthenware** often with a crudely modelled **bocage** resembling a few star-shaped bunches of oak leaves enamelled green with a central acorn and split acorn cup that tended to lose their identity and be coloured as flowers. Two or more sprays as illustrated overleaf formed the bocage. The name of the subject might be inscribed upon the plinth. A scrolling decoration in blue at the foot of the figure distinguished many Walton

designs, as illustrated on a typical base. This potter's most popular creation was the vigorously modelled sheep and lamb, the latter lying under a ledge in the rocky base. Walton also mady **toby jugs** which were marked. The name WALTON in a scroll impressed appears on the backs of many figures.

WARBURTON, JOHN (Hot Lane, Staffordshire)

A **salt-glaze stoneware** potter who established himself as an enameller of **earthenware** in the early 1750s and, with his wife Ann, was responsible for most of **Wedgwood's** early enamelling. When Enoch Wood developed liquid **lead glazing** Warburton made **cream-coloured earthenware**, and much of his work is confused with early Wedgwood productions. Their son Jacob (1740–1826) was a master potter and also a partner in the **New Hall China Manufactory**. The mark, rarely found, is WARBURTON impressed.

WEATHERING

Good quality **porcelains** and **earthenware** required their clays to be weathered in rain, frost and sun for about a year. The clay was piled to a height of no more than three feet and in such a way that rain-water drained away from it, carrying some impurities. The frost helped to break down and disintegrate the mass; the sun dried it for handling.

"WEDGEWOOD" MARK. *See* **William Smith and Company.**

WEDGING

An 18th-century process associated with **porcelain** manufacture. Two pieces of plastic clay were continually slapped together until all air bubbles were removed. Any air allowed to remain expanded in the kiln and escaped during the process of vitrification, disfiguring the surface of the ware with minute depressions known as "pig-skin pitting".

WEDGWOOD, JOSIAH (1730–94)

The most celebrated of all English potters, whose work was slavishly copied by contemporaries and whose enduring reputation still influences present-day production. He was a thirteenth child, son, grandson and great-grandson of potters. He was apprenticed to his elder brother in 1744 and in 1752 was in partnership with John Harrison at Cliff Bank Works, Stoke, where they made **agate ware** knife hafts and buttons. Two years later he was in partnership with **Thomas Whieldon**, recognized as the finest potter of his day. They made vast quantities of almost profitless **salt-glaze**: more profitable were **marbled** and **agate wares**, **tortoiseshell** and **Egyptian black** which greatly improved under Wedgwood's guidance. During his Whieldon partnership Josiah Wedgwood ceaselessly experimented with clays and glazes, having sensed the need to bridge the gap between delicate **porcelain** and the coarse **earthenware** and **stoneware.** In 1759 he perfected his now celebrated **green glaze** upon which he placed a sufficiently high value to warrant the risk of parting from Whieldon and establishing his own pottery at Ivy House Works, Burslem, where he made domestic ware until 1773.

Wedgwood's experiment book, begun in 1759 and still preserved by his descendants, tell in cypher the story of how his various ornamental wares came into being. The first of these was a refinement of the stoneware known as Egyptian black, made in Staffordshire from about 1700: the new ware he named **black basalt**, describing it as "a fine black porcelaine . . . equal in hardness to agate and porphyry . . . the black is sterling and will last for ever". This was quickly copied by competitors, and some fifty impress marks of other potters have been found on 18th-century black basalt. To exploit this Wedgwood opened a second factory in 1763 at Brick House, later known as Bell Works, Burslem. Here were made all his more spectacular productions, until Etruria was founded in June 1769, with Thomas Bentley as partner.

It was at Ivy House that Wedgwood evolved his celebrated **cream-coloured earthenware**, suggestive of old ivory and rivalling porcelain in form and decoration. This he christened **queen's ware** in honour of Queen Charlotte after she had accepted the gift of a combined breakfast and caudle set. Some kind of ornament was almost always introduced on this ware. This might consist of a raised rimband of leaves; or enamelling in colours by Ann, wife of **John Warburton**, Hot Lane, or from 1770 by artists employed at Wedgwood's decorating establishment in Chelsea; or it might be **transfer-printing** at the works of **Sadler & Green**, Liverpool, to whom the ware was sent—some being printed in outline and later coloured in by enamellers. The creamware business was carried on at Brick House until 1773 when it was transferred to Etruria. Thomas Wedgwood, Josiah's cousin, was his partner in this venture until his death in 1788.

Wedgwood was delayed in the production of **jasper** until 1774, and **dry**

bodies dated from about the same time. These consisted of five groups known as **rosso antico**, **cane ware**, **terra cotta**, drab ware and white stoneware. **Pearl ware** dated from 1779.

Josiah Wedgwood was elected a Fellow of the Royal Society in 1783 after inventing the first pyrometer capable of registering oven heat. Bentley died in 1780, but not until after the death of his cousin Thomas did Josiah take into partnership his sons John, Josiah and Thomas, together with his nephew Thomas Byerley. The style of the firm, which had been "Wedgwood and Bentley" from 1768 to 1780, and then "Wedgwood" until 1790, then became "Wedgwood, Sons, and Byerley". In 1793 his sons John and Thomas resigned from the firm which, until Byerley's death in 1810, was known as "Wedgwood, Son and Byerley".

Wedgwood marks always displayed the name. Pre-Etruria ware was rarely marked, but it is thought that the name WEDGWOOD impressed with irregularly placed type was used then. The first mark introduced at Etruria consisted of the names WEDGWOOD & BENTLEY arranged in a circle; or the same name with the addition of the word ETRURIA between inner and outer rings. The latter was impressed in circular seals which are found attached inside plinths of basalt vases, or on the pedestals of busts or large **figures**. The same mark was also impressed around the screws of basalt, granite and etruscan vases, as in the bottom right of the illustrations. The mark at the top right is of 1764–69, and is rare. The name WEDGWOOD & BENTLEY in two lines with a catalogue number was impressed upon intaglios, some very small ones being impressed W & B

with the catalogue number, or simply the number only. The name in upper case letters arranged in two lines and in various sizes was impressed upon busts, granite and basalt vases, figures, plaques, medallions and cameos. All the above marks dated between 1769 and 1780. From 1780 until shortly after 1795 the name Wedgwood or WEDGWOOD was used in various sizes. From 1769 to the present day the mark WEDGWOOD has been impressed or printed on queen's ware. The same stamp has always been impressed on ornamental jasper, black basalt, cane, and terra cotta. The mark ENGLAND was added in 1894.

Josiah Wedgwood never attempted to make porcelain, but from 1812 to 1822 Josiah II ventured into the **bone china** business, apparently with little commercial success. The Wedgwood pattern books show that no more than twenty-seven patterns decorated this ware. Bone china was always marked, usually with the name in red upper-case letters over the glaze; sometimes the mark was in blue, green, or gold. Manufacture of bone china was revived at Etruria in 1878, the printed mark consisting of a reproduction of the Portland vase and the name WEDGWOOD beneath it.

"WEDGWOOD & Co." MARK.

See **Ferrybridge** *and* **William Smith and Company.**

WELSH WARE

The 18th-century term for **combed** and feathered **slipware** streaked with yellow and brown **glaze**.

W H MARK. *See* **Hackwood.**

WHIELDON, THOMAS (Fenton Low, Staffordshire)

One of the finest potters of his day, operating from 1740 to 1780 when he retired a very rich man, living until 1798. **Josiah Wedgwood** was his partner between 1754 and 1759. Whieldon's ware falls roughly into five groups: **agate** and **marbled ware**; **tortoiseshell ware**; black glazed; **salt glazed** including **scratched blue; figures.** He made every type of Staffordshire ware fashionable during his period, however. None of the work was marked.

WILLOW PATTERN

A pseudo-Chinese design in blue underglaze **transfer-printing** introduced in about 1780 by Thomas Turner of **Caughley**. The original copper plates as used on **earthenware**, engraved by Turner with his signature in the margins, are preserved in the British Museum. In this Turner placed the pagoda on the right side of the design and surrounded by six types of conventional trees—willow, peach, fir, plum, the mysterious tree with dark circles, and the tallest tree of all bearing thirty-two apples arranged in three tiers. No figure appeared upon the bridge and the zigzag fence extended from the water to the right-hand edge of the design. On Caughley **porcelain** the design was different: the pagoda was on the left of the picture and the bridge had pointed arches: the sky and water were slightly shaded.

Thomas Minton, while an apprentice engraver at Caughley, cut many of the willow pattern copper plates and when he left to set up as a free-lance engraver in Stoke he designed and engraved variants for other potters, retaining the main motif, but altering the fence patterns, number of apples on the tree, and the rim and bouge designs.

Josiah Spode I made willow pattern from 1785 using a design resembling that on Caughley porcelain but applied to earthenware only. From about 1800 the original Caughley earthenware pattern was adopted with thirty-two apples on the tree. Wedgwood issued willow pattern from 1795, the design being a close adaptation of Caughley with the pagoda on the right, the fret on the fence different, and thirty-four apples in the design used on plates and more on dishes. In about 1830 the Wedgwood firm produced a small quantity of willow pattern earthenware printed in black and sometimes enriched with gilt bands.

William Adams of Greengates made large quantities of willow pattern, the tree bearing thirty-two apples and then fifty apples. **John Davenport's** trees bore only twenty-five apples: these dated from 1793 to about 1830. The **Swansea** willow pattern had thirty apples and might be printed in dark and light blues, also being found occasionally in black and brown.

There were nearly two hundred makers of willow pattern in underglaze blue by 1830 and the only way to attribute a piece definitely is by the mark or by comparison with a marked piece. **Leeds, Liverpool, Rockingham** and **Sunderland** made it. Willow pattern on soft porcelain or early **bone china** is rare.

WILSON MARK. *See* **Palmer.**

WINCANTON (Somerset)

Delftware made by Nathaniel Ireson (1686–1765). Dated examples prove manufacture between 1737 and 1748. Blue and white and manganese and white were used, and also a powdered manganese ground, sometimes with reserve medallions and through which lines were sometimes scratched. The mimosa pattern in trellis-work borders, also made at **Bristol,** has frond-like leaves and each flower consists of a dot within a circle. Some plates are edged with a fine brown line. Mark: WINCANTON impressed.

WIRKSWORTH (Derbyshire)

Soft-paste porcelain is believed to have been made here by **William Billingsley** during the early months of 1808, but no examples have been identified. Billingsley is known to have established a small decorating shop here at the end of 1807, assisted by his two daughters and Samuel Walker.

WOOD, STAFFORDSHIRE POTTERS

Aaron Wood (1717–85), Burslem, was celebrated as a block cutter, that is, a carver of alabaster moulds for **casting salt-glaze** and other ware. He worked for Dr. Wedgwood, Thomas Mitchell of Burslem, and **Whieldon.**

Ralph Wood I (1715–72), Burslem, was noted for **figures,** busts and **toby jugs** from 1760, at first in the Whieldon tradition, then in finer **lead glaze** and improved underglaze enamels. His mark was R. WOOD impressed.

Ralph Wood II (1748–95) succeeded his father. His mark was Ra

Wood, Burslem, impressed. He was succeeded in his turn by Ralph Wood III (1781–1801).

Enoch Wood (1759–1840), youngest son of Aaron, was renowned both as a modeller and as a master potter. After an apprenticeship with **Palmer** of Hanley, in 1783 he established a pottery with his cousin Ralph Wood as partner at Fountain Place, Burslem. In about 1790 he was joined by James Caldwell and traded as Wood and Caldwell. He bought out Caldwell in 1819 and then traded as Enoch Wood and Sons. He made a wide range of pottery including **cream-coloured earthenware,** enamelled and **transfer-printed, figures,** coloured and lustred, black **basalt,** and **jasper.** Enoch Wood was the first recorded collector of English pottery. The marks WOOD & CALDWELL and ENOCH WOOD & SONS are to be noted impressed. *See* page 149.

Other marks include an eagle and shield with ENOCH WOOD & SONS, BURSLEM and variants of this (the other marks in the sketch are of Ralph Wood I); and the mark below probably Enoch Wood's and mostly found on **bone china.**

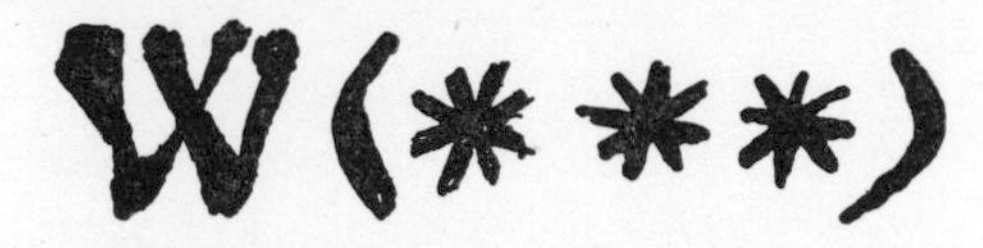

WORCESTER

The manufacture of **porcelain** was established here in 1751 at the **Worcester Tonquin Manufactory** by **Dr. Wall** (d. 1776) and fourteen associates who included William Davis, formerly of **Bristol.** Because of his practical knowledge, Davis was made works manager, a position he held until his death in 1783. The business was then bought by Thomas Flight, jeweller to the royal family and the firm's London agent, his son John becoming manager. The word "royal" was added to the firm's title in 1788, the works then becoming known as the Royal Worcester Porcelain Company. When Flight senior died in 1793 John took Martin Barr as partner and the firm was styled Flight & Barr. When the latter's son Martin Barr II joined the firm in 1807 it was re-styled Barr, Flight & Barr. In 1813 George Barr joined the business which then operated as Flight, Barr & Barr until 1840 when the concern was acquired by the firm of Chamberlain.

Robert Chamberlain, a porcelain decorator under Dr. Wall, had founded an enamelling establishment at Worcester in 1783, buying **porcelain** and **earthenware** in the white from **Caughley** and Staffordshire. After the death of Robert in 1798 his sons Humphrey and Robert launched into the manufacture of **bone china** early in the 19th century and were responsible for some exceptionally fine decorated ware. In 1828 the firm was owned by Walter Chamberlain and John Lilley who, as stated above, acquired the business of Flight, Barr & Barr in 1840, abandoning Dr. Wall's old premises, and transferring plant, moulds and stocks to their works at Diglis. The united firms traded as Chamberlain & Company until 1852. W. H. Kerr and R. W. Binns then acquired the business which, ten years later, was converted into a limited company known as the Worcester Royal Porcelain Company Limited.

Dr. Wall period (1751–83): soapstone porcelain was manufactured throughout the period, varying from a faintly bluish grey to a creamy-white and displaying a faintly bluish-green tinge if held to the light. The **glaze** early in the period was softly white with a suspicion of green, of even smoothness, glossy rather than brilliant. Late in the period the ware was glazed with a mixture of **grog** and oxide of tin: this had a faintly opalescent appearance and was evenly distributed.

Until 1763 production was confined to domestic ware which might be enamelled in **colours** but more usually was decorated in underglaze blue. The blue itself varied in tint from a clear bright sapphire to a dark indigo—sometimes almost a blue-black (*see* **Cobalt**). Moulding and finish were excellent. A notable change in policy took place in 1763, and Worcester began to cater for a richer clientele. Some of the finest of Worcester porcelain was made between then and 1783. In 1769 the firm was advertising porcelain ornamented with "beautiful Colours of Mazarine blue and gold, Sky-blue, Pea-green, French-green, Sea-green, Purple, Scarlet and other varieties of Colour" on dinner, dessert, tea, and coffee services.

The Worcester decorators now followed the vivid complexities of colour and pattern which characterized **Japanese** porcelain, modifying these and mingling them with the patterns and colours of **Dresden** and **Sèvres**: from the medley issued characteristic oriental Worcester, firmly established by 1770. Every fashionable design of the day was adapted by the Worcester decorators. Binns refers to "lovely exotic birds, those gorgeous ornithological fantasies of the imaginative painter, impossible but quite beautiful. Quaint posies of old-fashioned flowers—chrysanthemums, roses, carnations (generally striped) and picotees, the sweet blue nemophila and the dainty auricula in colours soft and harmonious; curious old landscapes in more than doubtful perspective, generally framed in turquoise husk borders shaded with black and gilt; rich and luscious-looking fruit; butterflies and insects, occasionally animals, and, apart from the Chinese style, rare figures." The Dresden influence was expressed in colourful birds, pink scale patterns, scattered posies and flower sprays, and bunches

21. Leeds cream-coloured earthenware: (*Top*) Teapots showing intertwined handles and a double teapot. Heights, left to right, $3\frac{3}{4}$ inches, $4\frac{3}{4}$ inches, $4\frac{1}{4}$ inches. (*Above*) Pearlware figures on square plinths, Mars flanked by Spring and Autumn, and two figures of musicians. Marked "Leeds Pottery". (*Left and right*) Perforated vases issued by Slee, who perpetuated the old Leeds tradition from 1888.

22. (*Top*) Cow milk jugs in mid-18th century earthenware. (*Centre*) Interiors of three loving cups showing modelled frogs in the base. (*Below*) Earthenware stirrup cups.

of fruit: even the Dresden marks were copied.

Queen Charlotte's pattern, used by Caughley (on the left in the sketch), has been described. This was selected by Queen Charlotte when she visited Worcester in 1788. It must not be confused with the more familiar queen's pattern with its alternating panels, often arranged spirally, of red on white, and white on blue, with gilding. This is found also on Derby and Lowestoft porcelain and on subsequent Chinese work.

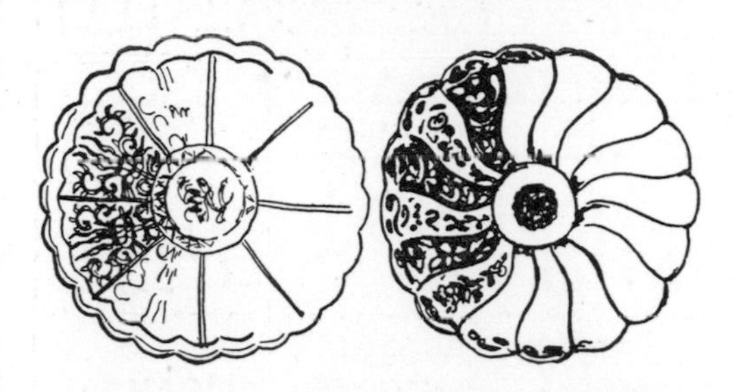

The blue grounds of Worcester are celebrated, the best known being salmon-scale blue, powder blue, **mazarine** or dark blue, and overglaze enamel blue. The device of breaking up a blue ground by diapering it with a close scale pattern known to some collectors as salmon-scale, dated from 1763. On early examples large scales were laboriously outlined and washed in: the later small scales were more speedily produced by wiping out the high lights of the pattern from a blue ground. Less frequently scale pattern is found in salmon-pink. These ground colours enclosed white reserves painted with flowers, fruits, birds, insects, figures.

Transfer-printing made its appearance at Worcester in 1757, a decorative style continued there until 1774. All manner of pictures were transferred to the porcelain, following the current vogues for pastoral scenes with shepherds and milkmaids, romantic ruins in classical landscapes, and subjects from sporting prints. Many patterns were copied from *The Ladies Amusement or Whole Art of Japanning*, 1760. The colour used was generally jet black, deep red, lilac or pale purple over the glaze until 1770, when underglaze transfer-printing in blue and sepia were introduced. Thereafter, transferred designs might be hand-decorated with bright-coloured washes of enamels, enlivened with touches of gilding. The **bat** process of transfer-printing was introduced in the Flight period (1783–93).

Marks used during the Wall period were many and varied, but no more than two may be regarded as true trade marks—the crescent, and the cursive capital or script W. The block capital W is found only on blue-printed wares. The crescent in various sizes is found in outline, with shading lines, and in solid colour, the small open crescent in blue underglaze being most frequent. A red open crescent is found on some enamelled porcelain from 1770. In varying forms the crescent appears to have continued until the end of the Flight period in 1793. The script W in blue and in several forms was used from 1755, sometimes

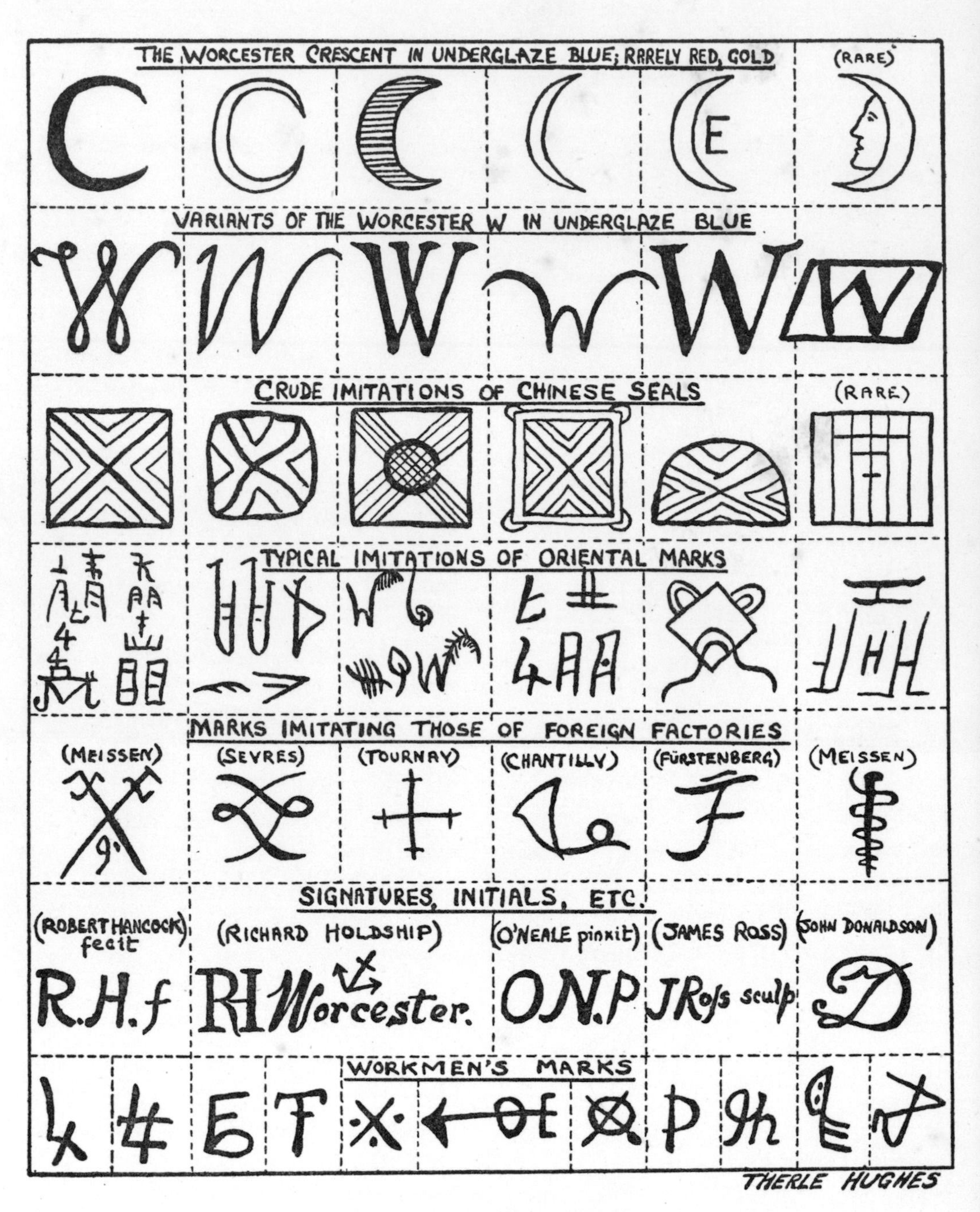

Worcester marks, 1751–1783

in association with a blue crescent. The "Chinese seal" in underglaze blue, a fretted square, appears in five different designs on ware printed in underglaze blue. Other varieties of the seal—square, round, semi-circular—are found on all classes of porcelain.

Flight, Thomas (1783–93): **Flight & Barr** (1793–1807); **Barr, Flight & Barr** (1807–13); **Flight, Barr & Barr** (1813–40): the soapstone paste and glaze were at once altered, now lacking the translucency of earlier Worcester and showing a faintly yellow tint if held to the light. Commercially, however, the paste was considered an improvement, even though there was no longer a harmonious blending of paste with glaze and decoration. Styles and designs were in the fashionable classical mood and decorators of pictorial panels developed a technique characteristic of Worcester, outlines being perfect and colours applied with precision. Ornament included landscapes, figure subjects, copies of celebrated paintings, allegorical pictures, illustrations of poems, and so on. Groups of flowers and finely painted shell patterns were in great demand. Less expensive decoration consisted of blue painted or printed flowers and blue bands, with or without gold decorated sprigs.

Flight and Barr from about 1800 began to manufacture bone china: the paste was hard-looking and faintly grey, less attractive than that made elsewhere. Pure whiteness and high translucency were achieved by about 1820. Meanwhile Thomas Flight's soapstone porcelain continued in production and shortly after Martin Barr II joined the firm in 1807 a great improvement was recorded in the texture and whiteness of the porcelain. Early in the 19th century decoration became simpler and enamel colours, cruder and harder than formerly, were used for naturalistic but mechanical flower painting. From about 1810 considerable quantities of flat ware were made, the borders and rims decorated with raised **rococo** moulding. These might be enamelled in full colours or in blue and gold. The introduction of Walker's muffle at this time gave finer results to enamelling.

The firm concentrated chiefly on table ware and vases, style and flamboyance of decoration resembling that of competitive ware, but with much more attention given to details. Trays intended to hold writing pens were a feature.

The earliest of Thomas Flight's marks was the name Flight in script, either above or accompanied by an open crescent in blue, red or gold. The name might be impressed in the paste. A crown was added to the mark in 1789. From 1793 to 1807 the name of the firm Flight & Barr appeared below a crown. The presence of an incised letter B indicates the piece to have been made from one of the experimental pastes initiated by Martin Barr I. From 1807 to 1813 the name Barr

1–4. Marks of Flight, Barr and Barr, 1813–40; (1) in red or black; (2) impressed; (3 and 4) printed in red or black.
5–6. Chamberlain's marks, printed in red: 5, 1816–1820; 6, 1820–1840.
7–11. Some of the marks used after the amalgamation of Chamberlain and Barr: (7) 1850–51; (8) 1840–45, printed in red, until the Coventry Street address was given up; (9) printed; (10) printed or impressed; (11) incised.
12. One of the marks of Grainger, Lee and Company after Lee joined Grainger in 1812.
13–14. Marks of Kerr and Binns, 1852–62; (13) on best-quality work, printed; (14) printed or impressed.
15. Mark of the Worcester Royal Porcelain Company Ltd. founded in 1862.

Flight & Barr was printed in red or blue underglaze accompanied by the firm's Worcester and London addresses. The impressed initials BFB surmounted by a crown belonged to this period. From 1813 to 1840 the mark, printed in blue, was Flight, Barr and Barr in script or FBB impressed.

Chamberlain's (1783–1852): until about 1800 the firm were decorators only. In about 1798 they began to make bone china with a slightly grey paste. By 1815 its translucency equalled that of **Spode**, but the paste was hardly so white. In 1811 they introduced a soft paste, very translucent and with a fine clear surface. Some magnificent matching dinner, dessert and breakfast services were made in this paste, known as "Regent China" and made until about 1820. A Chamberlain characteristic in bone china table ware consisted of borders in a chain or network design with carefully painted bouquets of garden flowers. From about 1821 many services were decorated with paintings of old castles, each piece displaying a different scene, with its name printed or impressed on the back. Japan patterns in red, blue and gold dated from about 1825. Vases lavishly gilded and painted with views of eastern towns belonged to the 1830s. The apple-green of Worcester was celebrated for the beauty of its tint.

The marks on Chamberlain Worcester always included their name, and few unmarked pieces were issued. Until 1808 CHAMBERLAINS or CHAMBERLAINS WORCS was painted in red script often accompanied by a pattern number. The same marks in purple dated from 1808 to 1820 and rare examples are found in gold. The first of the printed marks was CHAMBERLAINS WORCESTER & 63 PICCADILLY LONDON in red script and dated from 1814 to 1820. The usual mark from then until 1840 read CHAMBERLAINS WORCESTER & 155 NEW BOND ST LONDON. ROYAL PORCELAIN MANUFACTURERS. This was surmounted by a royal coat of arms or crown.

Chamberlain and Company (1840–52): the united firms issued a vast quantity of bone china articles, decorative and useful, in a wide range of patterns. *See* **Grainger, Lee & Company.**

WR (Monarch's cypher) MARK. *See* **Excise mark.**

WREATHING

Found on **hard-paste porcelain** from **Plymouth** and **Bristol.** This was the term given to the spiral ridging found on both interior and exterior of some hollow-ware and clearly visible when the porcelain is held at an angle against the light. Several incorrect theories, such as unskilful throwing, have been put forward to account for this feature. These wreathings were, however, purposeful. Because the paste softened at one period during firing, the ware tended to collapse beneath its own weight. The slight variation in thickness provided by wreathing was sufficient to prevent this.

Wreathing is also found in *Bristol* **delft** hollow-ware, such as drug jars and **food warmers.**

WS & S MARK. *See* **Isleworth.**

WT & CO MARK

Probably the impressed mark of William and John Taylor, late 18th-century potters of Burslem, Staffordshire, makers of **salt-glazed stone ware** and white **earthenware.**

YARMOUTH (Norfolk)

An independent enameller named Absolon operated here in premises known as "The Ovens" during the late 18th century and early 19th century, buying **cream-coloured earthenware** and **bone china** in the white from such firms as **Wedgwood, Shorthose, Leeds** and **Coalport.** He painted botanical flowers, monograms, landscapes and other popular motifs. Many of his pieces are signed in brown script ABSOLON YARM° followed by a number. Sometimes this is accompanied by an arrow in brown, probably the Shorthose mark.

ZAFFRE. *See* **Cobalt.**

SELECTED BIBLIOGRAPHY

ADAMS, Percy L. *William Adams, an Old Staffordshire Potter*. 1904.

BALLANTYNE, A. Randal. *Robert Hancock and his Works*. 1885.

BARNARD, Harry. *Chats on Wedgwood Ware*. 1924.

BARRETT, F. A. *Worcester Porcelain*. 1953.

BEMROSE, Geoffrey J. V. *Nineteenth Century English Pottery and Porcelain*. 1952.

BEMROSE, William. *Bow, Chelsea and Derby Porcelain*. 1898.

BEMROSE, William. *Longton Hall Porcelain*. 1906.

BINNS, Charles. *The Story of the Potter*. n.d.

BINNS, R. W. *A Century of Potting in the City of Worcester*. 1865.

BINNS, W. Moore. *The First Century of English Porcelain*. 1906.

BLACKER, J. F. *Nineteenth Century English Ceramic Art*. 1911.

BLUNT, Reginald (edited by). *Cheyne Book of Chelsea China*. 1924.

BRITISH MUSEUM. *Catalogue of the Collection of English Pottery*, by R. L. Hobson. 1903.

BRITISH MUSEUM. *Catalogue of the Collection of English Porcelain*. 1905.

BRITISH MUSEUM. *Guide to English Pottery and Porcelain*. 1923.

BRYANT, G. E. *Chelsea Porcelain Toys*. 1925.

BURTON, William. *A History and Description of English Porcelain*. 1902.

BURTON, William. *Porcelain: Its Nature, Art and Manufacture*. 1902.

BURTON, William. *A History and Description of English Earthenware and Stoneware*. 1904.

CHAFFERS, W. *The Ceramic Gallery*. 1907.

CHAFFERS, William. *Marks and Monograms on European and Oriental Pottery and Porcelain*. Fourteenth edition, 1946.

CHURCH, Sir Arthur. *Old English Pottery*. 1893.

CHURCH, Sir Arthur. *Josiah Wedgwood, Master Potter*. 1894.

CHURCH, Sir Arthur. *English Earthenware*. 1904.

CHURCH, Sir Arthur. *English Porcelain*. 1904.

CRAWLEY, James. *Potteries of Sunderland and District*. 1951.

CRISP, F. A. *Lowestoft China Factory*. 1907.

DILLON, Edward. *Porcelain*. 1904.

DILLON, Edward. *Porcelain and How to Collect it*. 1910.

DIXON, J. L. *English Porcelain of the 18th Century*. 1951.

DOWNHAM, E. A. *Blue Dash Chargers*. 1918.

DOWNHAM & GUNN. *English Pottery and Porcelain*. 1918.

EARLE, Cyril. *The Earle Collection of Early Staffordshire Pottery*. 1915.

ECCLES, H. and Rackham, Bernard. *Analysed Specimens of English Porcelain*. 1922.

ENGLISH CERAMIC CIRCLE. *Transactions of, from 1928*.

FALKNER, Frank. *The Wood Family of Burslem*. 1912.

FISHER, Stanley W. *English Blue and White Porcelain of the 18th Century*. 1947.

FISHER, Stanley W. *The Decoration of English Porcelain*. 1954.

FREETH, Frank, and Mrs. *Old English Pottery*. 1896.

GARNER, F. H. *English Delftware*. 1950.

GATTY, C. T. *The Liverpool Potteries*. 1882.

GIBB, William, and Rackham, Bernard. *A Book of Porcelain*. 1910.

GILLESPIE, F. Brayshaw. *Derby Porcelain*. 1950.

GRABHAM, Oxley. *Yorkshire Potteries, Pots and Potters*. 1916.

GRANT, M. H. *The Makers of Black Basalts.* 1910.

HAGGAR, Reginald G. *English Country Pottery.* 1950.

HAGGAR, Reginald G. *Staffordshire Chimney Ornaments.* 1955.

HASLEM, John. *The Old Derby China Factory.* 1876.

HAYDEN, Arthur. *Chats on Old English China.* 1906.

HAYDEN, Arthur. *Spode and His Successors.* 1925.

HOBSON, R. L. *Worcester Porcelain.* 1910.

HODGKIN, J. E. and E. *Examples of Early English Pottery.* 1896.

HODGSON, Mrs. Willoughby. *How to Identify Old China.* 1928.

HONEY, W. B. *European Ceramic Art*, 2 Vols. 1949–52.

HONEY, W. B. *Old English Porcelain.* 1928.

HONEY, W. B. *Wedgwood Ware.* 1948.

HUGHES, Bernard and Therle. *English Porcelain and Bone China.* 1955.

HUGHES, G. Bernard. *The Story of Spode.* 1950.

HURLBUTT, F. *Old Derby Porcelain and its Artist-workmen.* 1925.

HURLBUTT, F. *Bow Porcelain.* 1926.

HURLBUTT, F. *Bristol Porcelain.* 1928.

HURLBUTT, Frank. *Chelsea China.* 1937.

HYAM, E. E. *The Early Period of Derby Porcelain.* 1926.

JEWITT, Llewellyn. *The Wedgwoods: being a Life of Josiah Wedgwood.* 1865.

JEWITT, Llewellyn. *The Ceramic Art of Great Britain.* 1877.

JOHN, W. D. *Nantgarw Porcelain.* 1948.

KIDSON, Joseph R. and Frank. *Historical Notes of the Leeds Old Pottery.* 1892.

KING, William. *Chelsea Porcelain.* 1922.

KING, William. *English Porcelain Figures of the 18th Century.* 1925.

LANCASTER, H. Boswell. *Liverpool and Her Potters.* 1936.

LEWER, H. W. *Bow Porcelain Early Figures.* 1919.

LITCHFIELD, Frederick. *Pottery and Porcelain.* 1925.

LOMAX, Charles J. *Quaint Old English Pottery.* 1909.

LUXMORE, C. F. C. *Salt-glaze.* 1924.

MACKENNA, F. Severne. *The Chelsea: Triangle and Raised Anchor Wares.* 1945.

MACKENNA, F. Severne. *Cookworthy's Plymouth and Bristol Porcelain.* 1946.

MACKENNA, F. Severne. *Champion's Bristol Porcelain.* 1947.

MACKINTOSH, Sir Harold. *Early English Figure Pottery.* 1938.

MANKOWITZ, Wolf. *Wedgwood.* 1953.

MARRYAT, Joseph. *A History of Pottery and Porcelain.* 1857.

MAYER, Joseph. *On the Art of Pottery: with a History of its Progress in Liverpool.* 1873.

METEYARD, Eliza. *The Life of Josiah Wedgwood.* 1865.

METEYARD, Eliza. *Wedgwood and his Works.* 1873.

METEYARD, Eliza. *Memorials of Wedgwood. A Selection from his fine art works, in plaques, medallions, figures and other ornamental objects.* 1874.

MEW, Egan. *Old Bow China.* 1909.

MURTON, A. G. *Lowestoft China.* 1932.

NANCE, E. Morton. *The Pottery and Porcelain of Swansea and Nantgarw.* 1942.

NIGHTINGALE, J. E. *Contributions towards the History of Early English Porcelain from Contemporary Sources.* 1881.

OWEN, Hugh. *Two Centuries of Ceramic Art in Bristol.* 1873.

PARTRIDGE, Frank. *Ralph Wood Pottery.* n.d.

POUNTNEY, W. J. *Old Bristol Potteries.* 1920.

PRICE, R. T. *Astbury, Whieldon, and Ralph Wood Figures and Toby Jugs.* 1922.

PRIDEAUX, John. *Relics of William Cookworthy*. 1853.

RACKHAM, Bernard. *Medieval English Pottery*. 1949.

RACKHAM, Bernard. *Early English Pottery*. 1951.

RACKHAM, Bernard, and Herbert Read. *English Pottery*. 1924.

RATHBONE, Frederick. *Old Wedgwood: the English Relief Work of the XVIII century made by Josiah Wedgwood at Etruria in Staffordshire, 1760–95*. 1893.

READ, Herbert. *Staffordshire Pottery Figures*. 1929.

RHEAD, G. Wooliscroft and Frederick Alfred. *Staffordshire Pots and Potters*. 1906.

RHEAD, G. Wooliscroft. *British Pottery Marks*. 1910.

RHEAD, G. Wooliscroft. *The Earthenware Collector*. 1920.

SANDERSON, Arthur. *A Catalogue of a Collection of Plaques, Medallions, Vases, Figures, etc. in Coloured Jasper and Basalte, Produced by Josiah Wedgwood, F.R.S.* 1901.

SHAW, Simeon. *History of the Staffordshire Potteries*. Re-issued in 1900 by Scott, Greenwood and Company.

SOLON, M. L. *A Brief Description of Old English Porcelain*. 1903.

SOLON, M. L. *The Art of the Old English Potter*. 1883.

SPELMAN, W. W. R. *Lowestoft China*. 1905.

STRINGER, George Eyre. *New Hall Porcelain*. 1949.

TAPP, W. H. *Early Derby Ceramic Artists*. 1925.

TIFFIN, F. W. T. *A Chronograph of the Bow, Chelsea and Derby China Factories*. 1875.

TURNER, Donald C. *Leeds Pottery*. Published by Leeds City Art Gallery. 1951.

TURNER, William. *The Ceramics of Swansea and Nantgarw*. 1897.

TURNER, William. *Transfer Printing on Enamels, Pottery and Porcelain*. 1907.

VICTORIA AND ALBERT MUSEUM. *Catalogue of the Schreiber Collection*, Vol. 1 Porcelain, 1928; Vol. 2 Earthenware, 1930; Vol. 3 Enamels and Glass, 1924.

WALLIS, Alfred, and William Bemrose. *The Pottery and Porcelain of Derbyshire.* 1870.

WEDGWOOD, Josiah. *Letters of Josiah Wedgwood, 1762–1780.* 1903.

WEDGWOOD, Josiah, and Thomas H. Ormsbee. *Staffordshire Pottery*, 1947.

WEDGWOOD, Josiah C. *Staffordshire Pottery and its History.* 1914.

WILLIAMS, Isaac J. *A Guide to the Collection of Welsh Porcelain in the National Museum of Wales.* 1931.

WILLIAMS, Sydney B. *Antique Blue and White Spode.* 1943.

WILLIAMSON, F. *History and Classification of Derby Porcelain.* 1924.

WILLIAMSON, F. *The Derby Pot Manufactory known as Cockpit Hill, Derby.* 1931.